THE ROAD TO FIND OUT

A MODERN PILGRIM AND THE CAMINO DE SANTIAGO

For Kim —

With gratitude as

always ,

THE ROAD TO FIND OUT

A MODERN PILGRIM AND THE CAMINO DE SANTIAGO

Bruce H. Matson

Campbell & Parker

The Road to Find Out: A Modern Pilgrim and the Camino de Santiago

© 2016 by Bruce H. Matson
Published by Campbell & Parker Books

Produced with the assistance of Livingstone, the publishing services division of the Barton-Veerman Company. Project staff includes Dave Veerman, Linda Taylor, Larry Taylor, Claudia Gerwin, and Tom Shumaker.

ISBN: 978-0-9724616-9-6

Photographic images to accompany each chapter of *The Road to Find Out* may be found at wwww.theroadtofindout.com.

So on and on you go, the seconds tick the time out
There's so much left to know, and I'm on the road to find out.

Cat Stevens

Bay of Biscay

Santander

Bilbao

Saint-Jean-
Pied-de-Port

Sahagún
Calzadilla de la Cueza
Frómista
Hontanas
Burgos
Tosantos
Castildelgado
Nájera
Logroño

Rio Pisuerga

Carrión de
los Condes
Castrojeriz
Tardajos
Villafranca
Belorado
Santo Domingo de la Calzada
Navarrete
Viana

Pamplona
Zubiri
Roncesvalles

Rio Ebro

Zaragoza

Rio Duero

SPAIN

Tagus

MADRID

MAP OF THE ROUTE OF THE
CAMINO DE SANTIAGO
(Camino Frances)

Toledo

CONTENTS

DEDICATION &
ACKNOWLEDGEMENTS

This book is dedicated to my daughters Brooke and Amy with hope that it may encourage them to live an examined life, to walk always where the way is good, and to find rest in words and promises of our Lord.

This book is also dedicated to each of those individuals for whom I am grateful as identified and discussed in chapter 11 below.

In helping me to prepare this book for publication I want to acknowledge the contributions of and thank Carl Meyer, John McCauley, and Brooke Matson. For helping to analyze and graph the statistical growth of pilgrims on the Camino as found in the Appendix, I am grateful to Rob Smith and my friends at Protiviti and to Amy Matson.

A special word of thanks goes out to Dave Veerman (and his colleagues at Livingstone) who handled the hard work on the manuscript as well as the book and cover design.

Introduction

Let me recommend the best medicine in the world; a long journey,
a mild season, through a pleasant country, in easy stages.

James Madison

This book is about my journey on the Camino de Santiago—the Way of St. James—in April and May of 2014. It's about a walk, and sometimes a hike, of almost five hundred miles over thirty days—starting in southern France and finishing in the northwest corner of Spain. It's about the people, places, and things encountered along the way. It's about sleeping in crowded bunkrooms; walking through open, dry farmland; struggling with language barriers; and sharing communal meals with new friends. It's about hiking on through clouds and rain, meeting people from all walks of life and from all corners of the globe, enduring extended periods of time along monotonous roadways, and enjoying meditative walks through wheat fields and vineyards. And it's about pressing out the final five kilometers of long walks on hot and dusty paths, climbing up into and down out of medieval hilltop villages, exploring Gothic cathedrals and Romanesque chapels, and following rivers and mountain streams. It's about both tolerating industrial landscapes and rejoicing in the beauty of a perfect walk through a remarkable countryside.

This book is also about time on my feet and the thoughts and reflections that one has when given large blocks of time uninterrupted by meetings and calls and everyday obligations. Having reached a benchmark of sorts in my own life, I considered the Camino to be a great opportunity to look back and to look forward—to look back on more than fifty-five years at what I've accomplished and where I fell short, and to look forward and consider how to finish well. And it was time to consider more deeply the riddle of life and the big questions that confront most who take the occasion to reflect upon their place in the world.

Since the tenth century, a few million people have preceded me on this same route as they journeyed to the resting place of James the apostle for religious reasons. For them, the trip was a solemn pilgrimage: They were pilgrims. Today, people have a variety of motivations for heading out on the Way of St. James. Nonetheless, for me and for most undertaking the trip, the walk was still a form of pilgrimage— we were pilgrims (or, as they say in Spain, we were peregrinos). We were looking for something. We were on the way to find rest for our souls. We were on the road to find out. This book, then, is also about my observations and reflections about the spiritual aspects of such a journey—about the path life has taken, about the road not traveled, and about the trail ahead.

This is an invitation to come and see what I found on the Way.

Stand at the crossroads and look;
ask for the ancient paths,
ask where the good way is, and walk in it,
and you will find rest for your souls.

Jeremiah 6:16

Prologue: The End of the Earth I

World Peace or Bacchanalian Feast?

Pilgrims on the way to Santiago have the opportunity for personal reflection and prayer as well as enjoying the fellowship of other pilgrims from many different countries. The pilgrimage is an opportunity for spiritual renewal and growth in personal faith.

Oficina de Acogida de Peregrinos

(Website: Official Pilgrim Welcome Office)

Jacob stepped up on a nearby rock to give himself a modest pedestal from where, with hands waving, he gathered everyone's attention: "Okay, okay, okay. . . . Now, we're all going to offer a toast to the Camino—in our native languages." Jacob then led the group with his own testimonial, in Polish. The group was spread out against the whitewashed back wall of the famous "land's end" lighthouse at Finisterre, where—almost two hours earlier—my new friend Jack, from Australia, and I had initially sat alone, setting out bread and wine and cheese and waiting for the sun to set.

After we had settled in with our backs up against the lighthouse wall, a number of pilgrims, some alone, some in groups of two or three, joined us—each opening their plastic grocery bags of baguettes, sala-mi, fruit, cheese, and wine and offering it to the others, who in a very real sense were strangers but in a very real sense were not. We were all pilgrims who had completed a shared journey. The scene felt a little like the old children's story about making stone soup as others joined the group offering their own addition to the communion.

Next up on the rock perch was one of my new friends from Russia. Serge and I had been chatting earlier about his life and work in Russia and a little about Soviet–U.S. politics. Serge (honestly, his name was "Serge" and, to complete the caricature, he offered me some vodka he had brought along for the sunset) was convinced—in a serious way—that the Camino would be a way to world peace. In very good English he shared with me, "Everybody on the Camino are just people. We're all pilgrims. We're not Russians or Americans or Poles. Nations would not have any problems between themselves if they could meet on the Cami-no." And that is probably what he shared with the group, in Russian, after he mounted our rocky podium. The scene was fun, even funny, and probably a little crazy, but it was also genuine and serious—despite the fact that everyone probably had a little too much wine.

The gathering consisted of thirteen or fourteen pilgrims who had just finished the Camino de Santiago (some having also walked the three days to Finisterre). Like a holiday meal with my wife, Cheryl's, family, everyone moved effortlessly and comfortably around the group to visit with one another, each peregrino leaving his or her smaller group of friends to reach out to the many others. Jack and I, of course, had met weeks ago in Hontanas. Jacob and I had actually caused mis-chief together helping to prepare a communal meal back in Carrión. Another who came by and joined the group was "Mike from Wales," with whom I had shared a room at the hostel in Azofra, twenty-three days earlier.

Then Natalia gave her confession about what the Camino had meant to her, in Italian of course. She was not, however, from Italy, but from the tiny, independent country of San Marino on Mount Tita-no in north central Italy. Who knew? Just a few minutes earlier I had been speaking in perfect English with the forty-one-year-old Natalia (well, I'm not sure my English was perfect) about her homeland and her Camino experience. A medical doctor and a serious Catholic, she was almost as tiny as her country, which consisted of just twenty-four square miles and thirty thousand inhabitants. Natalie's toast seemed to be exceedingly cheerful and engaging. I wish I could have understood it.

As apparently the only spokesman for the United States at this international conference (I'm not sure what Hillary Clinton, then Secretary of State, would have thought if she knew), I started to ponder what I would say atop that promontory, because in a most entertaining, but *very* persuasive manner, Jacob was making it clear that *everyone* was going to speak. And, for me, my native language was the only one that everyone would understand. So, while everyone else's "public" confessions about their time on the Camino were essentially private although spoken out loud to an attentive crowd, I quickly figured mine would not be so "private."

The setting sun had been to our left as we faced the rear of the lighthouse, but a cloud cover had rolled in denying us the opportunity of experiencing the iconic sunset over the "end of the earth." Two hours earlier, I had walked the three kilometers from the center of Finisterre to the lighthouse, which sits on a finger of land stretched out into the Atlantic Ocean. I was alone. Dan, my friend with whom I had started the Camino, had flown back to the U.S. early to see a doctor about his injuries. David (the medical student) and Juliana, who had traveled with me to this ancient destination, had their own reasons to be alone. (David planned to propose that evening.) I had left my most recent pilgrim friends in Santiago. I was very early for the sunset, excited for and determined not to miss out. The day had been clear and beautiful, holding out promise for a great finish. The late afternoon sky continued to suggest that a beautiful sunset at the end of the earth seemed promising—for many pilgrims it would be the ultimate way to finish an adventure on the Camino. Before running into Jack near the lighthouse, I would have time to reflect on the journey.

In reality, however, it was nearly impossible to consider adequately what had transpired after heading out from the south of France a month earlier.

CHAPTER 1

THE GATEWAY TO SPAIN
(DAY 0)

I have always regretted that we could not find time
to make a Pilgrimage to Saint Iago de Compostela.
John Adams

Dan and I began "our Camino" in the south of France, deep in the Basque country. We had become friends a few years earlier in our hometown of Richmond, Virginia, when I trained for and ran my first marathon; Dan was one of my coaches. (For anyone who has read my earlier book, *The Race Before Us*, my Camino companion was different from my running buddy in that book, although they are both named Dan.)

Walking the Camino today retraces one of various routes medieval pilgrims took through Europe to reach northern Spain, as they under-took a difficult journey to the shrine of St. James at the cathedral in Santiago. In the Middle Ages, pilgrims could not take planes, trains, or automobiles. Thus, the journey began as soon as they stepped out of their town or village in Germany or France or Scandinavia. The routes they took, therefore, were varied and numerous, but they tended to work their way through France, converge in St.-Jean-Pied-de-Port, and follow a similar route through northern Spain—which route, not surprisingly, became known as the "Camino Frances" or the "French Way."

Only modern-day, recreational adventurers seek to traverse a mountain range by going over its highest peaks. Rather, like water, explorers and frontiersmen seek the path of least resistance, looking for "gaps" or "passes" in a mountain range. (Thus, settlers in the United States traveled through the Cumberland Gap in the Appalachians and through the South Pass in the Rockies, rather than attempting to summit Clingman's Dome or Pike's Peak.) Not surprisingly then, the Camino Frances takes the easiest route through the Pyrenees—the route that Napoleon used to invade Spain in 1807. St.-Jean-Pied-de-Port offered a more manageable way through the Pyrenees and into Spain. After thousands of years, therefore, St. Jean became an important settlement at this doorway to Spain—it became the gateway (or the "port") to Spain—a port at the foot ("pied") of the mountains.

It was this Camino route that Dan and I planned to take to reach Santiago. Indeed, St. Jean has become the most popular, modern-day starting point for people attempting to hike the Camino de Santiago.

Dan and I got a glimpse of this history during our stop in Bordeaux a couple of days before we arrived in St. Jean. During a tour of St. Emilion, our guide explained how the historic route passed just outside the village, in part because the namesake of the village was an eighth-century Benedictine, Aemilianus, who developed a monastic community there, which pilgrims used as a stopping point on their way to Santiago. Likewise, on a tour of the city of Bordeaux, our docent pointed out a brass emblem of the city with artistic representations of the city's past, including a scallop shell below a sky of stars, recalling both its Camino past and the continued commercial importance of the Garonne River cutting crescent-shaped banks through the city. (We had learned in preparing for our trip that the scallop shell was a primary symbol of the Camino de Santiago.)

To get to St. Jean, Dan and I flew from Richmond to Paris and took a train to Bordeaux in southeast France. We enjoyed a brief, two-day stop in Bordeaux and St. Emilion and then continued south by train to the resort town of Bayonne. After transcontinental travel and a diversion to see one of the world's premier wine regions, the two-hour train to Bayonne helped us refocus on the primary purpose of our trip. And if our thoughts were not enough, when we got off the train in Bayonne to catch a local train to St. Jean, we followed two women with backpacks, each adorned with a scallop shell. Later that day, we both confessed that our hearts had bounced a little in seeing the scallop shells as the reality of the journey before us was coming to the forefront.

Dan and I headed into the station to determine from which track our train to St. Jean would leave. We learned that a bus was replacing our local train to St. Jean because a few days of rain had caused some washouts affecting the tracks. Outside the train station in Bayonne, a dozen people loitered around the bus pickup. With backpacks (some with scallop shells) and walking poles, and considering the destination, there was little doubt that these travelers would very soon be pilgrims on "the Way" with us.

With perfect weather and tangible evidence that this journey was real, we were eager to get started. Before long the bus arrived. We stored our packs in its belly and found a seat; mine happened to be in front of Father Jim, an Episcopal priest from Seattle. Jim was tall and vigorous, which masked his seventy-plus years. The bus ride took us deeper into the foothills of the Pyrenees, but interesting conversation with Jim and spectacular natural beauty caused the travel to pass quickly, despite two hours of rolling and twisting roads through rural villages set among the hills and meadows.

Finally, the bus dropped this new class of pilgrim recruits at the St. Jean train station. We had to make our way into town. We had three primary objectives. First, we had to procure our "Pilgrim Passport," which served at least two related purposes. Without this document, we would not be identified as "pilgrims" on the Camino, and we would not be able to stay in the albergues (also, sometimes called *refugios*) or "pilgrim hostels." (An albergue generally is a dormitory-style overnight quarters offering little more than a bed and shared bathroom facilities.) Furthermore, if you make it all the way to Santiago, you must present your Pilgrim Passport (*Credencial)* at the Pilgrim Office (*Accueil des Pelerins*) next to the cathedral to receive a *Compostela*—essentially, your "certificate of completion" of the journey. Second, Dan and I needed a room for the night. And, third, we planned to pick up a few supplies, such as snacks and lunch for the next day.

The merry band with whom we walked from the train station all headed into the ancient town and up the main street—narrow, steep, and cobbled—to the official Pilgrim Office. The line of new arriving pilgrims spilled out on the street where we took our place. After a short wait, despite limited English, volunteers greeted us and helped us register for our trek. They issued to us our *Credencial*, gave us a scallop shell for our backpack, and wished us well. "That wasn't too hard," we both thought. Jim, Dan, and I went back down the narrow main street and stopped in an outfitter store. The proprietor was a wonderful guy who had walked a number of the different caminos. His shop had everything a pilgrim might want or need for the journey to Santiago. Father Jim picked out a walking stick, and I purchased a broad-brimmed hat. Then, it was time to get a room for the night.

We walked the rest of the way down the narrow, bumpy, stone-paved Rue de la Citadelle toward the River Nive. A couple of days later I would meet Jim and Debbie—an older couple from Australia who traveled the same exact steps as we did the day before Dan and I arrived. Jim and Debbie had walked from the train station, into town and up the rough cobblestones to the Pilgrim Office. Unfortunately, they did so with a heavy backpack/carrier system that was designed to permit them to wheel—or at least *try* to wheel—their packs along the streets as well as on their backs.

Being self-deprecatingly humble, they explained how they bounced and dragged those wheely-packs up the rough, narrow, main street, which caused some of the locals to comment and laugh out loud at the sight. The couple, after procuring their Pilgrim Passports, rolled back down the street to the outfitter's shop and proceeded to buy new equipment that would hopefully permit them to backpack the Camino. Apparently they had been told or thought the trail was smooth enough to permit all their personal gear to be wheeled, like airport luggage, all the way to Santiago.

At the bottom of the ancient road through the center of St. Jean, we turned right at the Eglise Notre Dame, but not before ducking into the fourteenth-century church, then through the Navarre gate to find the B & B where Jim had a reservation (and where friends of ours from home had stayed the night before their walk began the previous summer). Those coincidences convinced us to see if there was room at the inn for two more peregrinos, or in French, *pelerins*. Just outside of the old town center, we found the B & B, and as luck would have it, the owner had two rooms available, which Dan and I said we'd take. We dropped our packs and headed back out to run errands.

On a delightful day with bright sunshine and moderate temperatures, we took a tour of old St. Jean, which I found to be an intriguing and attractive town as it retains a medieval atmosphere. We climbed back up the cobbled main street, past the Pilgrim Office, past the prison, to the Citadel by walking through the Porte Saint Jacque, which served as a gateway through the town's fortifications. The fifteenth-century gate, which welcomed pilgrims arriving from throughout France, is now a UNESCO World Heritage site. Not surprisingly, the fort is at a high point, which provides a wonderful view back down into the medieval town, out over the modern suburbs and rolling countryside, and up into the Pyrenees Mountains.

As we walked about the ancient village, we openly discussed our first crucial, existential question about the long walk we were about to undertake: How do you pronounce *buen Camino*? Dan had learned that this was the proper way to greet other pilgrims encountered on the Camino. Obviously, in addition to being a greeting, it was a way to wish others a good journey, but we were unsure whether it was "b'wayne" or "b'wain" or "b'when." We certainly didn't want to appear as uninitiated as we actually were, so we debated which pronunciation was correct and, while doing so, practiced the expression. I reasoned that if *buenos dias* is pronounced "b'wayn-os" (or "boo-wain-os") should *buen Camino* be pronounced "b'wayne"? Yet, when I used the pronunciation tool in the Merriam-Webster online dictionary, it sounded more like "b'when." (I would say it inconsistently for days and continued to ask others I'd encounter. Eventually, I settled on "b'when" —as in "b'when Camino.")

We found a supermarket and bought some items for our lunch (and snacks) the next day. When we stopped at a sidewalk café to get some dinner, we were reminded repeatedly that on the Way no one local eats dinner until 8:00 or 9:00 p.m. Even though we were not yet in Spain, St. Jean was on siesta time as well. This inconvenience was obviously small compared with the challenges faced by pilgrims nine hundred years ago. The first guide for taking this pilgrimage to Santiago referred to St. Jean as a place where evil tax collectors attacked pilgrims with clubs, coercing payment of duties as a condition of moving along the Camino.

Without a restaurant eager to take our euros in exchange for a meal, dinner became a communal sharing of wine, cheese, and French bread over good conversation with Jim and Dan about the state of faith and the church in the United States. In retrospect, it was perhaps the perfect meal before starting on this pilgrimage. We made final arrangements to get started in the morning and headed to bed. As I settled in for the night, I was energized to know that we had reached the starting gate timely, safely, and prepared (or at least I thought so). Tomorrow the adventure would begin—it was an exciting thought, positive and free of apprehension. As my family would say, we were eager but not anxious.

CHAPTER 2

CLIMBING THROUGH THE PYRENEES

(DAY 1)

*Pilgrims are people in motion—passing through
territories not of their own—seeking something we might
call completion, or perhaps the word clarity will do as well, a
goal to which only the spirit's compass points the way.*

Richard Niebuhr

[St.-Jean-Pied-de-Port, France, to **Roncesvalles, Spain**]1
(25.1 kilometers—15.6 miles)

The first day on the modern Camino de Santiago is also the most difficult hiking day of the entire journey. My trip started by getting separated from my travel partner before we ever took our first steps. Leaving France and heading for Spain, I headed up into the Pyrenees during a cool, cloudy, and misty morning. The climb was significant, with little respite from the continual ascent and little relief from cold, clouds, and rain. After crossing into Spain, the downhill proved

---

1 **Bold** lettering designates the towns in which I stayed overnight in an albergue or hotel. [Brackets] identify towns I travelled through without an overnight stop.

to be even more difficult than the climb. The ancient convent in Roncesvalles, having been converted into a pilgrim hostel, finally offered rest for tired pilgrims completing Day One of the five-hundred-mile trek.

Tuesday, April 8 (Day 1)

[St.-Jean-Pied-de-Port to Roncesvalles]

Father Jim, Dan, and I enjoyed a nice breakfast at our B & B at 7:00 a.m. It was cloudy and misty in St.-Jean-Pied-de-Port as we made final adjustments to our packs. We had been urged to keep our pack weight to twenty pounds, but I'm afraid mine weighed in closer to twenty-five pounds or just over ten kilos. The temperature was in the mid-forties—actually good for hiking. I made final decisions about what I was going to carry (leaving two books behind for the next pilgrim to use this B & B room) and brought my backpack down from my room. The three of us gathered in the house's main room and confirmed we were ready to head off and start our adventure. Dan mentioned, "Perhaps I should use the bathroom one more time before we leave." I replied, "Take your time. We have plenty of it." Dan went back upstairs and Jim stepped back into his first-floor room. I started fiddling with my pack trying to properly attach my trekking poles to it. Concerned I might damage our host's carpet, I stepped out the back door a few steps away and onto the slate patio.

A few minutes later I stepped in from the back door just as Jim walked in from his bedroom. I said, "Ready to go?" He concurred, but I wondered where Dan had gone. With my brow furrowed, I ran up the stairs to tell him we were all ready to go. But I could not find him or his pack. I came back down and reported my findings to Jim. "Where could he be?" I asked, not really directed to anyone. Answering my own question, I said, "Maybe he's out front?" So I checked—no Dan. "Where could he be?" I repeated.

At this moment, the proprietor came in and offered a response, "I think he left."

"No," I said, "there's no way he left without us."

Jim said, "You know, when I was in my room, I thought I heard the front door close."

I stepped out the front door again and walked the short distance to the street—no Dan! I returned and said again to Jim, "There's no way he left without us."

Without needing to offer a word, Father Jim's face provided a clear reply: "Then where might he be?"

Later we all realized, like a scene from a Marx Brothers' comedy, when I stepped outside and Jim stepped into his room, Dan came down the stairs. Not seeing Jim or me, thinking we had left without him, Dan ran up, grabbed his pack, said goodbye to the proprietor, and headed out the door toward town and the beginning of the Camino. And, to complete the comedy routine, just as Dan headed out the front door, I stepped in from the back door and Jim stepped in from his room. And I said to Jim, "Ready to go?"

Unsure where Dan might be, I did not know what to do. Jim and I decided to start into town, buy our baguettes as planned ("Maybe he's at the bakery"), and see if Dan might be in town. Despite glancing around the streets of St. Jean near the Way-marked path out of town, we never saw Dan. Again, I was a little panicked and wondered what to do. Was I really going to leave St. Jean and start on the Camino? I knew Cheryl would be disappointed if I headed off without him, but again—what to do?

We decided finally that Dan knew where we were headed for the day, so hopefully he'd catch up to us or we'd catch up to him. Thus, Jim and I decided to start our trip to Santiago. Before doing so, we stopped outside the fourteenth-century Eglise de Notre Dame and received a blessing for the journey. Jim, a priest, had written his own blessing, which he offered. I wish I could recall the specifics, but I admit to being genuinely moved by his words. Here, though, is the "Pilgrim Blessing" included on the passport we received the day before (taken from a seventeenth-century edition of the *Codex Calixtinus*):

In the name of our Lord Jesus Christ, receive this rucksack, the habit of your pilgrimage, so that, having atoned, you hasten to prostrate yourself at Saint James' feet, where you yearn to arrive and, after having completed your journey, you come to us joyful with the help of God, who rules over the world without end. Amen.

Receive this staff as support for the journey and your efforts during your pilgrimage so that you are able to overcome the hordes of enemies and thus arrive safely at Saint James' feet and, after having completed your journey, you come to us joyful with the assent of the same God, who lives and reigns forever and ever. Amen.

My "rucksack" was a 36-liter Osprey Stratos Airspeed-ventilated technical pack and my "staff" was a pair of Black Diamond alpine carbon cork trekking poles. With these modern versions of the pilgrim's equipment and a blessing from Father Jim, I should have been physically and spiritually prepared to embark on, as Steven Curtis Chapman sings, "a great adventure."

As we left the front of the church and walked east through town, we passed through two, medieval, protective gates—first, the porte de Notre Dame and then the porte d' Espagne. (My high school French reminded me, of course, that *porte* means "door"). Being a fortress town, these gates had been used to seal up the town within its fortifications when needed to repel invaders. Considering its location and the "ease" of moving through the mountains from this point (recall we were taking the "Napoleon Route"), this town had seen many battles where warring factions claimed, lost, and reclaimed the town numerous times throughout its history. We passed through the "door to Spain" and were off.

As it turned out, Dan had left before us and walked very quickly trying to catch up to us. He proceeded that way up and over the mountains all day. Jim and I would not see him until we got checked into the albergue in Roncesvalles. We would learn that, for some reason, Dan thought we had left without him when he had gone back upstairs to use the bathroom.

To say the weather was disappointing would certainly be an understatement. The forecast for the next day was perfect. I seriously considered waiting a day and had mentioned the idea to Dan. But we were excited to get going so we had decided the night before, like Eisenhower before D-Day, despite the weather we would go forward with our plans and head out the next morning. Jim and I were dressed in rain gear as we walked north out of town in a cool, light mist. A few other pilgrims were milling about town and heading in the same direction. After just a few minutes, we reached a congregation of pilgrims, some holding guidebooks, looking at a fork in the road and trying to determine which route to take. *Wow!* I thought, *Is it going to be this hard?* We were on a paved road, we had only walked for ten minutes and were not sure where we should go.

Jim, Dan, and I had planned to take what is known as the Napoleon Route (as opposed to the Via Valcarlos or the Valcarlos Route, which remains on or close to the vehicle road over the mountain. Valcarlos is the name of the town that is the approximate midpoint of this alternative route and now is more intended for vehicular traffic). I glanced at a way-marker sign and for a moment wondered if we were heading in the correct direction. I was a little confused—and a little stressed. The sign pointed a certain way—the way I thought we were to go—but it read "Chemin to St. Jacques," and I knew we wanted the "Camino de Santiago."

I knew we did not want to take the Valcarlos route. Jim and I stood there with other Day One pilgrims who appeared equally confused. (I had forgotten that when looking for the Camino in St. Jean-de-Pied-de-Port—a French town—one needs to keep an eye out for the word *chemin*, the French equivalent of *camino*.) Just as my high school French was coming back to remind me that "Chemin to St. Jacques" translated means "Camino de Santiago," another pilgrim insisted that the road up and to the left was the Napoleon Route.

Jim and I followed this small band in the direction indicated as many tapped out a path with their trekking poles on the street and sidewalk, a sound that would become familiar along the Camino. A few minutes later, a sign pointing right and down a different road confirmed that the Valcarlos route was that way, a way we were not heading. So, fairly certain we were now on the route, we began to stride up the hill with more confidence and real excitement, despite the cool, misty air. Up into the Pyrenees we headed, toward France's border with Spain, and then on to Roncesvalles (or, in French, Ronceveaux).

Almost immediately the path was steep and unrelenting as it rose through fields and forest. Various other pilgrims were starting the Way of St. James this morning also. The fog and mist turned to a light rain. The walk was very much a climb—a long, steady, fairly steep ascent. The weather worsened with no relief from the relentless climb. Jim and I walked in a light rain with a dozen or so other pilgrims ahead and behind as different hiking paces began to spread us out along the route, which continued to be a narrow but paved road—yet with no traffic. We had begun in rain gear and our packs were covered, so we trudged onward and upward. Visibility was limited, so even though we were missing some beautiful vistas, the wisps of clouds rising up the ridges offered their own fascinating natural sight.

The light rain continued, as did the persistent incline. For at least the first two hours, the route did not level off to provide a brief rest from the unrelenting slope. When we came to bends in the road, the next vista was more of the same: a path that continued up and up at what appeared to be a forty-five-degree slope into a ceiling of clouds that limited our horizon. So we couldn't anticipate a break or where the peak might be. Just as the cool, wet climb was wearing on me physically and mentally, we came upon a modest building and signage telling us we had reached the albergue at Orisson. We had not taken a single break during that morning's hike through fog and light rain. The idea of taking a rest break was compelling, and to do so in a warm, dry spot was almost irresistible. Thankfully, Jim concurred.

Jim and I entered the albergue and were greeted by warmth and a room full of wooden tables occupied haphazardly by pilgrims in a variety of clothing with backpacks strewn about—lying on the floor, leaning up against walls, and propped up against the ends of benches, creating puddles wherever they stood. It was around 11 a.m., and we had covered about eight kilometers or almost five miles. We had not seen Dan and wondered if he might be resting in this warm, humid room of thirty-odd other hikers also out on their first day on the Camino. Looking around, however, we had no such luck.

I learned that this albergue at Orisson is the only one of the Camino where you can make reservations. Many less vigorous hikers break the climb over the Pyrenees into two segments: first, a steep hike up to Orisson and then the remaining fifteen kilometers to Roncesvalles the next day. So no one gets stranded trying to complete the entire St. Jean-to-Roncesvalles trip in one day, Orisson accepts reservations and provides an evening meal for pilgrims who recognize the limits of their hiking abilities. The ladies Dan and I met in Bayonne with their scallop shells dancing off their backpacks were planning to spend their first night here.

I would meet a couple from Australia the following night who planned to stay at the Orisson hostel but starting walking on the Valcarlos route. When Jim and Debbie Wood arrived in Valcarlos, they learned that the way to their albergue for the night was on the Napoleon Route. To get to their hostel for the night, they had to go 11.3 kilometers back to St. Jean and then eight kilometers back up the Napoleon Route. Exhausted, they had no idea how they were going to accomplish that, but a taxi happened to come by, brought them down the mountain, and then back up the proper route. When they were delivered to the albergue at Orisson they didn't have enough cash to pay for the taxi, but a local came out and paid the cab fare for them. If that wasn't a tough enough way to start your journey, this was the same couple that, the day before, had thought they could roll their luggage all the way to Santiago.

Jim and I spied an empty table in the back of the room, pulled off our rain jackets, and set down our packs. The bar at the opposite end was busy passing cups of coffee and bowls of hot soup to many of the pilgrims—both of which looked perfect for a couple more cold, wet pilgrims. Deciding to pass on the heated items, we pulled out our baguettes, fresh that morning, added salami and butter, and enjoyed an early lunch. We glanced at our guidebooks to confirm our progress and note what still awaited us. We more than welcomed a chance to rest, dry out, and refresh indoors. After a forty-five-minute break, we felt much better—warmed and almost dry, so off we went, enthused, into the cool mist to resume the seemingly relentless climb.

As we continued to gain altitude, the weather improved somewhat. The mist and rain began to lift, and the skies looked as if they might clear. We caught a glimpse of blue sky and, for a brief moment, we could look back from where we came and see a nearby ridge with wisps of white mist rising and dancing from below. We took a break at Pic D'Orisson, where a statue of the Virgin looks out over a valley (and where in medieval times a pilgrim hostel or "hospital" once sat). We could sense, but could not see, the majesty of the scene before us due to the mist and clouds. Guidebooks tell us that to the east we can see Somport Pass, another spot or "pass" where crossing the Pyrenees is more manageable, and thus, where the Camino Aragones runs before it joins the French Way in Puente La Reina.

Jim and I took off our rain gear. We both felt good. The drier air and cool temperature was quite good for our hike. While we lingered at the lookout, we met a couple from Seoul, and also met Gale and David Armstrong, who stopped and visited with us. Father and son, Gale is from Alaska, David is now from Austin, Texas, where he teaches college English. We had not caught Dan but learned from the them that Dan was ahead of us; Dan had walked along with them earlier that morning.

We walked with Gale and David for some time. I listened in as Gale and Jim discussed the Eastern Orthodox Church and their admiration for its emphasis on and use of music in worship services. The weather took a turn for the worse, but the rain did not resume. The heavy air and light mist never cleared—stated simply, we were walking through a cloud. Jim and I discussed the reports we had read about how change-able and dangerous the weather could be in the Pyrenees.

As recently as two weeks before we arrived in St. Jean, a serious rescue had occurred along this route because of a late spring snowfall. Jim asked, "What is the first thing one should do if lost or in weather crisis?"

Having been a canoe guide in the North Maine Woods, I thought I should know the answer. I thought for a moment, determined to get the right response, and then said, "You should sit down and assess your situation."

Apparently correct or close enough, Jim nodded and added, "A person can live three minutes without oxygen, three days without water, three weeks without food, and only three months without love." It sounded pretty accurate to me, even to some extent, the statement about love.

The hiking became less steep but continued upward. We left the narrow paved road and passed an emergency shelter (for those caught in "dangerous, changeable weather"). After another kilometer of fairly level hiking, we circled a prominent hill and came upon the border between Spain and France; however, it was not immediately obvious—the sign said "Navarra" and "Nafarroa."

The signage at the border reminded us that we were in Basque Coun-try with its history of fierce independence and a separate language. (The guidebook indicates that it is "the oldest living language in Europe.") We had entered the Navarre (*Navarra* in Spanish and *Nafarroa* in Basque), an autonomous political region in northern Spain that borders the Basque country. St. Ignatius of Loyola and St. Francis of Xavier, two of Christendom's greatest missionaries and founders of the Jesuit order, came from the area. Loyola is a castle in the Basque country where Igna-tius was born, and Xavier is a castle in Navarre where Francis was born.

Near this border is Roland's Fountain, a memorial to Charlemagne's nephew, who legend says sacrificed himself while protecting Char-lemagne's flank in 778 as they were returning to France (taking the Valcarlos route) after fighting the Muslims in Spain. (Another mon-ument to Roland is in Roncesvalles, which pilgrims can see along the

Camino path as they enter the small village.) While I had no recall other than the poem's title, this history is recorded in "Le Chanson de Roland"—an eleventh-century epic poem of chivalry I studied (or at least tried to read) in high school French class.

I knew little about the Basque country, just some about the separatist movement and violent protests that have arisen from time to time. Mostly, the ancient culture has resisted being assimilated (or eliminated) by both the French and the Spanish at different times in history. In response to what was seen by them as more repressive action by the government in the 1950s, a resistance group—known as the ETA—arose and often used violence to keep their drive for independence alive. In the 1990s and into the first decade of this century, pilgrims on the Way may not have been targets of the ETA, but prudence demanded caution when walking through this region. This was a concern of modern pilgrims until recently. German comedian Hape Kerkeling reported that during his time on the Camino in 2001, there was "a major attack in Logroño by the ETA." Since 2011, however, this primary Basque resistance group has maintained a ceasefire.

We left the open meadows and entered wooded terrain not long after crossing the France-Spain border. Visibility remained poor as clouds still blanketed the mountaintop. Jim decided to hang back to do some photography in the forest. Our guidebook explained that this beech forest is "one of the largest remaining" in Europe. While Jim saw beauty in the mist and trees, I remained more focused on the trail and making progress to Roncesvalles. (That night, Father Jim showed me some of his photographs from the beech trees in the mist, which were stunning.) I proceeded along and gently down with Gale and David. We slogged through mud, heavy leaves, drifts of snow, and portions of the trail that had turned into small, temporary mountain streams.

After rolling along at the top of the pass, the trail finally summited at a spot known as Col de Lepoeder, which is at approximately 1,450 meters or 4,757 feet—not as tall as Mount Washington on the Appalachian Trail at 6,684 feet. I had hiked that second-highest peak in the eastern United States during college. From there, we knew it was all downhill, so we headed off at a measured rate. After a short time, the Armstrongs stopped to rest. Still cold, I decided to move along, hiking by myself for the first time on the trip. This pattern would repeat itself for most of my journey—I enjoyed sharing the path with other pilgrims and meeting new friends, but I equally enjoyed having time to walk alone and be within God's amazing creation with just my thoughts and prayers.

Climbing down the backside of the mountains proved to be an even greater challenge as fatigue began to set in. The weather returned to fog and mist, which prevented me from experiencing the magnificent scenery I had seen in many of the blogs and websites I visited in preparing for the Camino—and again I wondered if we should have delayed our trip even just one day.

With less than five kilometers to go, the final descent into Roncesvalles became even more steep and monotonous—so much so that I had to ease myself down the path, more walking than hiking. I was ready for the day to end, but my enthusiasm for the first day of the trip carried me along. The misty cloud cover began to lift and the sky brightened some. Like taking a deep breath to make some final concerted effort, I stopped, took off my rain jacket, tightened my laces, and pressed on, conjuring a final dose of determination.

Without quite realizing I had completed the descent, I finally spilled out of the woods into an opening. I crossed a small stream and stepped into an empty parking lot just below the ancient convent—now converted into a hostel for those, like me, heading for Santiago. I could appreciate the words of Hape Kerkeling, who said about his first day on the Camino: "I feel as though I traveled through a foggy birth canal to get to Roncesvalles."

I followed yellow arrows up a slight hill, circled a collection of buildings including a historic chapel, and found my way to the albergue. Remarkably, this scene really was not much different seven or eight centuries earlier when medieval peregrinos climbed through the same mountain pass and found refuge for the evening at a hostel or "hospital" run by the local nuns.

The first pilgrim hostel opened in Roncesvalles in the twelfth century and, as captured in an ancient poem (reprinted in some of our materials), it welcomed anyone: "The door opens to all, sick and healthy, not only to true Catholics, but also to pagans, Jews, heretics, the idle and vagabonds." Even in the twenty-first century, most pilgrims stop at Roncesvalles after a twenty-five-kilometer hike from St. Jean because little daylight or strength (or even enthusiasm) remains after this first and most difficult day of the month-long journey to the northwest corner of Spain.

The hostel in Roncesvalles is the historic convent that welcomed pilgrims for hundreds of years, which today has been fashioned into a large, modern, organized, friendly, and clean albergue. Just before entering the reception area, Dan and I ran into each other—perhaps moderated by fatigue, we looked at each other with a grin, both thinking the same thing: *Well, things didn't start out quite as we planned.* Dan walked me through the registration process as I tried to ask him why he thought we might have left without him that morning.

I deposited my hiking shoes in a separate room reserved for that purpose, found my assigned bunk, and then took a much-needed shower. Father Jim arrived and was assigned a bed nearby. Dan, Jim, and I then went out into the small village with Ed Montgomery, whom we met earlier in the day, for a "pilgrim meal" together. We finished our dinner just in time to run to the pilgrim mass back at the chapel within the convent. Being almost completely in Spanish, it was hard to appreciate, but I was grateful for the priests who provided each of us with a blessing as they did every evening for pilgrims heading to Santiago.

After the pilgrim mass, I quickly retired to my bunk and tried to catch up on some email and blog updates, but the albergue's Wi-Fi (pronounced "wee—fee" in Spain) was not very useful. As I prepared for mandatory "lights out" at 10 p.m., I paused long enough to note briefly to myself what a remarkable day it had been, and again recalled how in many ways it had been similar to that experienced by millions in medieval times.

CHAPTER 3

WHO? WHAT? WHERE? WHY?

Our situation on this earth seems strange.
Every one of us is here involuntarily and
uninvited for a short stay, without
knowing the whys and the wherefores.

Albert Einstein

At the end of Day One on the Camino, I had checked into the only albergue in Roncesvalles where the friendly, efficient, and English-speaking staff and eager volunteers helped me get settled into the former convent and medieval pilgrim hospital. In addition to showing us where to leave our hiking shoes and collecting a ten-euro note for a bed, our host asked us to complete a questionnaire about our journey. Among the questions, set out in four different languages, was whether you were walking the Camino as (1) a religious activity, (2) a spiritual activity, (3) a sports adventure, or (4) for another reason. I paused and thought for a moment: Why were all of these people, from various parts of the world, carrying backpacks and walking almost five hundred miles to Santiago?

When I returned to the United States after my journey on the Camino de Santiago, I got three different reactions from most Americans. First, most had not a clue as to what the Camino Real was (as they often mis-pronounced it). I spoke with church pastors who had never heard of it. Second, some had a vague notion: "Is that the religious walk in Spain?" or "Wasn't Charlie Sheen in a movie about that?" (Well, almost—Martin Sheen was in such a movie, directed by his other son, Emilio Estevez.)

Then there was a third group: a small minority who knew something about the Camino and would inevitably ask right away, "Did you walk the whole thing (or the whole way)?"

Hmm, I'd think for a moment, *the "whole way"?* I knew what they meant, though. They were asking if I had done the five-hundred-mile walk from southern France to the city of Santiago in northwest Spain.

Historically, individuals undertook the walk to Santiago de Compos-tela as "a religious activity." Not just some general undefined religious activity, but a Christian activity—a journey taken by Christians for spe-cific reasons related to their faith. The destination for this pilgrimage of course was, and remains, the religious shrine of one of the apostles of Jesus Christ—the tomb of St. James at the Cathedral de Santiago de Compostela. Indeed, I was heading for Santiago, a city, but I knew also that Santiago was a person, St. James, for whom the city was named. As a reminder, I noticed that printed on my *Credencial* (the "passport" that allowed me to check into the albergue in Roncesvalles) is this Pilgrim's Prayer:

> *St James, Apostle, chosen among the first, you were the first to drink the cup of the Master and you are the great protector of pilgrims. Make us strong in faith and happy in hope on our pil-grim journey, following the path of Christian life, and sustain us so that we may finally reach the glory of God the Father. Amen.*

Long before Dan and I boarded a plane to Paris or a train to the south of France, I asked a lot of questions about the Camino de San-tiago. When I started to learn more about the journey to Santiago de Compostela, I could generally understand why a Christian might un-dertake a pilgrimage to Jerusalem (the "Holy Land") or even to Rome (the home of the Vatican and St. Peter's Cathedral), but I wondered (and I assumed that inquiring minds would want to know), "Why Santiago? Why walk to Santiago? What makes Santiago so important?"

I learned that "Santiago" was an old form of Spanish (*Sant Iago or San Tiago*) for "Saint James." James is an English variant of the name Jacob, which comes from the Latin, *Iacobus*. Hence, in many places, the journey to Santiago is referred to as the "Jacobean pilgrimage." So, perhaps we should pause long enough to ask—as I did before I took my first step on the Way—who was St. James? What is a pilgrimage to Santiago? Why would Christians walk to that destination? And why are pilgrims along the Way today?

The James of Santiago renown is the fisherman, son of Zebedee and brother of John, both of whom we meet in the New Testament. Jesus called them to be his disciples. Sometimes this James is referred to as "James the Greater," because another "younger" or "lesser" James was also a disciple of Jesus. Some tradition suggests that James the Greater may have first been a disciple of John the Baptist.

Church tradition says that, after Jesus' resurrection, James traveled and preached the gospel message around Galicia—what is today northwest Spain. A reference to James as the "great evangelist of Spain" by the official pilgrim website indicates scholarly and literary support for that tradition. It is not surprising that a Christian evangelist would concentrate his efforts in Galicia and the "end of the earth" because that region already held great spiritual significance. The earliest Christian evangelists would go not only to Jewish temples but pagan worship sites to preach the good news. Like Paul's presentation at the Aeropagus in Athens, Christian speakers found an audience receptive to the good news of Jesus in those already inclined to believe in God or a god. Some also believe that the Virgin Mary appeared to James when he was in the Iberian Peninsula and instructed him to build a church in Zaragoza. In fact, legend provides that the Iglesia de Pilar, which still stands today, is that church.

The Bible recounts that James was one of the first apostles martyred. King Herod Agrippa had him killed by the sword in A.D. 42 as part of an early persecution of the Church. Tradition says that James' disciples (Atanasius and Theodore) then brought his remains to the ancient port of Iria Flavia in Padron, near present-day Santiago, and buried them in Galicia. For hundreds of years, history records nothing about St. James in this area, which was under Roman control for two hundred years prior and hundreds of years after the birth of Christ.

Early in the eighth century, a faction of Visigoths traveled to Islamic Africa to seek support for their regional conflicts on the Iberian Peninsula. With the fall of the Roman Empire, the area had been unstable politically for many years. The Muslims who came from Morocco, referred to by the Iberian inhabitants as "Moors," arrived in strength and ultimately conquered most of what we think of today as Spain. The presence of the Islamic people from Africa on the Iberian Peninsula would play a key role in the future of Spain and in the rise of St. James as the patron saint of the country, particularly as it concerned the "Reconquista"—the effort by Christian kings to take back control of Spain from the Moors.

In the ninth century, St. James would be reintroduced to the Spanish people in a very significant manner. Tradition holds (recorded in the *Codex Calixtinus*) that a hermit or shepherd named Pelayo had a vision of a bright star that led him to a field where the body of St. James was discovered. To be sure, the local bishop confirmed the find. (Some date this event more precisely to the year A.D. 813.) Hence, the area acquired the name Compostela (or "campus stellae") meaning "field of stars." Now, of course, the area is a city called Santiago de Compostela.

Upon locating the remains of St. James, King Alfonso II built a chapel to the saint, probably at the burial site. Some sources indicate this first shrine was established in A.D. 829. At this same time, Christian kings were attempting to retake control of Spain from the Moors. In 844, during the Battle of Clavijo, St. James is credited with appearing in a vision on a white horse to help defeat the Moors, which led to referring to St. James as "Santiago Matamoros," or the "Moor-Slayer." This and other victories in the Reconquista attributed to his "appearance" confirmed James as the patron saint for the region; however, historians generally agree that the Battle of Clavijo itself is pure legend. Yet, James remains the patron saint of the Spanish people today.

With a reawakening of St. James' presence in Galicia and the success of the Reconquista, pilgrimages to Santiago began. Pilgrimages to Jerusalem and Rome were already popular by the ninth century. (Many historians point to Emperor Constantine's mother—Helena—as the first to make a pilgrimage to Jerusalem, which she did in the fourth century.) The first recorded pilgrimage to Santiago was by a French bishop from Le Puy who led a group of Christians in 950. Presumably to encourage such journeys, King Alfonso VI abolished tolls along the Camino in 1072. Resolving to establish a more appropriate shrine to St. James, local kings and the Church began construction of the current Romanesque cathedral as early as 1075, completed in the 1120s. The Cathedral de Santiago, of course, has been renovated and embellished since that time, including the addition of the baroque façade in the eighteenth century.

Pilgrimages grew in the eleventh century and exploded in the twelfth century. Perhaps the most crucial step in fueling an increased interest in this pilgrimage occurred in 1122 when Pope Calixtinus II granted the city of Compostela the privilege of giving plenary indulgences to those completing the pilgrimage in a Holy Year (when Saints Day falls on a Sunday)—a status equaling that of pilgrims traveling to Jerusalem or Rome. The website of the Official Pilgrim Office confirms these developments as follows: "Though a few pilgrims to Santiago are recorded in the 10th century, and many more in the 11th, it was in the early 12th century, and particularly under the energetic promotion of Archbishop Diego Gelmírez (1100–1140), that Santiago came to rank with Rome and Jerusalem as one of the great destinations of medieval pilgrimage."

Also in the twelfth and thirteenth centuries, the French helped to popularize the Camino for commercial and political reasons. Around 1139, a French priest—Aymeric Picaud—produced the *Codex Calixtinus,* a five-volume work about St. James and the Camino de Santiago. It was named after incumbent Pope Callixtus II and is often referred to as "The Book of St. James." The fifth book was a travel guide—a "Michelin Guide"—for pilgrims heading out along the Way. By providing specific details about the route—river crossings, accommodations, shrines to various saints, local customs, dangers, and the like—the *Codex* helped spurred a rise in pilgrimages to Santiago.

The idea of taking a pilgrimage to Santiago thus gained broad popularity and the number of pilgrims grew considerably. Monastic and other religious orders like the Benedictines, Augustinians, and Cistercians developed "hospitals" and other infrastructure to care for and support individuals on their journey. Spanish kings saw benefit as well and commissioned road improvements and institutions along the route. Also, religious-military orders like the Knights Templar arose to protect pilgrims from violence and thievery often encountered on the Way of St. James. Historians believe that over half a million pilgrims made their way on the Camino each year during the Middle Ages, especially in the twelfth and thirteenth centuries, which is sometimes referred to as the "golden age" for pilgrimages to Santiago.

With these developments, St. James took on a different image—one of a pilgrim, "Santiago Peregrino" as opposed to the Moor-Slayer, "Santiago Matamoros." Thus, the symbols representative of this more humble personage are a walking staff, robe, wide-brim hat, and scallop shell.

Due to significant doctrinal issues raised by the Reformation, the number of pilgrims heading out on the way to Santiago inevitably declined. Many Protestant theologians saw pilgrimages as improperly emphasizing man's role in salvation, whereas a key tenet of the Reformation was salvation "by faith alone" apart from works—and a pilgrimage sounded a lot like man's "works." Inevitably, the Enlightenment also helped to undermine interest in the historic pilgrimage as modern society increasingly saw reason and science as replacing faith and God.

By the eighteenth century, the annual number of pilgrims on the Way to St. James apparently had fallen to around thirty thousand. Perhaps consistent with that estimate, when John Adams visited Santiago in 1779, having been sidetracked on a mission to Paris to raise funds for the American Revolutionary War, he observed, "Upon the Supposition that this is the place of the Sepulcher of Saint James, there are great numbers of Pilgrims, who visit it, every Year, from France, Spain, Italy and other parts of Europe, many of them on foot." Typically thought of as being more pious than his "enlightened" rival from Virginia, Adams noted his disappointment that he did not "find time to complete a Pilgrimage to Sant Iago de Compostela."

Most historians suggest that by the nineteenth century, walking the Camino de Santiago essentially died out. With the world being consumed by two world wars and a devastating depression, it is not surprising that the historic pilgrimage remained but a footnote. What happened late in the twentieth century, however, few could have predicted. No one could have foreseen the resurgence of interest in walking the Camino. Although the number of pilgrims recorded in the 1970s never exceeded more than a handful, by 1999 over 150,000 appeared at the Pilgrim Office to receive their *Compostela*. A rebirth had certainly occurred. Thousands throughout the world began to think about heading off on a pilgrimage to Santiago.

Like the two marathons I ran in the late 1970s, my decision to walk the Camino did not occur as a great, original thought. Perhaps similar to the running boom that occurred when I was in college, I was attracted to a new phenomenon whose popularity was on the rise. Maybe, then, I was just caught up in a new fad. That said, something made the idea quite compelling. Was it the challenge of a long hike? Other than a walk to a historic, holy place, was a trip on the Camino de Santiago something else, something more? Was it a pilgrimage, and how might I understand exactly what that is?

I turned my attention back to the form I had been asked to complete—religious activity? Sports adventure? Thinking of the people I had encountered on my first day, the reasons did seem diverse from what I could pick up in our conversations. Jim was a priest. Gale and David talked openly about their worship at the Eastern Orthodox Church—their journey seemed to be a "religious activity." Religious motivation may have been part of Jeff's or Carol's or Ed's purpose for climbing over the Pyrenees, but it was not open or obvious. From my investigation, the reasons people walked the Camino in the present day were considerably more diverse that in medieval times, when it clearly was a religious activity. People on the Camino then were true pilgrims.

The official website of the Pilgrim Office in Santiago (where I would get my *Compostela* after completing the trek) says the following about "Why People Walk Camino":

> *We urge you to think about your motives for wishing to make the pilgrimage to Santiago. Traditionally these fell into three categories: from a personal desire; to complete a vow; or in atonement for sins. Some people may be attracted to the cultural aspects of the journey. These entirely complement the religious heart of the Camino and indeed making the Way often leads the pilgrim to draw closer to God.*
>
> *Here are some of the reasons which pilgrims give for making the pilgrimage:*
>
> * *To find oneself*
> * *To find the meaning of one's life*
> * *To find a favourable environment to think and reflect*
> * *To fulfill a promise*
> * *To meet other pilgrims*
> * *To follow millions of others that have done the Way over the centuries*
> * *To learn more of the culture and art along the Way*
> * *To honour St James, one of Jesus' Apostles*
> * *To deepen and enrich faith in God*

I had finished Day One. As Steven Curtis Chapman sings in "Long Way Home," I had "set out on a great adventure." I had to ask myself, though, was it a religious activity? Was I on a pilgrimage?

For me, I considered it a pilgrimage. Just six months earlier I had published a memoir (*The Race Before Us: A Journey of Running & Faith*) about running and the exploration of religious faith. The book's primary title attempts to evoke thoughts and purpose similar to pilgrimage. In becoming convinced of the truth of Christianity, the next step was to gain an even deeper understanding of what such realities meant for every aspect of life. For me, then, my time of the Camino was another *journey*—a physical trek, but primarily time to reflect more deeply as to how I should live the rest of my life. To do that, I wanted to have some prolonged periods of solitude so I might "look forward and look back" at my life, and to genuinely consider how a Christian worldview informs life's biggest questions.

I checked the appropriate box, finished the other questions, and handed the form back to the volunteer host.

CHAPTER 4

"790 KILOMETERS"

(DAY 2)

The idea of taking a six-week walk is totally foreign to most Americans. But it's probably exactly what we need.

Emilio Estevez

[Roncesvalles—*Burguete, Viscarret,* **Zubiri]**
(21.9 kilometers—13.6 miles)

In some respects, the trip to Santiago begins as you leave Roncesvalles. The climb over the mountain pass through the Pyrenees is a special journey complete in itself. No day on the Camino would come close to the first day—a considerable test by itself, an initiation. The expression, "There's no turning back now," takes on special meaning with an exclamation point when you have successfully crossed over not just a border between two countries but a mountain pass with severe slopes both coming and going that you are not likely to want to repeat anytime soon. In fact, I learned that many Spaniards begin their journey here rather than St. Jean. One of my best Camino friends, Carmen, from southeast Spain (with whom I would walk into Santiago), started her adventure at Roncesvalles, the same day I awoke in the albergue there. (I would not meet Carmen, however, for eleven days.)

Wednesday, April 9 (Day 2)

[Roncesvalles to Zubiri]
(21.9 kilometers—13.6 miles)

A few steps out of Roncesvalles is a road sign for vehicular traffic that reads: "Santiago de Compostela—790 km." Because the Camino walking path west runs right by the street here, many pilgrims take a photograph next to this sign, as did Dan and I. Early morning dew hung in the air, but we could see that the rising sun would soon clear the air. Work and commitments actually felt as far away as they were. Eager and excited, we headed off together.

Not long before Dan and I stopped by the "790 km" road sign, we were asleep in our bunks back in the former, medieval pilgrim hospital. I woke around 5:30 a.m. Most of hostel was still asleep, so I quietly used the bathroom and brushed my teeth. Within thirty minutes, however, everyone was up and about. As I was packing, Dan came by and said he was ready and wanted to get started early.

We met at the front door of the albergue around 7:00 a.m. The air was cool and the sun was still hidden, but the forecast was exceptional. We headed into the darkness but saw an optimistic red glow at the horizon. We took the road sign photographs, donned our headlamps, and stepped off. The pleasant, earthen path underfoot took us through light woodlands. My trekking poles clicked lightly as we moved along. I was excited to be walking again and the forecast filled me with an even greater enthusiasm.

After an easy three kilometers, Dan and I reached the small Navarra village of Burguete (apparently frequented by Ernest Hemingway) and stopped for coffee—actually café con leche. The "coffee" in Spain proved to be exceptional, the first day and every day. Americans, like me, generally drink what others call "filtered coffee." To over-simplify, Europeans generally start with pure espresso and either drink that as is or add steamed milk to it to create *café latte* (in France) or café con leche (in Spain). As my Camino continued, almost every morning, I enjoyed—thoroughly enjoyed—a cup or two of café con leche, which could be obtained at almost any bar in any town. I quickly realized that a "bar" in Spain served the traditional function Americans likely think of for a bar (a place to enjoy alcoholic beverages and socialize) as well as serving as a morning café (a place for coffee, light breakfast items, and socializing).

The morning was great for walking—cool, dry, and bright. The initial eight kilometers were relatively flat, punctuated occasionally with a few serious, but brief, uphill climbs. Three or four kilometers after Burguete, we walked through Espinal, another quaint, Basque town and then back into some light wooded areas alongside farmland. Dan was a few steps ahead. Without saying anything to him, I stopped to shed a layer of clothes. An opening in the trees beckoned me to take in the broad expanse of farmland with the foothills of the Pyrenees as a backdrop. I gave into the temptation, soaked in the scene, and took some photos—it was really magnificent. I delayed even longer when two teachers from England popped through the same opening in the woods and came out into the same morning beauty. We visited for a few minutes. They had only two weeks for the Camino.

When I departed from these ladies I was on my own—Dan was many minutes ahead, but I was not eager to rush. I could not believe how majestic this early April day was. I seemed to enjoy a heightened sense of awareness. The usual stress of the day had been vanquished by international travel and a stern climb over the border mountains. I found myself slowing to notice in greater detail than usual the evidences of spring that seemed to be reaching out to me, crying for notice: trees just beginning to bud, overactive songbirds fighting for airtime, and wild flowers blooming all about. I sensed something different, or at least more intense—something I can describe only as a real, inner joy and calm. This special morning of walking remains among my most vivid memories of the journey, perhaps because the prelude had ended and the symphony of the Camino was just beginning in earnest. When I look back upon it now, that morning holds together almost as a lyric poem. I certainly cannot put myself in C.S. Lewis's shoes, but

I've wondered if my morning out of Roncesvalles was anything like his experiences where he was "surprised by joy."

I came out of my communion with God and His creation as I caught up to and met Justin (from Seattle) just outside of a tiny hamlet. We walked into town together to find Dan waiting for me. Justin was having serious blister problems, which surprised me because he had been telling me about a 1,400-kilometer pilgrimage walk to eighty-eight temples in Japan he had taken the previous year. I enjoyed another cup of coffee and other half of the baguette I bought on the first morning (right after Dan went AWOL). We rested at a picnic table and met an older American, who had just come in from Persian Gulf where he did ship repair, and a young American woman who had come to Spain via Madagascar. Dan headed out again without me while I relaxed and visited with my new friends.

After a twenty-five-minute break, Justin and I walked out of town together into the Basque countryside. The day was still incredibly cool and pleasant. I climbed some modest hills and then caught up with Jeff from Scranton, whom I had met the previous afternoon on the backside of the mountains coming down into Roncesvalles. As we enjoyed pleasant hiking through dense, mixed woodland, we talked about his work as a state trooper. This walk included a number of short but steep hills followed by some immediate descents. If we had been trying to summit a mountain, the numerous descents neutralized any progress we made climbing the hills.

We walked by a monument reminding us again that Charlemagne and Roland had passed that same way, and then through a couple of small villages, including the tiny hamlet of Linzoain where the local thirteenth-century Romanesque church is named for Saint Saturnino. Curiously, Saturnino is a French saint, which seems odd until we are reminded that the French played a significant role in developing and popularizing the Way of St. James—and that we are on the Camino Frances.

Eventually we came to a clearing next to a road where a couple of plastic tables surrounded by bright red plastic chairs sat by a food van, set up to sell sandwiches and drinks to pilgrims. A number of pilgrims, including Carol (Jeff's wife) were there relaxing. Jeff and I ordered a chorizo sandwich and a cervesa. We sat and visited with the group. Perhaps recalling the magnificent morning, I decided I needed more solitary hiking, so after a pleasant visit, I headed out on my own.

Like a number of our new friends we met in Roncesvalles, our destination that day was Larrasoana. I came to a bridge that led pilgrims off the trail and into the town of Zubiri. Larrasoana was another five kilometers down the path. I wondered if Dan was there or had moved on to Larrasoana. I had run into and was walking with two French women who were heading into Zubiri. I followed them, thinking I'd check to see if Dan might be there.

Crossing the River Arga on an impressive Gothic bridge (the Puente de la Rabia), I entered Zubiri ("village of the bridge"). The abutment of the bridge was said to contain relics of St. Quiteria. Tradition says a person could rid livestock of rabies by driving them three times around the central pillar of the bridge—hence, "Bridge of Rabies." I found Dan immediately, or I should say, he found me. Resting on a bench outside an albergue, Dan spotted me coming over the stone footbridge.

I checked into the albergue in Zubiri that Dan had selected and took my bunk below him. Across the room—yet close enough that, lying on our bunks, if we reached out our arms we could touch hands—were two twenty-something women from Germany. We talked about their hometown and their travel on the Camino to date. Also in the room, almost as close, were an older couple from Australia and a middle-aged couple from Korea. I introduced myself to the older woman Dan had told me was from Australia. "Hi," I said. "I hear you're from Australia. My name is Bruce."

Immediately she gave a big, welcoming smile and a laugh and said, "Oh come on—what's your real name?"

I said, "Bruce. Really, my name's Bruce."

"Oh," she replied. "I thought you were pulling my leg because many tease people from Australia that everyone's name is Bruce. You know, 'Hi Bruce,' or 'Yeah, I'm Bruce.'" She finished, a little embarrassed, by adding, "I'm Debbie. My husband is Jim. He just stepped out to check on something with the manager."

We laughed about my name and its apparent use as somewhat of a generic (like, "You can call me Joe...") in Australia, but I quickly added (in part to reassure her), "It really is 'Bruce.' My ancestors came from Scotland. I'm a 'Campbell' and 'Bruce' is very Scottish—remember Robert the Bruce, the first king of Scotland?"

Dan and I decided to finish the beautiful day with a celebratory drink. The albergue's proprietor recommended a nearby restaurant with a pilgrim menu. We enjoyed an afternoon beer outside and decided to stay for dinner. It helped that our server Natalia spoke fairly good English and could explain the menu choices. I followed Natalia's recommendations and had the most local dishes—white bean, tomato, and chorizo soup, grilled cuttlefish (similar to calamari), and milk custard for dessert. The meal also came with water, wine, and bread. The meal was exceptional and, for ten euros, a tremendous bargain. Little would I know that this would be one of the very best "pilgrim meals" I'd enjoy or that the opportunity to discuss the menu with the server would be so rare. We would soon learn that most local merchants along the Camino did not speak English.*

We returned to the Albergue Zaldiko and our cramped quarters with the German women and the couples from Korea and Australia. Before the mandatory lights out, I worked on my journal and my blog. All in all, particularly when compared with the weather and the climb the previous day, Day Two was a fairly easy day of rolling forest pathways and ever-present mountain streams. For me, the day's walk had been exhilarating, as we gently had exited the foothills of the Pyrenees while enjoying a special day in northern Spain as spring continued to reveal itself with every step.

CHAPTER 5

NEW FRIENDS AND NEW ROUTINES
(DAYS 3–4)

An early-morning walk is a blessing for the whole day.

Henry David Thoreau

[**Zubiri**—*[Larrasoana]*, **Pamplona**, *[Cizur Menor]*, *[Zariquiegui]*, *[Alto de Perdon]*, *[Uterga]*, *[Eunate Church]*, **Puente La Reina**]

(44.5 kilometers—26.7 miles)

After a physically challenging first day and a spiritually exhilarating second day, I started to fall into a routine. Days three, four, and five were not days of intense inner or outer journeys. Rather, I began to develop new friends from all parts of the world as we headed in the same direction and began to enjoy the Camino and all it offers. In particular, we walked out of the Pyrenees on forested paths, through modest towns, and into Pamplona, our first major Camino city. We also began to experience the interesting history set before us along the Way as we both climbed the Alto de Perdon and visited Puente La Reina with its famous, namesake footbridge—two of the iconic stops for modern pilgrims. In Puente La Reina, I enjoyed dinner with fifteen other pilgrims from seven different countries—I was the only American.

Thursday, April 10 (Day 3)

[Zubiri to Pamplona]
(20.3 kilometers—12.6 miles)

At 4:30 a.m., our bunkroom of Germans, Aussies, Koreans, and Americans was very quiet, but I was awake. I used the bathroom and went back to sleep and didn't wake again until after 6:00, when most everyone else was packing up. Dan and I went a block to get our morning coffee. Dan ordered eggs and I had a granola bar. My Pennsylvania trooper friend was there and introduced me to a sixty-year-old man wearing a Minnesota Vikings cap who was explaining how he got too tired at the top of the mountain and never made it to Roncesvalles for the first night. He spent the night at the emergency mountain shelter, one that I had walked by the previous day just before crossing the border into Spain. When I ordered a second cup of coffee, Dan decided to start out alone. I was going to just be five or ten minutes behind, but I had forgotten to make my blog post the night before. I stopped at the albergue to use the Wi-Fi to photo-stream first-day photos and post a description of "Climbing over the Pyrenees" on my blog. With that, I had fallen behind Dan.

I started hiking alone but quickly caught up to and made "little-while friends" with Elsa from Holland; Claude from Stuttgart, Germany; and Clara, also from Germany. While the walking path was pleasant, just after leaving Zubiri we passed an ugly magnesium factory. It reminded me of my hometown of North Branford, which also hosts a large plant with similar types of very large metal sheets bent into and around machines processing some kind of rock or mineral with large columns of steam rising into the sky. As we walked, I asked whether they thought many pilgrims came from Germany. Elsa explained, "The countries with the most pilgrims on the Camino are Spain, Germany, France, Italy, and Korea—in that order."

That seemed interesting, so I responded, "Really? Why Germany… and why Korea?"

Clara added, "It's probably because of Hape Kerkeling's book. He's a well-known comedian in Germany."

Claude injected, "Kerkeling's book was very popular in Germany, and it caused a lot of us to think about doing the Camino."

Interesting, I thought. I had not heard of Kerkeling or his book. But just as quickly I wondered and asked, "But what about Korea? Why are so many Koreans walking to Santiago?"

Elsa said, "I understand a woman in Korea walked the Camino and wrote a book about it that became very popular. Apparently, it's even become a valuable résumé item back in Korea." And, with a smile, she added, "I've heard that there's a joke on the Camino that each morning you can see young Korean women with backpacks waiting at the bus stops to go on to the next stage stop." Hence, the joke, like the cynic, paints these young women as caring little for the Camino experience but rather rushing along the Way by bus to get their Credencial stamped and eventually "improve" their résumé. (I also discovered that the popularity of the Camino in South Korea arose in part after Korean journalist Kim Hyo Sun published three different books on the Camino. It continued to be fueled by other books and attention brought to the pilgrimage when a well-known businessman in Korea completed the Camino in 2011.)

I read Kerkeling's book *I'm Off Then* after I returned from my trip to Santiago. I appreciated some of his candor. His inner or spiritual quest seemed to be genuine, if disjointed and haphazard. At the outset he does confess, "I'm drawn to the idea that the pilgrimage will help me find my way to God and thus to myself. That's certainly worth a try." Even though the mantra from the Appalachian Trail should apply to the Camino such that everyone needs to "walk their own walk," I was surprised when Kerkeling writes, "Still, I have no desire whatsoever to join up with other pilgrims." Really? I loved my time alone on the Camino, but I equally loved the numerous others I encountered along the Way. Kerkeling also took buses and skipped portions and seemed to engage little with the history and heritage he was constantly passing through. Again, I guess "to each, his own," but it appeared as if we took completely different trips to practically different destinations.

After a little while, Claude and Elsa stopped to rest, but Clara and I decided to walk along together, which we did for the morning. We bypassed Larrasoana, deciding not to cross the medieval bridge and visit the town. We did stop in Irotz, where we wished local children *buenos dias* on their way to school, refilled our water bottles, and, while we rested briefly, examined (and photographed) the Romanesque church there—Iglesia de San Pedro. During our walk around St. Jean on Day Zero, Father Jim had sensitized me to some of the history of architecture we would see along the Way. Romanesque architecture, which was replaced by Gothic, would apparently be the most common form we would see throughout the village communities of northern Spain. This stop in Irotz was one of the first opportunities to consider the topic more intensely.

Shortly, outside of Irotz, Clara and I climbed a steep hill up to Zabaldica and the thirteenth-century Iglesia de San Esteban. Based upon the architecture lesson Father Jim had given me, I could see that this church was of Romanesque vintage with its rounded arch entranceway, thick walls, and small windows. Its bell tower, we learned, still holds the oldest known church bell in Spain, dating to 1377. The sisters of the Society of Sacred Heart, who care for the church and the albergue next door, welcomed us and a few other pilgrims who had arrived just before us. When I dropped my pack to begin to tour the church and take photographs, Clara decided to move out on her own. We said goodbye and thanked each other for the pleasant company we had shared. (I would see Clara a few days later and learn later that whenever Clara took a break, which she really rarely wanted to do, she never removed her pack because "it's too hard to get it back on.")

The weather continued to be majestic, warming somewhat as midday approached but never turning hot. I ran into a group from Ireland walking together with daypacks—they were out for two weeks and used vehicle support to shuttle their gear to each overnight town, something I was unaware you could do. I then ran into Jeff and Carol from Scranton again just as we reached a medieval bridge that was to take us into the town of Trinidad de Arre. The bridge sat just upstream from an impressive set of waterfalls. The physical beauty of the falls with the bridge and a cloudless sky serving as a backdrop was stunning. We removed our packs and took photographs for one another. After walking most of way through Trinidad de Arre, Jeff, Carol, and I stopped for a *bocadillo*—basically Spanish for "sandwich" and one of the most useful words on the Camino. The rest and nourishment helped prepare us for the less attractive, suburban march on paved roads into Pamplona, the largest city on the Camino and the day's planned destination.

Pamplona is an ancient fortress city, originally settled by the Romans in the first century before Christ. The pilgrim's approach to the town is over the magnificent, fourteenth-century Magdalena Bridge. From there, Jeff, Carol and I followed the thirty-foot city walls, on both our left and right, that led us around to the portal de Francia (the French gate) and across a drawbridge before we could finally enter the city proper. John Brierley's guide, *A Pilgrim's Guide to the Camino de Santiago*, says this gate is a "reminder that Pamplona has always opened its doors to pilgrims coming from France since medieval times." We followed the yellow arrows deeper into town until we found signs for the large, municipal albergue (Jesus y Maria Albergue), where I was scheduled to meet Dan.

Jesus y Maria is an albergue or "albergues de peregrinos." The Brierley Guide goes to significant lengths to explain the difference between the various albergues: municipal, private, parish, convent (or monastery), or association. I would stay at each of these types of albergues but did not make special note of unique characteristics. They seemed to be more alike than different—rooms with bunks and shared bathrooms. The newer, private hostels often did have the best facilities, but that is to be expected. The municipal ones were typically larger in terms of the number of pilgrims they could accommodate on a given night. The monastery and Christian association hostels typically (but not necessarily) were a little more spartan, but they also had a more communal feel or life—they tended to offer communal meals and make some organized efforts to engage people with the inner aspects of the journey on the Camino.

Dan had arrived at Jesus y Maria three hours before me, but I ran into him immediately upon stepping up to the registration desk and showing the warden or *hospitalero* my Pilgrim Passport. Dan began to tell me about his visit to the local hospital to get care for his feet—his Achilles tendon was causing severe pain. He explained that the doctor wanted him to stay here and rest for two days. Before I could get out that I had no idea he was so hurt, he continued by saying he had decided to rest one day and that I should go ahead and let him catch up. I told him I would be happy to wait, but he insisted. After some debate I realized he might not rest if he thought he was holding me back, I agreed to move ahead the next morning while he rested at the albergue. (Typically a pilgrim may stay only one night in a hostel, but they make exception for illness and injury. Dan had already cleared this with the hostel's warden.)

Not only was Dan injured, but it seemed like over half of the pilgrims I met were hurt. Everyone seemed to have some leg, knee, or foot problem. A young woman, who had accompanied Dan to the hospital to speak Spanish for him, had herself been to the hospital for a leg injury from walking the Camino. The most common problem, however, was blisters, some of which were severe. The pilgrims were certainly the walking wounded, but somehow, I had avoided these problems—at least thus far. My good fortune is probably best explained because of the care I took in selecting my hiking shoes, in breaking them in, and in using a liner sock under a thicker hiking sock.

In addition to being injured, many were exhausted physically, and it was only Day Three for most of us! Evidently, a surprising number of pilgrims were not prepared for twenty-five kilometers of hiking each day. Moreover, many had grossly over-packed and were trying to lug thirty-five or forty pounds (or more!) along the Camino. I started to hear people talk about the option of taking a bus for a stage or two and possibly using a transport company to shuttle packs to the next destination. I was feeling quite good. I never considered either option. I guess I was a bit of a purist—I thought you were to do the Camino on your feet with all your belongings on your person, as the medieval pilgrims had done.

I got settled in to the albergue, as did Jeff and Carol. Father Jim was there, too. I met Josh and Briana from Susquehanna, Pennsylvania (ages twenty-two and nineteen who were starting the Camino the next day). I showered and then headed out into the city that is probably best known for its annual "Running of the Bulls" (made famous by Ernest Hemmingway in *The Sun Also Rises*). Almost thirty-five years earlier, I had planned to see the bulls run in July during the Fiesta de San Fermin while I backpacked through Europe after college gradua-tion, but my plans changed. I never made it to Pamplona. I would not see the running of the bulls on this visit either, but I did have time to take in the old city and its narrow streets. Its impressive cathedral and cloisters, which appeared to occupy the highest ground in the city, was also the site of the city's original Roman citadel. The cathedral was fifteenth-century Gothic, but its façade did not look anything like the Gothic cathedrals I'd see in Burgos and León; it was "Neoclassical," having been added during the eighteenth century.

I returned to the albergue after touring the historic church, and after picking up a replacement electrical adapter (having left mine in the wall in Zubiri), I met Dan and Jim for dinner. We had trouble finding a pilgrim meal. Dan returned to the hostel for a massage. Jim and I settled on a beer and a small, incredibly average baguette sandwich of bacon and cheese. So far, my intake of bread and pork products was setting new records, and I had only been out for three days. Father Jim and I returned to the hostel for journaling, blogging, and bed.

Day 3 had been much like the second day—extraordinary weather and a reasonable footpath as we covered twenty-one kilometers and continued to leave the foothills of the Pyrenees in our rearview mirror.

I felt as if I was off to a great start. I was eager for another day and excited for the larger journey as well.

Friday, April 11 (Day 4)

[Pamplona to Puente La Reina]
(24.2 kilometers—15.0 miles)

Despite doctor's orders, Dan decided to try to hike again when we woke the next morning in Pamplona. We left the albergue around 7:00 a.m. with Josh and Briana from Pennsylvania. Josh had been to Ukraine recently doing evangelism work and was to start Bible college after the Camino. Briana is a pastor's kid. We walked through the old city, taking note of the streets and the turns where the bulls run in July. Leaving Pamplona, we walked along the old citadel through attractive, local parks, along some city streets, and finally across a modest footbridge. The four of us then headed west out of the city and down into a small valley. We knew from our guidebooks that the day included a major climb—not quite like climbing over the Pyrenees but a substantial climb up to an iconic spot on the Camino. We would be hiking up one of the most famous sites along the Way of St. James—the Alto de Perdon.

Before that, however, we enjoyed a pleasant walk as we left the outskirts of Pamplona. The four of us then climbed a reasonable hill into the bedroom town of Cizur Menor. Dan and I stopped for coffee and eggs at a bar where we ran into Jim and Debbie Wood with whom we had shared a bunkroom in Zubiri our second night. After breakfast, Dan was eager to get going, and again he struck out alone while I again stayed back and socialized. I was very focused on taking my time and "smelling the roses," but little did I know then that it would be the last time I'd see him on the Camino.

Jim and Debbie rested a bit longer as I headed out alone. Greeted again by brilliant sunshine, I looked out and up at the terrain ahead, toward the Alto de Perdon. In the distance I could see a long string of pilgrims making their way up the well-marked path on this famous ridge outside of Pamplona. I was headed toward them on a trail of smooth dirt with small, loose rock as I climbed up through the small village of Zariquiegui and then onto to a long, continuous climb up to Alto de Perdon. During this climb, which remained pleasant despite the bright sun due to a cool breeze, I ran into Andy (a woman from Washington state), Jeff and Carol again (which meant I had seen them on each of my first four days), a woman walking alone from Italy, and Father Jim. We covered three hundred meters of elevation over 2.4 kilometers before reaching the top of Alto de Perdon. The climb was steady and continuous but not too long, serious but not severe. I dropped my pack at the top to enjoy the views and take photographs, but I was not particularly tired.

At the top of the Alto de Perdon is a fairly new (for Camino purposes) metal sculpture of pilgrims walking and on horseback on their journey to Santiago. Nearby are some enormous windmills or wind turbines placed on either side of the Camino stop along the high ridge. The weather remained brilliant, so the views from the top of the ridge were spectacular, which I enjoyed with a dozen other pilgrims who also paused at the top for rest, refreshment, and great photographic opportunities. Part of the pilgrim lore is that pilgrims were pardoned of their sins if they made it at least this far on the Camino—hence, the origin of the name of this high spot, Alto de Perdon. The guidebooks say that a basilica, a pilgrim hostel, and a hermitage were all once atop this ridge in medieval times although it was hard to see where adequate room existed on the narrow ridge for such buildings.

Some of the most difficult climbing of the trip was coming down from the top of the Alto de Perdon where the path was mostly loose, sliding gravel and various-sized, rounded rocks on a severe decline. Slipping, sliding, and falling were real possibilities. I proceeded slowly and carefully, easing myself down the steep terrain—slipping and sliding, but not falling. I followed a tall, young man (who turned out to be Matt, the son of an Australian couple whom I'd see for most of the rest of the trip) down and down until the path leveled off and worked its way through some wheat fields. (Although I navigated the hill successfully, I would discover the next day that the constant stress of the steep incline caused swelling and a minor injury to my right knee.) I moved on to a great lunch spot at Uterga, which would prove to be among the best such stops on the Camino. I ordered lunch. Matt and his parents arrived and enjoyed some rest with a number of other pilgrims, who had also earned the privilege to sit outdoors, soak up the sun, and prepare for the next part of the journey.

From our modern, outdoor café in the tidy hamlet of Uterga, I headed off to Muruzabal, where pilgrims must choose the more direct path to Puente La Reina (the Queen's Bridge over the River Arga)—our destination for the day—or add some distance and take a detour to Eunate Church. As I walked down off the high ground of the tired and worn town of Muruzabal, I could see Father Jim a few hundred yards ahead as he also had decided to take the detour. The next kilometer and a half was hot and dry amidst early spring agricultural land—plowed dirt without any green growth breaking through the earth yet.

Jim and I arrived at nearly the same time followed by Jim and Carol from Scranton. Father Jim explained the history and legends surrounding this unique, octagonal church. More specifically, he explained that we were looking at a twelfth- or thirteenth-century Romanesque church, likely constructed by the Knights Templar and probably modeled after the Church of the Holy Sepulchre in Jerusalem, but added, "The building is not adorned with any outward Christian signs." In addition to its obvious octagonal shape, it featured a freestanding outer porch wall—a gallery—with twin pillars and thirty-three arches completely surrounding the church. The Basque name for the church means "house of a hundred doors." Jim explained further that it contains architectural elements from Muslim and Jewish traditions, and that the thirty-three arches may reflect Muslim prayer beads. Finally, Jim explained that some religious historians have speculated that worshipers here may have circled the church three times using each arch as a "door" before entering the main church door as the one hundredth door—hence, the Basque name.

After our brief visit and Father Jim's architecture lesson, Jim, Carol, Jeff, and I decided to walk what Brierley indicated was the more "pleasant" route into Puente La Reina. Very quickly we found ourselves on hot pavement with cars driving by frequently—definitely not pleasant. After a little over a kilometer, however, we took an old dirt road that rolled through agricultural land that eventually dropped us into town but exactly where was not immediately clear. I was tired—the first time since Day One. I was not sure where I was. I was planning to find Dan in this city, presumably at one of the albergues, but we had not said which one. I used the tallest church steeple to help get my bearings and headed right for it. (I had already observed that often albergues are near or even part of a church complex.) When I got to the church and looked at my guidebook map, I realized there were two prominent churches in town. *Which one am I standing under?* I wondered. Once I knew, I could use the map to orient myself accurately. But how could I figure that out?

Unsure where I was and unable to speak Spanish, I pointed at the church and said to two ladies walking by, "*Santiago?*" They apparently understood and responded, "*Si.*" I was where I thought I was—at the Church of Santiago in Puente La Reina. Then, thinking that it would be the likely place for hostels to be located, I looked at my map and headed toward the river and the twelfth-century Romanesque bridge that gives the town its name. With its history, six arches, and five pillars, it is often said to be the most famous bridge on the Camino. The bridge was constructed expressly for the pilgrim traffic coming through this town and needing a safe route over the river.

I reached the river and the bridge. With a further glance at the map, I quickly realized that I had probably gone the wrong way if I wanted to find Dan. Almost every hostel was located at the beginning of town where pilgrims arrive if coming into town by the direct and traditional path. My detour and arrival in a different part of town had kept me off balance as to my location. I was tired and now a little frustrated. Dropping my pack, I sat by the famous footbridge to try to assess the situation. My guidebook indicated that a private hostel (Santiago

Apostle) was just across the bridge—my decision was made. I was too beat to walk back to the other side of town to try to find Dan or the albergues there.

I headed across the footbridge and took a right turn—the yellow arrows pointed the opposite way, toward Santiago, but within a hundred yards I saw a sign for the hostel and headed up its driveway. The drive continued and continued, up and up. I caught up to two bicyclists. The entrance drive was so steep and long that they had dismounted and were walking their bikes. *What have I gotten myself into?* I wondered. I feared I'd never reach the albergue or maybe I was headed the wrong way. Hot and tired, I was getting grumpy, if not angry, for what I started to think of as a misrepresentation about the location of this hostel. Finally, the Santiago Apostle albergue came into sight and finally, I walked in despite being a little wobbly on my feet.

Two women from Australia were at the bar when I stumbled in and checked in to secure a bed. Without dropping my items at my bunk or even washing up, I order a beer and give out an audible sigh. Whew! I was happy to be sitting and enjoying a cold drink. I talked with the girls from Down Under, who agreed to sell me some euros because I was so low. I figured I should be able to resupply the next day based upon the intended route, the size of the towns to be encountered, and the information in the guidebook.

Thankfully, the hike was worth the effort. The albergue was nice and pretty quiet. It appeared to have been built to sleep about a hundred, but only a quarter of that amount were booked to stay the night. After negotiating my foreign currency transaction and enjoying conversation with my new Aussie friends, I sought out a bed. There were several available, so I chose one in my own little corner. The hostel was modern and clean with good facilities for showers and laundry. It also served dinner, which was good considering its location on a mountaintop. Who would want to venture back into town? When I checked in, I had also paid the warden for dinner that night.

After washing up and washing some clothes, I headed back into the main room for dinner. As I entered, I almost ran into Clara, the nineteen-year-old German woman I walked with on Day Three just outside of Zubiri. Twenty of us, almost everyone who was spending the night there, sat together for a pilgrim meal. At one large table, I joined Frank from Austria, a young woman from Italy, a lawyer from Switzerland, the Aussie women, a young man from Korea, Clara, and a few from England. We ordered off the albergue's pilgrim menu, which offered five choices for each of a starter, a main course, a dessert, and a beverage.

My starter was a simple, but adequate, soup. Clara had a wonderful dish of spaghetti with marinara sauce that I admit I started to covet. I mentioned to her, "How did you get that? I didn't see it on the menu."

She replied, "I just ordered it. It was right there as one of the choices—'tomato macaroni.'"

"Tomato macaroni," I repeated, recalling that I had chosen not to order that item because I assumed it was cold macaroni salad with chopped bits of tomato mixed into it. Now, partly exasperated, I said one more time with a different intonation, "That's tomato macaroni?" *Oh well,* I thought. *I'll know next time.* But, I would have enjoyed it considerably at that moment.

I was more tired than I had been on any other day so far—even Day One. I was eager to get some sleep. Just before turning in, Clara asked if I would walk with her in the morning. She knew I liked to get an early start, as did she, and she explained, "I promised my father I would not hike alone if it was dark." As a father of two daughters, I certainly understood and I said I'd be happy to head out with her in the morning. We left for our bunks and planned to meet before 6:00 a.m.

CHAPTER 6

CLARA AND SOCRATES

The tragedy of the modern man is not that
he knows less and less about the meaning of his own life,
but that it bothers him less and less.

Vaclav Havel

I met Clara early in the morning on my walk to Pamplona on Day Three. My friend Dan was a few minutes ahead of me. Clara was a recent high school graduate from Germany. Recalling the questionnaire from my stop that first evening at the albergue in Roncesvalles, I asked her, "So why did you want to walk the Camino? Did you come by yourself?"

The eighteen-year-old blonde responded in excellent English, "I wanted to think about what I was going to do next, what I was going to study at University."

"And you're here by yourself," I asked.

"Yep," she responded.

"Your English is quite good. I'm afraid I cannot speak any other language," I said.

Clara smiled briefly, perhaps slightly embarrassed, and said, "Thanks, but I do not think it's that good. I need to practice more often."

"I don't know. It's awfully good to me." And I added, as I let a smile form on my lips, "It's dramatically better than my German. And where did you learn to say 'yep'?"

Clara confessed that she had improved her speaking and learned a lot of American expressions and slang from her year abroad in Santa Fe, New Mexico, a couple of years earlier.

Clara and I had a wonderful walk that magnificent, spring morning. We talked about Germany and Richmond and about our families. I heard about how German high school girls were little different than American high school girls—how clothes and "boys, boys, boys" were all her friends talked about. She told me that all they wanted to do was party and hang out with the "boys, boys, boys." She seemed to want something different, something more in her mind anyway. She enjoyed school. She liked studying Latin and history and most subjects, for that matter. She loved her year abroad. Clara had good friends and family relationships. She was no loner or outcast. Boys were fine, but at the right time and in the right amount. She wondered why her friends had interests that were so limited.

Clara wondered about what life would bring her. Of immediate concern was a decision she had to make about college, or "university" as most Europeans would say. She loved history and thought very seriously about studying that. I shared that history was my love and what I had studied. Clara was also interested in medicine. "I'm interested in most things," she said. "I think about doing a lot of things. I'm just not sure what I want to do," she said. After a couple hours of walking and talking she offered, seemingly a little frustrated with herself, "sometimes I think I think too much."

Socrates is famously quoted as saying "The unexamined life is not worth living." Clara was examining life. Wise beyond her years, she was confronting questions of life and living that often elude many of us for many years and often never seriously enter our minds. Clara was looking for answers. In a very real sense, Clara was searching for truth. Socrates viewed truth as the highest goal, the most worthy of pursuits. Clara was on the Camino to think about her future, about life and its essential questions. Some of those questions inevitably would change with the years, but I could tell, Clara would have "a life worth living."

Like Clara in some respects I too was "on the road to find out." A primary reason for my time on the Camino was to think about my own life—"to look back and to look forward." In some crucial respects, Clara and I appeared to be walking to think about life. Was that a "religious reason"? Were we on a pilgrimage?

Since the Biblical times, pilgrimage has been marked, if not defined, by difficult physical movement to a place accompanied by an inner or spiritual objective. Perhaps it should not be surprising, then, that Abraham—the patriarch of three world religions—went into the wilderness on a most important of physical and spiritual journeys. Though pilgrimage is now of limited significance within Judaism, it is still important in other major religions such as Islam, Hinduism, Sikhism, and Buddhism. One of the "four noble truths" is the "noble path"—the idea of eliminating suffering and gaining insight into the true nature of reality by journeying through something known as the "Noble Eightfold Path." Hindus have four great pilgrimage sites or *dhamas* and their *Kumbh Mela* sends as many as thirty million on a journey every three years to bathe in a sacred river. Similarly, one of the pillars of Islam is the Hajj—the requirement that every Muslim make a pilgrimage to Mecca at least once in his life. Hajj means, "to intend journey" and connotes both the outward act of a journey and the inward act of intentions.

Americans have a popular point of reference for this idea of pilgrimage by annually recalling the "pilgrims" of Plymouth Rock and the "first" Thanksgiving. (The quotation marks are for my wife and other Virginians who point out that an earlier "Thanksgiving" was held at Berkley Plantation in colonial Virginia in 1619, at least two years prior to the northern version. As a transplanted Connecticut Yankee, I am conflicted on this issue but satisfied that the Civil War is over.) While the motivation of these founding fathers is obscured today by candy corn, pumpkin carving, and a Charlie Brown television special, we should remember that these pilgrims endured long, arduous travel to a new, remote land (their physical journey) to find a new home where they could worship freely (their religious purpose or inner journey). Indeed, they understood their journey in those terms. The group's leader, William Bradford, wrote this about the group: "So they left that goodly and pleasant city which had been their resting place near twelve years; but *they knew they were pilgrims,* and looked not much on those things, but lifted up their eyes to the heavens, their dearest country, and quieted their spirits."

A decade later, my great-great-grandfather, Sgt. Thomas Matson, captained one of the thirty ships that accompanied John Winthrop to Boston as part of that initial wave of what is often referred to as the "Great Migration." These "Puritans," as history recalls them, were also expressly on a journey of physical and spiritual dimensions—they were on "an errand into the wilderness." And the reference to "wilderness," recalling Abraham's journey, was anything but incidental. Discouraged by the developments in the English Protestant Church, the Puritans came to the colony of Massachusetts to "purify" the church by establishing, as their leader John Winthrop wrote, a "city upon a hill"—a model for the proper worship of God. Again, this idea of pilgrimage—physical movement with a religious purpose—was intentional. Hence, unlike the Thanksgiving celebration itself, the notion of pilgrimage for these founding fathers was neither romantic projection nor revisionist history.

The idea of pilgrimage, I believe, remains relevant today for most anyone who is curious about life or searching for meaning or truth. While Merriam-Webster defines pilgrimage simply as "a journey to a holy place," scholars have more recently defined pilgrimage as "a journey, a search for something, a ritual, a commemoration, perhaps something the pilgrim cannot express in words, perhaps even something the pilgrim does not fully perceive."

Not only is a broader concept of pilgrimage relevant today, something in the human heart longs for pilgrimage—so much so, that journeys of inner discovery and quests for meaning have been the subject matter of some of the greatest works of literature. In fact, no theme in philosophy or religion is more common than man's search for truth and, considered properly, such stories are about pilgrimages. Plutarch expressed this idea by saying, "The soul is in exile and a wanderer." Chaucer, Dante, Bunyan, Melville, Twain, and others purposefully coupled physical journey with spiritual inquiry and discovery. (Tradition is that both Chaucer and Dante walked the Camino, although it is not known if it was prior to their famous works focused on pilgrimage.) There is deep within us—but very real and existential—something restless, something that stirs our souls to wonder. We ask for answers and clarity, but lacking the immediate or obvious, we look for moments of solitude, we long for time of reflection. We were made for pilgrimage.

In *Moby Dick,* Ishmael went to the sea to try to soothe the "damp, drizzly November in his soul." In using the name "Ishmael" (the name of Abraham's son), Melville intentionally invokes the allusion to wandering and searching in Genesis. Like Ishmael, we all want "rest for our souls."

Huck Finn was on a journey as well. In Twain's novel that takes place on a raft floating through unknown territory, Huck confronts something he knows, but does not fully perceive at the core of his being, is not right. In setting the slave Jim free, Huck discovers what is right and true, despite what society is telling him. ("Alright then, I'll go to hell.")

And in *The Wizard of Oz,* Dorothy and her companions were certainly on a journey—to Oz—but they each had an inner or spiritual purpose behind the adventure. Most notably, Dorothy thought there was "no place like home." The idea of being "home" is likewise an eternal quest—being "home' is how and where we find "rest for our souls."

Like Ishmael, Huck, and Dorothy, something tells us that all is not right—we are not at peace. Our souls are not at rest. We express or define this disquiet in a number of different ways. Some people say, "I just want to be happy." Others seek truth and meaning and ask, "What's it all about?" Still others express this desire in terms of wanting life to have some purpose, "Why am I here?" or "Who am I?" Through the years many have embraced a belief in, or at least a search for, God.

Others write about being lost or searching for something in which we can become grounded, something we can believe in, something we see as true. The Transcendentalists dismissed traditional religion and looked for answers in nature. Perhaps appropriate for the Camino, Henry David Thoreau, in his essay on "Walking," wrote:

> *So we saunter toward the Holy Land, till one day the sun shall shine more brightly than ever he has done, shall perchance shine into our minds and hearts, and light up our whole lives with a great awakening light, as warm and serene and golden as on a bankside in autumn.*

Likewise, physical movement has always been an important aspect of the search, of the journey—as early as Moses' wandering and Homer's odyssey and as modern as Melville and Thoreau. Much like the growth in the popularity of the Camino, this notion shows no likelihood of disappearing or declining. In fact, upon my return from Spain, Cheryl recommended and I read *The Unlikely Pilgrimage of Harold Fry*, a novel that has been broadly read and widely acclaimed where the protagonist heads out on a long walk for a purpose that does not, at least initially, appear clear. Thus, something about the actual movement, typically including hardship along the way, leads to spiritual revelation. As I have learned and as classic writing has shown us, one of the crucial aspects of facing hardship is learning that we are neither invincible nor purely self-reliant.

Thoreau's use of the word *saunter* is not only very intentional but tied historically and philosophically to walks like the Camino de Santiago. He explains the word is derived from people of pilgrimage:

> *I have met with but one or two persons in the course of my life who understood the art of Walking, that is, of taking walks, who had a genius, so to speak, for sauntering; which word is beautifully derived "from idle people who roved about the country, in the middle ages, and asked charity, under pretence of going à la sainte terre"—to the holy land, till the children exclaimed,*

"There goes a sainte-terrer", a saunterer—a holy-lander. They who never go to the holy land in their walks, as they pretend, are indeed mere idlers and vagabonds, but they who do go there are saunterers in the good sense, such as I mean.

That Thoreau would use the reference to "holy land" in expressing these ideas is fascinating. To "saunter toward the holy land" then is to be "on the road to find out—to be questioning, wondering, searching—to be examining life."

Thoreau suggests an alternative explanation or etymology for the word *saunter*. He suggests, "Some derive the word from 'sans terre,' without land or a home." This "alternative" derivation, though, is really just a variation on his preferred origin because seeking meaning or truth is really no different than "seeking rest for our souls" or longing to be "home." Thoreau also writes that "every walk is a sort of crusade. ..." Hence, a "saunterer" is someone who, like Ishmael, is wandering— ultimately hoping to find rest, to find one's home. By understanding his use of "saunter" then, Thoreau both clarifies and emphasizes the importance of pilgrimage. Sauntering then is seeking answers—the objective is truth, which Thoreau identifies as "the holy land."

In his classic book *The Screwtape Letters,* C. S. Lewis also identifies the value of taking a solitary walk. In Letter #13, the devil chastises his apprentice for permitting the person, whose soul the devil has targeted, to take a walk in the woods. The devil is direct in his criticism saying, "You allowed him to walk down to the old mill and have tea there—a walk through country he really likes, and taken alone. ... Were you so ignorant as not to see the danger of this?" The problem here, as explained by the devil, is that it provides the walker with "a touchstone of reality." The walker did something for the pure enjoyment of it as opposed to advance some cause or earn some recognition. In other words, this "reality" is the truth that we seek—truth devoid of selfishness that permits us to see what is most important in life.

For me, I think we come closer to finding answers—to an awakening (or some might call an "epiphany")—when we see that our own will must be subordinated. This often can be difficult in a culture that stresses self-reliance and success over individual initiative. Similarly, what society values most highly is not what Jesus stressed as most crucial. In fact, it was just that challenge or choice that set mankind up for the Fall. In seeking to be God himself and rejecting the need to obey, Adam set the stage for each of us to "saunter." As the writer of Hebrews tells us, we are all "strangers and aliens on this earth" and we are "seeking a homeland."

Most of us, at one time or another, probe these questions—the "big questions of life." Many of us ask them all the time. Sometimes they are in the forefront of our thinking and sometimes they run in the background, but even when not right in front of us, we typically know they are there. The question is to what extent we act on that longing or instinct. Hape Kerkeling, author of *I'm Off Then* wrote, "The Camino is not one single path, but thousands, and it poses only one question to each of us: 'who are you?'" To embark on pilgrimage, even when not fully perceived, is a response to the longing of the human heart. In Melville's terms, it is a reply to a "damp, drizzly November in our soul."

Sometimes we pull these questions or thoughts out from the back of our mind and wrestle with them like Hercules, in a very existential way. Sometimes they are active, intentional dialogs, even while constrained within our own mind. Sometimes we fear that our inquiry looks more like an endless hill to climb rather than a finish line to clear—we see ourselves and our search more in terms of Sisyphus than Nike. Sometimes life's events or just the cycles of life bring these questions clearly out into the open, screaming for answers. In a very real way, then, most of us have been or are "on the road to find out." To mix our metaphors, when we're on the road to find out, we are seeking "rest for our souls," we are hoping to find "happiness," or we are searching for "meaning." These questions are at the essence of pilgrimage—yesterday and today and tomorrow.

Most people who walk the Camino acknowledge that the trek involves a spiritual or inner journey as well as a physical challenge (hiking almost five hundred miles with a twenty-five-pound pack on your back). The Brierley Guide, in fact, has a section in every chapter (set up by recommended daily distances) discussing both the physical journey, which the author calls the "Practical Path," and the inner journey, which the author calls the "Mystical Path." This inner quest, or "search for something," is very real on the Camino. While some people were following yellow arrows for a sports adventure, most had a spiritual or religious purpose for undertaking the journey to Santiago—even though for some it was not readily or openly articulated, or even acknowledged. While not clearly or openly religious in a traditional sense, apparently a nagging, internal voice followed them and challenged them along the Way.

The day before I met Clara, walking between Roncesvalles and Zubiri, remains one of my most memorable days on the Camino. Following a tough and challenging day mentally and physically (due to the severe climb and the difficult weather), something made me uniquely attentive to the beauty of the creation. I had what I can only explain as an unusual, heightened sense of wonder and excitement as I walked along. I loved being on the Camino and in nature. The sky was a brilliant blue. The sun streamed through trees, danced on the leaves, and illuminated the undergrowth. The usual stress of business or life was nowhere. I loved the time on my feet alone—time to think. I paused to examine the new growth of buds emerging and the earliest spring wildflowers. Something was slowing my step and helping me, literally, to stop and smell the flowers.

The walking path was perfect—soft, earthen and pleasantly rolling through woodlands and alongside fields with horses grazing. The air was cool without being cold. My step was light. I could barely feel the weight of my pack. While it sounds somewhat trite or cliché, in its most intense moments it felt like an inner sense of peace. Even more so, it might be best expressed as a palpable sense of joy. Were these glimpses of the divine? I recalled C. S. Lewis being "surprised by joy" (also the title of his autobiography) and wondered if my experience was the type to which he referred.

I had planned to use much of my time walking the Camino to think and reflect. The physical challenges of Day One crowded out much opportunity for reflective thought. This time of wonder, awe, and joy seemed so rare and appeared as a gift to be savored and absorbed, a gift from God, my family, and my firm—all who made this journey possible.

Another way to think about Day One was that the spiritual or religious aspects of the trip had taken a back seat to the immediate task of climbing through the Pyrenees. So I was encouraged to be greeted so immediately by such exciting insights concerning the inner journey. The time away from the usual commitments and distractions coupled with the simplicity of daily life provided me also with crucial "space" and valuable time to pursue the spiritual journey as well. By the time I met Clara on Day Three, I was, in a very real sense, on a pilgrimage. Like the words of a Cat Stevens song, a favorite singer-songwriter of mine in the 1970s, Clara and I—like most others on the Way of St. James—were pilgrims, we were "on the road to find out."

CHAPTER 7

BECOMING A PILGRIM

(DAYS 5–8)

Nothing is harder on mortal man than wandering.

Homer

[**Puente La Reina**—[Cirauqui], [Zarapuz ruins], [Irache Monastery], **Villamayor de Monjardin**, [Los Arcos], Viana, [Sansol], [Torres del Rio], [Logroño], Navarette, [Nájera], **Azofra**]

(100.0 kilometers—62.1 miles)

Having settled into a routine, I was more comfortable with the Way of the Camino. Exploring and sharing why others were walking along with you was easy and natural. These days continued to offer unique Camino experiences including the free wine fountain, a communal meal offered by a Christian association from Holland, and the opportunity to experience extraordinary art and architecture. Yet, these days also involved the stress of running low on cash, the realization that not everyone on the Camino is honest and generous, and the amusing embarrassment of ordering and trying to consume a meal where the local language remained elusive.

Saturday, April 12 (Day 5)

[Puente La Reina to Villamayor]
(25.3 kilometers—17.7 miles)

Clara and I left in the pre-dawn light. Just after descending the steep hill from our albergue, we saw signs for "Camino Aragones" (one of the ancient routes referenced in the *Codex Calixtinus*, which begins at Somport, France, in the Pyrenees and joins the Camino Frances in Puente La Reina) reminding us that there are other established routes to Santiago. Because we rose early and were heading west to Santiago, we watched the sun rise and had it at our back most of the day—every day! It was another perfect morning. Once again, I had a magnificent day for walking. We had the path to ourselves with a brilliant red-purple sky back over our shoulders. It was just the fifth day, but so far, the cool mornings had been exceptional for hiking, and remarkably, as the sun got higher in the sky, a modest but steady cool breeze arose each day to moderate the afternoon temperature.

Right away Clara and I encountered two serious climbs of five hundred meters each through red clay hills. We then took more of a modest roller coaster walk through the countryside and farmland between Puenta La Reina and Estella. Well rested, we were ready to conquer the hills and, while doing so, enjoyed songbirds, other signs of spring, and interesting conversation. Clara was between high school and "university." She explained how she was walking the Camino to give some serious thought to whether to pursue medicine or some other discipline. I felt much like a father listening to a daughter's views on life.

After another steep climb up and into the town of Cirauqui (which apparently means "viper nest" in Basque), we passed through a Gothic archway, an access point through ancient city walls, where we picked up a stamp for our Pilgrim Passport. We then looked for a place for our morning café con leche. I was starting to notice that many of these older villages are located on hilltops, presumably because such a location made them easier to defend in earlier times. We selected a bar and were pleased to find Jim and Debbie Wood from Australia inside.

We treated our Aussie friends to coffee and wondered how they got to this bar before Clara and me. I had last seen Jim and Debbie in Trinidad de Arre where they told me of their troubles in St. Jean with the heavy and awkward "wheely-packs" and about taking the wrong route through the Pyrenees on their first day. I knew their hiking pace. They could not have passed Clara or me. In fact, Clara kept quite a vigorous pace (she would complete the Camino two days before me). I asked how the hike was going. Jim explained that Debbie was having trouble carrying the full backpack (even after they resupplied in St. Jean), and he had hurt his leg. They had taken a bus from Pamplona to Cirauqui and now were trying to let Debbie walk with a daypack while a transit company brought their big bags ahead to the next town. And Jim was trying to hike every other day with Debbie and resting alternately.

After our coffee break, we had an easy six-mile walk to the modest town of Villatuerta where my guidebook indicated an ATM. The walk this day with Clara was simply majestic. Part of our walk was on an old Roman road and across an old Roman bridge where we walked briefly with Jim and Debbie. Considering that the Romans had conquered and occupied the Iberian Peninsula two hundred years before the time of Christ, I had to pause and remark with amazement at the history around us—a *Roman* road and a *Roman* bridge—imagine farmers, merchants, soldiers, peasants, traders, pilgrims, and others traveling thousands of years ago on this same way, on this same path! In Villatuerta, we would also have to decide whether to take a more rural, alternative path or stay on the route leading pilgrims into Estella, a small city. Before I left Virginia, after doing some advance reading, I had decided to take the "detour" or the "road less travelled" whenever the option presented itself on the Camino. I had done this when I visited the Eunate Church with Father Jim. This was another such detour or alternative route, one that Brierley said was a route "virtually unused."

I tried unsuccessfully to get money in Villatuerta. If I were going to take the older detour, I'd have to borrow some euros from Clara to cover the cost of my albergue that night. The alternative route bypassed the large town of Estella, which almost certainly would have had a few

ATMs. Clara wanted to take the more rural hike, as did I, so we headed off that way. Historically, pilgrims walked directly on this path to the Irache monastery, bypassing Estella as we were doing. On the detour, Pete from Cornwall, England, joined us for the walk after appearing out of some ruins of a medieval monastery at Zarapuz. (Clara knew Pete because they had taken the same bus to St. Jean a few days earlier to start their Camino.)

As we marched along together, it felt like the Scarecrow, the Tin Man, and Dorothy heading off to the Emerald City. Pete, Clara, and I were all on the road to find out, and it dawned on me that in many respects that's exactly what the characters in the *Wizard of Oz* were pursuing. After visiting for a while, I signaled it was time to move along by saying, "We're off," which led me to sing out briefly as we started to hike again, with no obvious objection, "We're . . . off to see the wizard, the wonderful Wizard of Oz." This touch of fantasy and mirth was reinforced by our stop at the Irache ("free wine") Fountain, where the monks (and now a commercial producer) have offered wine free to pilgrims for hundreds of years. Before we could enjoy that visit, however, we had to maneuver our way from the "detour" route back to the "main" route, which we accomplished only after walking through a suburban neighborhood and asking for directions. The guidebook indicated it would be much easier than that.

After refreshments at the wine fountain, we walked by the Monastery of Santa Maria la real de Irache, which dates to the tenth century and where its monks supported a pilgrim hospital since the eleventh century. We then journeyed another seven kilometers to the small village of Villamayor de Monjardin. Again we had to climb a steep hill into the town. As we picked our heads up to see our way, above the town stood castle ruins at the top of Monjardin where once the "castile" stood sentinel protecting the town. From a distance the nearly perfect, conical-shaped hill upon which the castle ruins sat looked like a tiny volcano. Interested in such things—perhaps I think too much—I wondered what geologic forces created that scene. Certainly it was a feature that "stood out" (pun intended) among the otherwise expansive, rolling agricultural topography.

Entering the town, we passed a new, private hostel, but circled around to the back of town and decided to stay at an old albergue run by Christian volunteers from the Netherlands. The older one was five or six euros cheaper. Pete wanted to save money. I wanted to stay at the first one (thinking it might be cleaner, better equipped, etc.), but did not say so. We received a friendly greeting, checked in (Clara paid for my bed and dinner) and were assigned a bunkroom.

The hostel showed its age but featured a communal meal. At my table for dinner were ten people from England, Germany, South Africa, Netherlands, Canada, and Richmond. Yes, sitting across from me was Sue from my hometown of Richmond, Virginia—amazing. The meal, the conversation, and the camaraderie made the evening special (a good thing because we were twelve to a room in very tight quarters). It was not lost on me that if I had insisted on staying at the modern albergue I would have missed this remarkable gathering.

Before time for lights out, I met a husband and wife—Wayne and Barbara—from Boston. When Wayne heard I was from Richmond, he asked if I knew of Hermitage Country Club where he visited each of the last twelve years to play in its member-guest golf tournament. I responded simply by saying, "I play in that tournament. I'm a member of that club. What a small world!"

Sunday, April 13 (Day 6)

[Villamayor de Monjardin to Viana]
(29.8 kms—8.5 miles)

The Dutch Christian Association provided breakfast at the hostel—a generous spread of fruit juice, salami, cheese, breads, and coffee. Pete, Clara, and I started out at 7:15 and stayed together as the sun was rising on another perfect day—a cool, beautiful, clear morning with sun rising at our backs. Not surprisingly, Clara wanted to stay close to me; I owed the recent German high school grad 23 euros she had to front me for dinner, bed, and breakfast at the Villamayor hostel. (I had not yet found a use for a credit card and only 20 percent of the villages had ATMs—and some of those, like the one I tried to use in Villatuerta, apparently have never heard of the Bank of America.)

Pete, Clara, and I enjoyed an easy, pleasant walk as we discussed movies and literature. Clara also told us more about her friends and family. We arrived in Los Arcos around 9:30 having travelled over twelve kilometers at a relatively fast pace. We found nice outdoor seating in the Plaza de Santa Maria next to a church by the same name where we sat and enjoyed pastries and coffee. The Dintaman Guide (*Hiking the Camino de Santiago* by Anna Dintaman and David Landis) advised me that the church was an amalgam of Romanesque and Gothic features but that the bell tower was Renaissance. Looking up at that tower I captured one of my best photographs of the trip—a hawk gliding by the top of the tower caught perfectly (luckily) in full frame.

A few fellow pilgrims from South Africa and Germany joined us in the church square. When these new friends learned I was an attorney, they wanted to know my thoughts about the guilt or innocence of Oscar Pistorius, whose trial for murder was right then being held back in Pretoria. Pistorius was famous for participating in the 2012 Olympic Games as a sprinter despite having had both legs amputated, but at the time he was facing trial for the alleged murder of his girlfriend. Like the protest over Trayvon Martin, or the *Today* show poll about whether Edward Snowden was a patriot whistleblower or a despicable traitor, I wondered how people could hold certain opinions—or ask me mine—where none of the people supposedly expressing an opinion about guilt or innocence had the benefit of hearing the testimony or seeing the other evidence. (In September, Pistorius was convicted of "culpable homicide.")

I finally got some euros and repaid Clara, which seemed appropriate when I read in Dintaman that in medieval times Los Arcos was a crossroads of trade routes and "a place for toll collection and changing money." Looking for some time alone, I considered resting in Los Arcos when Clara and Pete headed back down the Camino. So I said goodbye to them but would not forget how thoughtful and mature my young German companion had been.

I found a shop to buy a baguette and then followed Clara and Pete toward Logroño. I was thirty minutes behind them, purposefully. I looked forward to some time on my feet alone. I passed by a cemetery at the outskirts of Los Arcos and, for the first time on the trip, I slipped on my ear buds, turned on my iPod, and started stepping out toward the city of Logroño—the commercial center of the La Rioja region. Day Six would be my last full day in Navarre. I would enter Rioja shortly before reaching Logroño. I listened to James Taylor. I'm a big fan, and I enjoy how he delves often into life's big questions, with songs like "That Lonesome Road" and "The Secret of Life." And sometimes his tunes just fit the mood, such as "Walking Man" and "Wandering." I walked along and took in the music and lyrics.

I enjoyed my midday hike as I was left alone with my own thoughts and the words of songs sung by James Taylor and other artists. Just before I climbed up into the small village of Sansol, I stopped to take a photograph of the local vineyards. Another pilgrim walking alone came up to me, said something in Spanish, and motioned that he would take the photo so I could be in it. When he finished I offered my best *gracias* to which he pulled out a piece of paper and said what someone had written for him: "It is nothing" (which of course is the literal translation of *de nada*—a common response in Spanish to *gracias*). Juan was practicing his English. We both laughed. We exchanged names—I thought he said "Juan," but when I saw him a few times later over the next two weeks and greeted him with "Juan," he seemed to correct me by saying something like "Juan Ho," but I never seemed to understand. Later in the trip, it was explained to me by someone else that he was saying, "JuanJo" as an abbreviation of "Juan Jose," which I also learned is very typical in Spain. (JuanJo checked into the same hostel in Carrión right behind me—the sixth time we'd run into each other since that photo session. Just something that happens to everyone almost every day on the way to Santiago.)

Right after my photo session with JuanJo, I caught up to Sue from Richmond (who had sat across from me at dinner the previous night) just a few hundred yards outside of Sansol. We stopped in town for some cold drinks. We briefly discussed issues of faith. Sue taught religion back in Virginia, but quickly assured me that she was an atheist. She emphasized problems with "evangelicals" and "fundamentalists," especially as it concerned her beliefs about homosexuality. Sue moved on to Torres del Rio, just a kilometer away to secure a bed for the night at the albergue. I pulled out my baguette and butter, bought another drink, retrieved the code for Wi-Fi pass access, took off my shoes and socks, put my feet up, looked out over the vineyards of Rioja, and relaxed for almost an hour on a magnificent afternoon.

I wasn't eager to disrupt the tranquil scene, but I finally decided to move on. Walking alone, I climbed down out of Sansol and immediately back up into Torres del Rio, which featured an octagon-shaped twelfth-century Romanesque church thought to have been built by the Knights Templar, much like the Eunate Church, also based on the plan of the Church of the Holy Sepulchre.

I planned to get a private room in Viana, which I did after a challenging late afternoon walk. The temperature rose, but there always seemed to be a cool breeze. The hike was pleasant but not without some work, which included many steep ups and downs, including a significant walk down into and then out of a ravine known as the "mule killer" ("Barranco Mataburos") followed by another—the climb up into the old Roman settlement known today as Viana. The climb did not kill me, but fatigue did start to set in. My walk this day, in terms of mileage, would be my longest yet.

Like Viana, many of these older villages are located on hilltops. One Camino website indicates that the "formidable walls" of Viana are an indication of the town's importance as a heavily fortified frontier town, and that "despite the fortifications the town was often besieged, occupied (once by Pedro the Cruel), and bounced between the kingdoms of Castile and Navarre." It became important, though, as a Camino stop. The first pilgrim hospital was built there in the thirteenth century, and by the fifteenth century, Viana supported another three hospitals to aid individuals on their pilgrimage to Santiago.

After climbing up and into Viana, I finally rolled into town around 5:00 p.m. on a very busy Palm Sunday afternoon. Crowds milled about the church squares and people packed the local bars. After a little map reading challenge and some backtracking through a maze of narrow city streets, I found the Pension San Pedro. A very pleasant woman, who did not speak English, checked me into my room. The timing of my first hotel stay was good. I was ready for the quiet and the rest. I enjoyed a great, long shower and recalled the value of some private space. I called Cheryl and worked on my journal before easily falling to sleep.

Monday, April 14 (Day 7)

[Viana to Navarette]
(22.7 kilometers—14.7 miles)

The pleasant monotony of beginning a day's hike in the cool of the morning while the sun rose at my back continued. I could hardly believe how blessed I was each morning to be greeted by a perfect sunrise and perfect walking weather. I had enjoyed my first non-hostel room in Viana the night before and was enthusiastic to move ahead on the journey. Even though I left much later than usual, it was largely solitary. I ran into sisters from Florida and cousins from Holland and Minnesota, both pairs hiking the Camino together. Coming upon and walking through the commercial prelude just outside of Logroño, I decided to listen to music again.

I was glad to have these tunes to distract me from the uninspiring, light industrial landscape I had to pass through approaching the city of Logroño. The lyrics of many of my favorite singer-songwriters coupled with uninterrupted time on my feet offered a time to think about some of life's big questions. Shortly before reaching this city, by a busy city bypass road, I passed the border between Navarre, which I was leaving, and Rioja, another autonomous political division and perhaps Spain's best-known wine region.

The ten kilometers from Viana to Logroño passed quickly as the Way-marked path was relatively flat or gently downhill (except for a modest hill around the highway bypass) until just before entering the city. Before the river Ebro, where pilgrims walk down a fairly steep hill, Brierley tells us we will encounter an iconic Camino personality there who greets those of us on the Way. Felisa continues the tradition started by her aunt (also named Felisa) many years prior. In addition to a hearty *buen Camino*, she has a special stamp for the Pilgrim Passport, offers refreshments, and sells Camino-themed jewelry at her modest path-side stand. I had a short visit with Felisa.

Arriving at and crossing over the river reveals a clean, modern, and pleasant city. History indicates that Alfonso VI built the first bridge here to maintain Logroño as an important commercial center that was fought over for centuries, which suggests why so few medieval monuments remain today. One resource suggests that the charter (*fuero*) granted to Logroño was the template for future such charters in Castile. The tempranillo grape and Rioja wine dominate the business of the area and this city, which is headquarters to over five hundred wineries. If you enjoy Spanish wine, it probably came from this region.

In contrast to Pamplona, Lagroño looks and feels like a very modern city—little of its older heritage (other than a few churches) remains. Yet, like Puente La Reina, this was a crossroads town where people "on the Camino" from the Mediterranean met up and joined the Camino Frances. Although no evidence remains today, the Knights Templar established a monastery or "priory" in Lagroño in 1144.

I walked a little over four miles when I decided to stop for a break outside the Church of Santiago for water and to look at my guidebook and map. After easing off my backpack, I enjoyed a rush of cool air against my back, which had started to sweat from the rising heat. As I pulled my water bottle out for a drink, a man speaking English with a strong accent that sounded German approached and tried to explain that his ATM card broke into pieces when he tried to use it a few minutes earlier. He was looking for a "fellow pilgrim" to lend him some money. "Austria" and "money at the embassy another day" were a few of the scattered words I picked up.

The vibe and story did not feel right. I said something like, "Well, the great thing about the Camino is there's no need to rush and you will have your money tomorrow." I quickly gathered my things and walked on. A few minutes later, deeper into the city, I stopped for an early lunch at a café. Within a few minutes Inae ("eena") Choi, a twenty-five-year-old Korean woman, joined me. We recognized each other because we had crossed paths and stayed in the same hostels a few times since starting in St. Jean. Inae was between jobs back in South Korea. After our lunch, we left together and made the long walk out of the city on sidewalks and through city parks.

We walked by a reservoir also used for boating and swimming and treated ourselves to an ice cream novelty. We hiked by Wayne and Barbara from Boston and then were back in rolling vineyards. The afternoon was warmer and we had a few hills to climb on our way to Navarette. Inae, who wore a broad, floppy hat and gloves to protect her fair skin from the bright sun, started to tire at the end, but we finally made the final climb into the ancient town. Inae was exhausted, so I walked with her to the first hostel we came to and got settled. For an additional ten euros I had a private room (but shared the bathroom facilities in the albergue). I headed out for supplies and to explore the village.

Navarette was built in a semi-circle into the base of a hill with a prominent church at its center. I headed directly over to the sixteenth-century church, which is not only the most prominent structure in town but also its inside features a magnificent, Baroque *retablo*. For the price of one euro, I was able to illuminate the expansive and remarkable altar piece of brilliant gold. The dazzling showpiece reminded us not only of the enormous wealth amassed by Spain particularly in the sixteenth and seventeenth centuries but prepared us to learn more about the extraction and export of gold from Galicia where I'd be in a couple of weeks. After purchasing some bread and cheese, I returned to the albergue to be greeted by my Aussie friends who were grabbing a bunk nearby. Andy, Jane, and Matt would walk a very similar pace as me all the way to Santiago.

After hiking out of the Pyrenees and its foothills, the terrain for the second three days was more gentle and rolling, yet it had numerous hills that raised my heart rate. The landscape was more open and the trail less protected by tree cover. The pilgrim experienced a different look and feel as we left the piedmont for wheat fields and vineyards punctuated by medieval villages, many with Roman walls and all with a Romanesque or early Gothic church. The cynic or critic might note that every day seems rather the same—walking through fields and vineyards and then spotting a village with a church tower in the distance and then climbing up into those medieval hamlets. That has considerable truth, but I was still enjoying every day and had not experienced any sense of boredom or monotony—other than the same, magnificent morning sunrises.

Tuesday, April 15 (Day 8)

[Navarette to Azofra]
(22.2 kilometers—13.8 miles)

Probably because I had a private room within the hostel, I didn't hear some of the early morning rustling of eager peregrinos preparing to depart. I slept later than usual but found myself easing my way down the steep hill upon which Navarette sits by 8 a.m. Just ahead I could see Inae, my traveling companion for the previous afternoon, and beyond her was a large group of pilgrims appearing to be walking together. The morning was cloudy and the air was unusually humid. The paved road passed a cemetery and then headed through typical Rioja vineyards on dirt and gravel roads but near a busy roadway. I peeled an orange as I walked, turned on my iPod, and enjoyed a wonderfully peaceful and easy seven kilometers on my own. I listened to a variety of lyrics... "I've been wandering early and late, from New York City to the Golden Gate, and I don't think I will ever stop my wandering" and ... "talk of poems and prayers and promises, things that we believe in ..."

The trail headed gently and modestly uphill. I continued to follow Inae and caught up to her as we entered the small village of Ventosa where my Australian family friends (Andy, Jan, and Matt) were sitting enjoying bacon, eggs, and coffee. Inae and I joined them for breakfast. We also enjoyed some conversation with a young couple from New Zealand and a young Spanish woman hiking with her dog. Then, as it so often was with the Camino, JuanJo (who took my photo the prior day just before entering Sansol) came into town and we shared a brief hello.

After breakfast, Inae and I walked together and ran into the large group we had seen and had been following during the early morning. The cluster ahead turned out to be three families from Barcelona taking their spring break on the Camino. As Inae and I caught up with them, the families formed two spirit lines on either side of the trail and, with appropriate arm movements, cheered, *Buen Camino!* as Inae and I passed through. For a moment we were like players running through a tunnel created by lines of cheerleaders at an American football game.

I then walked for an hour with Marina, one of the moms and her two boys. She was their trip organizer, taught Spanish and "Catalan" at a Barcelona university, and not surprisingly spoke excellent English. I learned that Catalan is a separate language used primarily in Valencia and Barcelona (and is the official language of the tiny country of Andorra). As my time on the Camino increased, I noticed that the Spanish identified themselves with their home region—Galicia or Barcelona or Alicante—more than their nation. While I wondered initially what historical developments might have led to this, I realized that their preferred affiliation might not be that different from those of us in the United States where we might proudly say we were from Texas or New York or Virginia.

Marina explained that individuals, families, or other groups in Spain walk the Camino a portion at a time (like a "section hiker," I thought, on the Appalachian Trail). For this group of families, this was their fourth year walking the Camino and in two more years they would finally get to Santiago and complete the journey from Roncesvalles. (Many in Spain start in Roncesvalles rather than St.-Jean-Pied-de-Port. For someone starting in Spain, Roncesvalles is easier to access than St. Jean, but I also wondered if the reason the Spanish might not want to travel the additional twenty kilometers had more to do with nationality than the severity of the climb over the Pyrenees.)

The next significant town we came to was Nájera. I ran into— again—my Aussie friends. I had beer with them and joined them as we walked into the center of Nájera. I said goodbye as I stopped at a supermarket for shampoo, nuts, and Oreos. I marveled at the cost of local wine in the store—I could buy a bottle for two or three euros.

Resupplied, I crossed a river at the west side of the city. I noted that this part of the town was wedged between a red rock wall and the river. Also, the feel was completely different—so much so that when I try to recall my time in Nájera, I am often confused because of conflicting images. The half I came to and walked through first was commercial and more modern in look and feel; its other half featured historic government and church buildings set against a red rock wall. These sectors are best recalled by remembering that a river separates the two. After crossing the Rio Najerilla but before leaving town I decided to stop for lunch. I wanted something different and more interesting than another baguette with cheese or salami. I splurged by sitting down and ordering a real lunch.

I selected a bar that looked nice enough and had a name I thought I had read somewhere. After looking over the selections written in Spanish, a very helpful bartender walked me through the menu with better than just passable English. He seemed happy to be able to practice his language skills. Not fully understanding the explanations and getting embarrassed by my delay (and noting to myself that this special lunch had seemed like a good idea when I sat down), I finally ordered the fish platter. It came with fried calamari, some fried fish, and a pile of fried sardines (or some similar tiny whole fish). I usually subscribe to the theory that "when in Rome, do as the Romans do," but after trying a couple of the tiny fish I just couldn't eat them all. Not wanting to embarrass my host (or maybe not embarrass myself), I wrapped them in my napkin and hid them in my hat.

Nearby the bartender was enjoying his own lunch. He came over to visit with me and offered a bit of what he was eating. He said it was "tapas." Confused, I tried to explain that I thought everything on the menu was "tapas." This confused him, but as I tried a piece of what he was eating on the end of a toothpick, I finally figured out that he was trying to say "octopus." Realizing what it was as I chewed, and despite some apprehension, I swallowed the "pulpo" bite. I thought it tasted fine.

Having finished lunch but carrying a hat full of fried sardines, I headed out of town. I discarded the tiny fish in the weeds along the dirt path that rose steeply between a gap in the red rock. After that initial climb, the trail descended fairly severely before leveling out and rolling on through more vineyards, mostly on paved but quiet roads. I was greeted by a pleasant surprise when I caught back up with Marina's group of families as I walked with Wayne and Barbara from Boston. The assembly gathered in a nearby gazebo and sang to us (with synchronized clapping) as we passed. The day warmed and the sky cleared. I continued on and enjoyed another hour or so of gentle hiking among the vineyards of Rioja.

While the terrain was not difficult, by mid-afternoon I started to feel the weight of my pack as a pain developed in the lower left side of my back. I found that this nagging ache would appear most days, which I typically tried to combat by using my pack straps to readjust the weight and relieve whatever muscle was being strained.

After a twenty-three-kilometer day, I reached the village of Azofra and headed for the only albergue in town, which proved to be one of my favorites, especially for a municipal hostel. As I entered the property, pilgrims were gathered around a comfortable courtyard featuring a small pool of *very* cold water apparently used mostly for soaking tired feet. I spotted a group of three from Italy (who, for me, would become the "Italian Trio") whom I had leapfrogged with a day or two earlier, and waved. After checking in with the hostel warden and collecting a stamp for my pilgrim passport, I dropped my items on my bunk and cleaned up. It was beautiful and the albergue's courtyard was a lovely spot to relax, read, visit with others, and soak my feet. While I was hanging out with twenty other pilgrims, my Aussie friends arrived. I called Cheryl to keep her up to date on my travels, but before doing so I spoke with Wayne and Barbara from Boston, with whom I had walked earlier in the day and whom I had first met in Villamayor de Monjardin.

My friends had walked the same distance as I had that day having also started in Navarette. So I asked them if they had seen the incredible golden *retablo* at the church that had made such an impression on me. Wayne replied, "We didn't have a very good stay in Navarette." I could tell something had not gone well and the topic did not seem out of bounds, so I inquired. Wayne explained that when they had come into the center of Logroño, a man wearing a backpack had approached them claiming he needed money because of problems with his ATM card. He went on to say that they were uncomfortable with the situation so they walked on, yet when they arrived in Navarette, the same man confronted them again, but this time he had changed his clothes. Wayne commented, "He had to have driven or had someone drive him there."

They again walked away from this man and went to find a hostel. At the albergue, the individual appeared again and spoke to the warden as if he knew him. Twenty minutes later, after Wayne and Barbara got settled in a private room at the hostel, Wayne stepped into the hallway outside his room and found the German-speaking man standing there. Apparently, he had the room next door. Quite disturbed by the developments, they checked out immediately, got a refund for their room, and found a more formal hotel to stay at for the night. Not surprisingly, then, they did not tour the town and explore the church and its fantastic, Baroque gold altarpiece. When he finished his story, I mentioned how I had probably encountered the same unsavory character.

The sleeping arrangements in Azofra might have been the best of the trip for a pilgrim hostel—two to a room, which was nice of course, but very unusual. And, who was my roommate? Mike from Wales, the fifty-five-year-old I had met the prior day in a town thirty kilometers east. After a great rest in the albergue courtyard, I walked the three blocks into town to try to find some Wi-Fi. I ran into Jan sitting at a table on the village's main street. I joined her for a beer when she explained that the bar's Wi-Fi was working well. I had seen Jan as well as her husband Andy and son Matt, "my Aussie friends," a number of times already over the last few days. We were obviously walking at a very similar pace.

Andy and Matt returned, and we all enjoyed a "pilgrim meal" together. I had Cuban rice, veal, and ice cream as well as wine, bread, and water—all for ten euros. My roommate Mike joined us at the end of the meal, and we shared observations and plans after our first week on the Camino. We all walked the short distance back to the albergue and headed for our bunks—another fun and varied day on the Way of St. James.

CHAPTER 8

JEFF AND THE DEVIL

All that is gold does not glitter.
Not all those who wander are lost.

J.R.R. Tolkien

I met Jeff as we both tried to make our way down the backside of the mountain into Roncesvalles on Day One of the Camino. Three days later, walking between Pamplona and Puenta La Reina, I had come upon Jeff partway up the climb to the Alto de Perdon. Obviously winded and tired, Jeff paused at the foot of a steep hill for a brief rest. We were both walking alone. I said hello. We both had that moment of recognition as we re-introduced ourselves. Jeff had just retired from a long service as a Pennsylvania state trooper, one of the few Americans I met on the Way. We continued the hike up to this famous ridge, which that day featured enormous wind turbines on either side of the pass through which the Camino travels over this terrain.

Shortly before reaching the summit, the traveler comes upon the Fuente Reniega, which means "spring of renouncement." As we passed by this spot, I said to Jeff, "Did you read about the tradition concerning this spring?"

"No," Jeff replied, "I don't think I did."

I briefly told him what I had learned, "Tradition provides that in medieval times a pilgrim reached this point exhausted and dying of thirst. The devil appeared and offered him water if he would renounce his faith in God. The pilgrim rejected the proposal, at which point St. James then appeared and showed him to this spring. The pilgrim quenched his thirst using a scallop shell as a drinking cup."

Jeff responded, "That's a nice story, but I can't believe that really happened." He added, "Things like that . . . ," he seemed to pause to find the right word, ". . . the miraculous . . . make it really hard for me to believe in God." Jeff also noted that there were a number of stories about improbable events along the Camino.

I made note of Jeff's comments. I had to agree, believing the story was difficult and accepting a multitude of similar stories was a challenge. Not only did such accounts seem to reduce the seriousness or sincerity of the pilgrim quest, but they also portrayed events that do not—usually—happen. In preparing for my journey on the Camino, I had read about many of the traditions and miracles associated with the pilgrimage. I had not made any judgment at the time, but the amateur historian in me noted that historically most walking the Camino believed in the God of the Bible and were predisposed to accept the supernatural events that are part of the history of the pilgrimage to Santiago. Many modern pilgrims, however, were on the Way for a variety of reasons with an array of belief systems.

A few days later, I arrived in the town of Santo Domingo where I thought of this encounter with Jeff as I was reminded of perhaps the most famous of Camino traditions—the story of the hanging of the innocent and the judge's chicken dinner (which I recount below in the chapter—"Burgos and Timeless Camino Towns"). In another couple of days I'd be in Carrión de los Condes, which has its legend of a hundred virgins. While under Moor occupation, the Christian King Mauregato was required each year to surrender a hundred virgins to the Moor rulers. The Christians prayed to be free of this burden—and a herd of bulls attacked the Moors and chased them off, freeing the Christians from the obligation.

Still another legend comes from the mountaintop village of O Cebreiro. Tradition holds that after the local priest mocked a pilgrim for walking through a snowstorm to receive Communion, the elements of bread and wine turned into the actual body and blood of Jesus, while the twelfth-century statue of the Virgin Mary turned her head to get a better view of this event. Late in the fifteenth century, Pope Innocent VIII validated the accuracy of this event as an official miracle of the Church, which is the point here—these traditions typically are stories of, as Jeff said, the "miraculous."

For some, these traditions appear to be far too odd or impossible to be true. For many, acceptance of these stories, like believing in Noah and the flood or the parting of the Red Sea, becomes a stumbling block to faith. Some, like Jeff, may be attracted to the figure of Christ or the elegance of Christian theology but have trouble coming completely to faith because of the miracles in the Christian tradition. For them, the need to accept these miraculous events brings the entire belief system under question. For many atheists, the view is less charitable. They contend that believers abandon reason to accept as true the events recounted in the Bible or religious tradition that they believe violate the natural order.

I wondered what these stories mean for today's pilgrims—modern people on the road to find out. Some like Jeff find them to be irrational baggage that taints or undermines confidence in God. Some cannot accept such miracles and, as a consequence, conclude that belief in God is irrational. But, I thought, are those the only choices? Must a person accept as true the various Camino traditions involving miraculous events to believe in God? It seems too quick and simplistic to dismiss the larger question just because of doubt over a story of the devil appearing to offer water to a pilgrim. To me, whether that happened or not does not seem dispositive of the ultimate question. If many have accepted and repeated a tradition that in fact is just a fanciful story, it does not follow logically that God does *not* exist.

In the same sense, if such stories or traditions are fanciful or just hard to believe, does that mean they are not true—or cannot be true?

Is it possible that they actually occurred? Could they be true? Almost all religious traditions adhere to various miraculous events, whether it is God dictating the Quran to Mohammed or causing the hand of death to pass over the Jews. The skeptic or atheist would say simply that these traditions violate the "laws of nature" and cannot then be true. As he famously said in his essay titled, *Of Miracles*, David Hume wrote,

> *A miracle is a violation of the laws of nature; and as a firm and unalterable experience has established these laws, the proof against a miracle, from the very nature of the fact, is as entire as any argument from experience can possibly be imagined.*

Relying on a strict view of the weight of evidence, Hume essentially eliminates the possibility that *any* miracle might exist based upon the definitions and methodology utilized. ("Nothing is esteemed a miracle, if it ever happen in the common course of nature.")

Oxford University mathematics professor John Lennox, however, takes issue with Hume noting: "When a miracle takes place, it is our knowledge of the laws of nature that alerts us to the fact that it is a miracle. . . . If we did not know the [laws], we should never recognize a miracle if we saw one." Stated differently, unless you know a rule—a "law"—you cannot identify the exceptions to that rule. For Lennox, the laws of nature are particularly useful because they describe the regularities that God has built in to the cosmos. Hence, "it is therefore no act of violation if he intervenes in his own creation. For such intervention breaks no laws."

But, what did *I* think of miracles? Did I think the devil actually met the pilgrim at the spring near the Alto de Perdon? Likewise, did St. James appear to offer the pilgrim drink? We can see these as fanciful embellishments and nice stories to accompany pilgrims on the way to Santiago, but did I really think they were true—or could be true? And, if I rejected them, like Jeff, what did that mean?

Because of our typical reaction to and use of sensory experience, Hume's view seems compelling. We are more comfortable drawing conclusions from what we see or hear or feel. The apostle Thomas certainly had that same, initial reaction: "Unless I see in his hands the mark of the nails, and place my finger into the mark of the nails, and place my hand into his side, I will never believe" (John 20:25, ESV). Do I really believe that a chicken could come back to life after having been roasted for dinner? It seems very unlikely. Yet I wondered, somewhat like Plato, if there was one event—one miracle—that I genuinely accepted and believed to be true, might that help in considering other "miraculous" events, such as the traditions along the Camino?

For me, one such event that appears so compelling, both philosophically and existentially, to be categorized as a miracle is the creation of the world. In *The Race Before Us,* I analyzed this issue, sometimes known as the "cosmological argument," for the existence of God. The question essentially is: How did the entire universe appear from nothing? The creation of the cosmos was a miracle event, but one that I believe did occur.

Current scientific thinking almost universally assents to a "big bang" theory, which emphasizes that at a single point in time all time and matter was created. Philosophically, if something begins to exist at a certain time, it did *not* exist prior to that time. And, of course, if something (i.e., the universe) did not exist and exists now, something or someone had to act to create or cause what it is that now exists. Many think of that "something or someone" as god—or, as Pete introduced to us, a person behind a design—the "man with the plan."

Once we acknowledge that God exists as a necessary condition to the creation of the world, logically we must be open to the possibility of other miraculous events. Stated differently, if God can create the entire universe—which I believe He did—something as incidental as bringing a chicken back to life seems readily achievable. In fact, after recognizing the enormity of creation, what other miracle would seem *impossible*? In the Christian context, and of obvious interest for the Camino, if God can create the world, why can't He raise Jesus from the dead? (The question of the truth of the resurrection is another subject concerning which I devoted significant time and ultimately an entire chapter in *The Race Before Us*.) And if God could raise Jesus from the dead—which I believe He did—why couldn't St. James appear to a thirsty pilgrim on the Camino?

Having considered the particular issues deeply a few years earlier, these thoughts raced through my mind. I wanted to share it all with Jeff, but most of all I wanted to at least point out that even if stories like the devil at the Fuente Reniega are not true, it does not mean that God did *not* create the world or that God did *not* raise Jesus from the dead; and, of course, it would follow that, even if those tales are not true, it does not mean that God does *not* exist.

CHAPTER 9

BURGOS AND TIMELESS CAMINO TOWNS

(DAYS 9–11)

Pilgrimage—this is beyond walking.
This is walking with the intention of searching the soul.

Stephanie Dale, *My Pilgrim's Heart*

[**Azofra**—[Ciruena], [Santo Domingo del Calzada], [Grañón], [Border: La Rioja-Castilla], [Villamayor del Rio], **Belorado**, [Villafranca Montes de Oca], [San Juan de Ortega], **Ages**, [Atapuerca], [Cardeñuela], [Castañares], **Burgos**]

(88.1 kilometers—54.7 miles)

After completing a week on the Camino, I was very comfortable with a new routine. I continued to meet new pilgrims daily and enjoyed the company of these many new acquaintances. In the days leading up to Burgos, I continued to be exhilarated by hiking through country dominated by vineyards and farmland but dotted with curious medieval towns. Those days would also feature walking through a modern ghost town, appreciating both modern and historic aspects of the ancient journey, suffering an attack of bedbugs, witnessing timeless traditions of Easter in northern Spain, and learning more about Gothic architecture while touring one of the world's great cathedrals.

Wednesday, April 16 (Day 9)

[Azofra to Belorado]
(38.1 kilometers—23.7 miles)

I was out walking before sunrise once again, even a little earlier than usual. It was still dark as I followed my new friends from Boston out of town with my Italian trio not far behind. During the first thirty minutes, we at time had some navigation problems and had to use our headlamps and flashlights to find the Way-markings in the tall grass of the dark fields. Yet, it was beautiful, cool and with the sun rising behind us while a full moon still hung in the sky before us.

Initially we had a gentle morning climb, which finished with a steep, final kilometer up and into Ciruena, a modern ghost town. Not unlike towns after the end of the gold rush in the American West, this town had completely constructed, fairly high-end single-family residences, apartments, and condominiums. In a town with 131 people, to see perfectly good housing for another four thousand just sitting there completely unoccupied was quite odd, to say the least. I was an actor in one of those nuclear holocaust movies, walking through a town whose residents had fled after witnessing a mushroom cloud upwind. And, perhaps even more out of place is the Rioja Alta Golf Club—a course that was described as the "Augusta National" of northern Spain. What we walked through with an odd quiet was a stunning example of the excess that preceded the international credit crisis of 2008. Spain still had not recovered. Unemployment remained very high. A few seemed to have arrived to play golf, but no one had come to Ciruena to begin occupying the fine housing that had been built out of rampant speculation.

I caught up with Wayne and Barbara just as we reached the only part of town with any life. We enjoyed morning café con leche and croissants together and talked about our time on the Camino so far, mostly about the physical challenges. We did not revisit the story of the Austrian having ATM problems and their disturbing encounters with him in Navarette. Both in their mid-sixties, Wayne and Barbara had retired just a few months before starting out from St. Jean.

We had been hiking for over eight days. Wayne mentioned, "It's been hard for us carrying these heavy packs. When we got to Pamplona, we mailed three kilos of gear each to Santiago to lighten the load. And yesterday we sent another three kilos there to be picked up at the end of the journey."

I said, "My pack is heavier than I wanted it to be, but every time I look at my gear I cannot decide what to get rid of. How did you get rid of six kilos?"

Wayne explained, "We got rid of our sleeping bags yesterday."

"Really!" I replied with a real sense of surprise. "How can you do without a sleeping bag?"

"Some hostels have blankets, and if we get cold we just put on and sleep in more clothes," he explained further.

I loved their resourcefulness and determination. They were going to *walk* all the way to Santiago. Hopping on buses or sending their gear ahead each day by transport company was an option but not one suited for them and their Camino. Remember, we all needed to "walk our own walk."

I paid our bill and headed off ahead of them. Before leaving Ciruena, I ran into JuanJo who had stayed at the "miserable" albergue in that town, as he described it. Apparently he had to sleep on a thin mattress on a wood floor without any heat. I later spoke with someone who also stayed in this mostly abandoned town who raved about the hostel and its hostess. These disparate reports made little sense until I realized there were two albergues in this town, despite its deserted feel and its population of just 150.

After descending from the ghost town, I enjoyed my walk on a farm track through rolling fields. In my ears James Taylor sang about "the secret of life" and Gordon Lightfoot sang about the "wherefore and the why."

I was enjoying my time alone. I had another five kilometers before reaching Santo Domingo de la Calzada, a noted Camino town named for Saint Dominic, who is credited with improving the path of the Camino and with expanding services along the Way in the eleventh century. Many local miracles are also attributed to Dominic. I found that I needed to remind myself constantly that these towns and villages on the Way cared for Christian pilgrims over a thousand years ago. I made a very brief stop at a very unhelpful tourist office, but found my way to the center of this ancient but still lively city by following the brass, scallop-shell markers stamped into the walkway. As in every town, the Way-marked path takes pilgrims past the town's famous cathedral, which houses one of the oddest attractions on the Camino.

When I was preparing to take this trip, I tried to read as much as I could so I would not miss (and might better appreciate) many of the important or historic places on the historic way. Reading the Brierley Guide I ran across a strange but notorious story about an unjust hanging and a chicken dinner. Here is how the guidebook explains this tradition:

A German family (father, mother, and their only son—Hugonell) were on a pilgrimage. In Santo Domingo they stayed with a farmer's family, and the farmer's daughter tried to seduce Hugonell, but as a pious pilgrim, he refused her. She became so angry that she hid some silver items in his pack and after he left called the authorities and accused the boy of theft. Upon finding the items in his pack he was found guilty and hanged.

His grief-stricken parents continued on to Santiago but stopped to see their son's remains on their return journey (thieves were left to rot on the gallows as a warning to others). They were delighted to find that he was still alive, claiming that Santo Domingo held him up so he did not die.

The parents hurried to the Magistrate and asked him to cut down their son, as he was clearly innocent. The Magistrate, who had just sat down to a hearty chicken dinner, shouted, "Why,

he is no more alive than this roasted chicken I'm about to eat."
At this, the cooked chicken stood up on his plate, miraculously
brought back to life, feathers and all, and crowed.

For hundreds of years, live chickens have been kept in a coop at the rear of the Cathedral of Santo Domingo to venerate Dominic and to commemorate the miraculous event. The story itself, not to mention the live birds in the sanctuary, was just a little too much for me. Perhaps that was why I did not linger long in Santo Domingo but started walking west again. I was still hiking alone. I enjoyed that solitude. It was more "time on my feet" to look back and to look forward. Having just left Wayne and Barbara (whom I would not see again), I was starting to exceed the pace of many of my early Camino friends. (I had left Jeff and Carol, Jim and Debbie, Father Jim, and others.) Yet some, like Dan and Clara and Pete, had likewise left me in the dust. I did not stress either development—it was how it was meant to be. I put on earphones, turned on my iPod, and selected some songs by Alison Krauss, Cat Stevens, John Denver, Josh Radin, Mary Chapin Carpenter, and probably some more James Taylor. My focus on the lyrics always seemed more intense when a song matched my mood or challenged my thoughts.

As I hiked the Camino, I thought about my life's time
I thought about my life and what I've done well
And what I have left unfinished
I know I'm going to hate to see it end.[2]

I thought intently about the music. Too often I hear the music but do not *listen* to the lyrics. Time on the Camino, especially when there was a sameness of the landscape, helped me concentrate on the words. Songwriters are poets, and many modern songs intend to convey serious thoughts and timeless themes.

---

[2] Due to copyright laws I cannot include the specific song lyrics to which I listened that encouraged contemplation of some of life's great questions, so the editor and I have tried to capture the idea with some made-up lyrics that are placed in various places to signify times of walking and thinking.

Mary Chapin Carpenter, another of my favorite singer-songwriters, has written some thought-provoking songs about relationships, social issues, and life generally. I focused on the lyrics to "Stones in the Road," a song about a time in my era that makes us think about how fortunate most of us are, but also challenges us about the moral choices we make ("A thousand points of light or shame—baby, I don't know"). I thought about life's obstacles, but also about the good fortune I've experienced. Those thoughts were not just about being grateful but about why, and what it means, and what the response should be to such blessings.

I felt good and strong as the Camino path went through modestly rolling, broad, agricultural land. My guidebook indicated that very soon I would leave La Rioja and enter Castilla y León or "Castile," the largest autonomous region in Spain and the "county" in which pilgrims spent the largest amount of time while on the Camino. I did not have a planned or particular destination in mind for the day, and thinking about that was liberating rather than disconcerting. I was relaxed, reflective, and not in any hurry.

> *On the Camino as I walked every day*
> *I thought about the secret of life*
> *I thought about the passing of time*
> *I thought there had to be more to life than that*
> *I didn't know if we had reached the top of the hill*
> *I thought about the secret of life.*

Distracted by the contemplative music, the beautiful morning, and a buoyant mood, I unknowingly strayed from the Way-marked trail, veering left when I should have stayed, as my new British friend Pete would have said, "straight away." With no interruptions or distractions, I walked on, deeper into the farmland and farther from the Way-marked path of the Camino. After a while, still merrily listening to the iPod and walking through the fields, I saw a farm tractor heading for me on the farm road. I moved to the side, almost standing in the crops that were just pushing out of the ground, so it could pass. I expected it to move past so I could return to the farm road and continue on my hike, but the tractor stopped right next to me. I looked up a little in wonder at a man atop a big, green piece of farming equipment.

The farmer behind the wheel was waving and pointing. He was saying something, and it was hard to hear because of the noise of the tractor and because what he said was all Greek (well, Spanish) to me. Yet, despite the language barrier, he communicated well and quickly—I had left the Camino path and ventured well into his farm. Without a moment's hesitation, he tapped on the fender above the big tractor tire inviting me to step up and on the tractor. The farmer then drove me all the way back to where the path had split and I had taken the road not traveled by pilgrims.

I was just outside of the town of Grañón. Up the hill not too far ahead was a familiar trio—in fact, the group had been behind me since leaving Azofra early that morning. I climbed the hill on which the village sat and looked for a place to rest and refresh. The Italian gang (two guys and a woman, who all appeared to be in their thirties) was settled into a table just outside a bar and motioned for me to join them. They explained excitedly that they had seen me take the wrong turn into the farmland, that they had waved and whistled and yelled, but could not get my attention. I showed them my iPod and earphones, explaining why I did not hear their cries. I thanked them nonetheless for trying to set me straight. I bought a beverage in the bar, pulled out some snacks, and joined them for a midday break.

There are some special and some iconic locations. I had just come from one—the Cathedral in Santo Domingo (with the live chickens). Another of the unique stops is in Grañón. Unfortunately, I had not recalled it when the day started out. Thus, even though I toured the Church of Saint John the Baptist there, I did not consider spending the night at its albergue. Despite the clear, bright day, the church seemed very old, damp, and dusty when I toured it briefly. It did not seem very inviting, and I wasn't ready to stop for the night, but I should have inquired further when I ran into Mike from Wales (my roommate from the previous night in Azofra) as I was leaving the church. He said he was staying there for the night even though we still had a half a day of hiking time on a beautiful day.

Much later on the trek to Santiago, some new friends, who had stayed at the basic, parochial hostel, told me about their special night's stay there. The sleeping arrangements were on mats on a wood floor in the attic, near the church bell. A communal meal was served and the *hospitalero* led the pilgrims through a program where the overnight pilgrims explored the inner aspects of their journey on the Camino. The fee for staying was a donation of their choice and the box used to receive that "payment" said "give what you can, take what you need." Like many others, Mike knew this parish albergue was a special Camino experience. Sadly, I did not know. I moved along and missed one of the special experiences on the Camino—obviously my pre-trip preparation could have been better.

Almost three kilometers outside of Grañón, I met two women, sisters from Germany, on a hilltop rest spot by a large sign announcing that we were entering Castilla Y León. Jan (with whom I had enjoyed dinner the night before with her husband Andy and son Matt) showed up by herself while I was speaking to the sisters. Jan's family had decided to spend a few days walking alone and to reunite in Burgos. Jan and I moved off into Castile together. We walked through open fields beside an asphalt road and through a couple of villages as the path rolled up and down some reasonable, but not difficult, climbs. The day was warm without being hot. The temperature rose as the day moved on, but a light breeze kept us comfortable. By late afternoon, we decided to stop and stay in the small town of Villamayor del Rio. However, when we finally hunted down the only albergue, there was no activity, no sign of life. For no apparent reason, this hostel was closed.

Now tired, we nonetheless had to carry on another five kilometers to get to the next town, Belorado. Fortunately the walk was easy. We passed the first albergue and picked out a private hostel in the middle of town. Jan and I were the last to arrive. This albergue was very busy, but we were pleased when we were assigned beds in a quiet, overflow room. The hostel, El Caminante, also offered pilgrim meals. Arriving at the latest hour thus far on the trip, it was an easy decision to sign on for dinner. We joined an older couple from Denmark and enjoyed a good meal and a great evening visit with them. I was pretty tired, having finished an aggressive hiking day (my longest to date), which included climbing up and down three hilltop villages with little respite from the bright sun. With my "detour," I actually walked an additional two kilometers making the day's total right at forty kilometers or almost twenty-five miles. I was most happy to settle in for the day in Belorado. I all but collapsed into the bunk after dinner.

Thursday, April 17 (Day 10)

[Belorado to Ages]
(27.9 kilometers—17.3 miles)

Unlike most albergues I had visited, El Caminante also offered a breakfast. Jan and I left pretty late (almost 9:00 a.m.—my latest morning) after breakfast of cereal, bread, juice, and coffee. With the Camino's increasing rise in popularity, many private hostels have popped up in various towns along the way to supplement the traditional parish, parochial, and municipal albergues. The private are typically for-profit, so not surprisingly the owners might want to supplement bed income by selling breakfast or dinner or both. Before we resumed chasing after yellow arrows, Jan and I briefly toured the old, pilgrim town of Belorado, which dates to Roman times. The town appeared old and tired, but was home to the fascinating sixteenth-century Iglesia de Santa Maria, which was built against a red rock wall and has become a nesting place for numerous storks.

In the Middle Ages, pilgrims would overnight in caves hewn out of that rock behind the church. In fact, at one time San Caprasio had lived as a hermit in the caves. Because of his martyrdom, he became the patron saint of the Via Francigena, which is the name of another historic Christian pilgrimage—a walk through France to Rome. It was curious to consider how much more vibrant this city was six hundred years earlier when it featured eight churches and numerous pilgrim hospitals on either end of town.

Belorado had been settled in Roman times, I felt as if I could imagine the town's gradual development almost like Kingsbridge in Ken Follett's novels set in medieval times. Closing my eyes, my mind settled on a specific scene—a thriving commercial center holding its annual wool fair in the thirteenth century, made possible only after acquiring a coveted charter from the king, no doubt only after some persistent effort, graft, and persuasion. That scene vanished as quickly as it came by walking through the empty streets as we headed off toward Burgos. On a given night, especially during a Holy Year during medieval times, as many as twenty thousand pilgrims would seek refuge, while in April 2014 there might have been eighty or ninety in a town whose population had dwindled to two thousand. The morning Jan and I visited its center square—its Plaza Mayor (many towns had a plaza mayor and a camino mayor)—we saw no one stirring.

Jan and I had another perfect day for hiking as we traveled through other small towns with a couple of quick breaks to take our packs off and get some refreshment. In Villafranca Montes de Oca, we discovered a beautiful garden courtyard of a former "hospital" (a place medieval pilgrims could rest, obtain some basic food and aid, and often, medical care on their way to Santiago) that is now an upscale hotel. Again we were struck by the changes wrought by five hundred years of history. Although the guidebooks indicate that Villafranca has only 147 inhabitants today, in the seventeenth century the hospital there hosted as many as eighteen thousand pilgrims each year. And, our waiter spoke great English. We relaxed there and enjoyed an early lunch.

The climb out of Villafranca Montes de Oca was a very steep incline followed by a longer, steeper descent. My left knee was crying out. I apparently hurt it trying to ease myself down the Alto de Perdon a few days earlier. I only had some real pain when I was hiking terrain similar to what caused the injury. Once I managed the steep but thankfully short downhill, the walk was a long, straight and somewhat monotonous path through the woods between Villafranca to Ages, an area where robbers once attacked pilgrims on their journey in medieval times.

We passed my "Italian trio" friends, who had settled in for an afternoon nap in the woods just off the path. We visited with a father and son biking on the Camino between Atapuerca and Belorado and then again a few hours later when they made the return trip. The father was a prosecutor in Burgos and the son was a medical student. They both had a welcoming and playful spirit. They were proud of their region, and we had fun learning a little more about this area of northern Spain. Although we did not take this three-kilometer detour, we learned that Atapuerca, where our new Spanish lawyer friend has a country house, is home to prehistoric caves and an ongoing archaeological site where the oldest known human remains were discovered, establishing human activity going back over nine hundred thousand years.

We finally ended our long, straight march of twelve kilometers through heavily wooded but relatively flat terrain when we came upon the large open square that appeared to constitute the entire village of San Juan de Ortega. We stopped there for a rest. While we took off our packs and filled water bottles, we met and spoke with Janina and Lucia, a couple of thirty-something women from Germany who were doing a week on Camino. Jan and I carried on to Ages and got settled in the surprisingly crowded village. The albergues were pretty full, but we were shown bunks in the auxiliary "Hay Loft," where I ran into the Crazy Englishmen. As I would discover a few days later, the Hay Loft was appropriately named as I was attacked by bed bugs that night in Ages. At dinner, we realized the increased activity in Ages was a result of Spaniards heading out on the Camino for Holy Week. Thinking back to my own faith tradition, I noted that we had spent Maundy Thursday evening in Ages.

Not only would the next day be Good Friday, but also it would mark a change, as I would reach the great cathedral city of Burgos, after which it was on to the meseta. After coming out of the foothills of the Pyrenees, I had settled into a routine of walking vineyards and farmland, rolling through broad fields and scattered woodlands punctuated by steeper climbs up into and back out of interesting hilltop villages. I had been blessed with wonderful hiking days of perfect sunrises, cool mornings, and brilliant, but mild days. I still looked forward to and was excited to start each day. The physical journey had been largely fun. The time on my feet for personal reflection had been meaningful. Being reminded that thousands of pilgrims had walked these same trails through the same towns that are over a thousand years old (which had much larger populations when the Camino was in its original heyday) recalled the remarkable history of this way to Santiago. I looked forward to the destination, but I had much to do before getting there. I was in no rush.

Repeating platitudes like "it's the journey, not the destination" has become commonplace. Ralph Waldo Emerson is credited with saying, "Life is a journey, not a destination." It sounds nice, maybe even clever—some would say, profound—but I wondered, what does it really mean? How often do we travel or journey and care more about the trip than the destination? How often do we stop short of the gates to Disney World and tell our children it was really just about the journey, not the place where we are headed?

Metaphors work because there is a relationship between the mundane and the profound—meaning that a comparison with everyday things illuminates a greater understanding of something more profound in life. So, I ask myself again, "Do I really care more about the journey than the destination?" I think what people mean by that quip is that journeying in its profound sense is a process of changing by reflecting on and reacting to the physical aspects of the travel. I think I get that, what change? Any change? Is change good in itself? I think what most read into that journey of change is finding answers, resolving issues, discovering meaning or truth. The answers, the truth, really matter, not the process to get there. Baking a cake might be fun—many may enjoy the process—but most bake a cake for the result, the cake.

Not many, or at least not many that most of us would think of as sane, bake a cake just to toss it in the trash and feel good about the experience. So shouldn't we care a little more, if not a lot more, about the destination? How many of my fellow pilgrims did not care about arriving in Santiago? That, of course, was their outer or physical journey. But just as they hoped to complete that journey, didn't they also want to finish—reach the destination—of their inner journey? How many of us would say, "I'm eager to explore the meaning of life, but I don't really care if I find the answer?"

I think this is what C.S. Lewis meant when he wrote, "When we are lost in the woods the sight of a signpost is a great matter, but when we have found the road and are passing signposts every few miles, we shall not stop and stare." You see, to him, and I think to all of us, when we think about it, the destination really did and really does matter. The signposts are only important, and we only take time to wonder about the signposts because they help us toward a destination. In fact, one could say that Lewis's point is that if the destination is important and we are on the right path, we need to hurry along the way because the destination is of such precious worth. As pilgrims heading out on the Camino de Santiago, were we not on the road to find out?

Friday, April 18 (Day 11)

[Ages to Burgos]
(22.8 kilometers—14.2 miles)

The day started like so many before—a cool, brilliant morning with the sun arising at my back. Jan and I planned to stop in Atapuerca (the town with the archaeological dig and evidence of earliest human beings) for coffee, but nothing was open. We continued on another six kilometers to Cardeñuela, which involved a pleasant hike through farm fields and a gradual but serious climb out of Atapuerca. The first bar we came to in Cardeñuela provided our reward—fresh-squeezed orange juice (something very prevalent on the Camino), typically great coffee and, even better, homemade cheese Danish. Slipping off our backpacks, we enjoyed a particularly refreshing stop.

Opting for a more rural route, we first had to hike around a private airfield and then on to the town of Castañares. Pilgrims opting to take a slightly more direct approach to Burgos must walk along busy streets for almost five miles, which we heard were more harrowing than boring. Castañares was within an hour and a half of Burgos. The rural approach brought us to Burgos by following the River Arlanzón. We leapfrogged with a young Spanish couple all day but saw few other pilgrims. With each step as we approached Burgos, the trail went from wild to rural to well-worn until we were on brick pavers in a formal city park. And, likewise, with each step, we saw an increasing number of people until reaching the edge of the city where people young and old were everywhere. Initially we were surprised at what could be described as crowds of people, but eventually recalled that not only was it Good Friday, but in this dominantly Catholic country it was also a major, public holiday.

After first spying the cathedral towers in the distance, we felt as if we would never actually reach that destination. It recalled a story a comedian once told about waking in Paris one morning and glimpsing the Eiffel Tower. He decided to walk to the iconic site. It looked close enough, so he decided just to keep it in his sights and start walking toward it, much like I was doing this midday. After walking for an hour, just looking up and heading for the tower, it did not appear any closer. Continuing to walk along, he all but became convinced that the Eiffel Tower had been placed on wheels and with each step his family made toward it, someone was rolling the historic monument a few steps farther away. Likewise, I started to wonder if we'd ever actually reach the center of the city and its famous cathedral.

The walk along the river, including through a beautiful city park, was easy, pretty and pleasant, but having seen where we were headed for what seemed like a full day already, I was ready to be there. Finally, Jan and I walked through an old city gate where the historic Gothic cathedral revealed itself immediately. Despite the distraction of the swarms of people and sounds of a religious procession nearby, the majesty of the cathedral, at least for a few moments, captured my focus and seemed to drown out any noise or activity around me.

We circled around the cathedral and very quickly and easily found our way to the large, well-run, municipal albergue. Jim and Debbie (friends from Night Two in Zubiri) and Janina and Lucia, the German women from San Juan de Ortega, were already there. I also spoke briefly with the very tall Nick, whose acquaintance I made in the showers the night before at the Ages albergue. Nick seemed even more familiar, though. As I walked back to my bunk, I realized he was the "Crazy Englishman."

Earlier in the journey someone had referred to Nick, without knowing his name, as "the Crazy Englishman." He earned this trail name (like one on the Appalachian Trail) because as Father Jim, the Armstrongs, and I had ascended the Pyrenees on Day One, a very lanky, fully bearded hiker walked by us talking to himself and mumbling a bit about being unable to see anything because of the fog. Nick, a name I'd later attach to this image from Day One, continued down the mountain in a direction we clearly understood to be the wrong way. He walked farther on and back down the mountain. Like an apparition he disappeared from sight as the mist and clouds enveloped him. Nick would repeat the climb the next day so he could enjoy the physical beauty of crossing over the Pyrenees. It seemed crazy because the climb is very difficult, but it reminded me of my uncertainty as to whether to wait a day and start off the next day in the perfect weather that was forecast.

The afternoon had been planned as time for laundry, rest, and sightseeing, which is exactly what I did. Jan went out to try to find her family. While my clothes tumbled dry, I worked on my journal and researched the city for its historic sights. I ventured out alone and toured the town, including the cathedral. Both for modern as well as medieval pilgrims, the "magnet" drawing walkers into Burgos is clearly its famous cathedral, named by UNESCO as a World Heritage site. After traveling through a variety of villages with simple, twelfth-century churches, the Gothic styling displayed by the Burgos cathedral, I learned, reveals the march of architecture as it replaced the Romanesque.

Prior to Gothic design, architects had to use much thicker walls to support the height of the structure. Such building methods permitted only rounded arches and modest windows. The genius of Gothic architecture was the ability to build taller structure but with simpler walls, allowing for the large and long windows permitting much more light into the churches, emphasized by the use of stained glass. Architecture historians remark how "Our Lady of Burgos" is a living exhibition of the evolution of Gothic architecture. While early aspects of Gothic remain, the more obvious elements of the cathedral—the church spires—exhibit a "high" or later Gothic with its significant ornamentation.

After touring the cathedral, I went out into the city to explore. I ran into Janina and Lucia, enjoyed a glass of wine with them, and had an impromptu lesson on the finer points of Spanish, and particularly, "Iberico" ham. Then I climbed to the highest point and looked down on the city and its cathedral and out on the meseta. I watched a Good Friday procession at the cathedral, notable in part for the processional dress: robes and tall, pointed headwear, which looked eerily similar to ones pictured in history books about cross-burning and lynching by the Ku Klux Klan.

When I returned to the albergue, Jim and Debbie, who must have caught a few shuttles since I saw them with Clara a few days ago, sat at the outdoor café just outside the hostel. I was happy to join them and hear how they were doing. They were fun to visit with and always had the best disposition. Later Jan and her son Matt joined us. Recalling that Jan had been in the bunk above me (and thinking I was Jay Leno), when Jan's husband Andy showed up, I asked him if he wanted to sleep with his wife that night—because, as I continued, I'd swap bunk assignments with him if he did.

As I turned in for the night, I noted that it had been quite a day, with two distinct halves. While viewing the cathedral, witnessing the religious processions, and touring the city, I could hardly recall that earlier that same day I had enjoyed a twenty-three kilometer hike just to get there. I had been forewarned that the meseta, which started the next day, would be a challenge. I needed to get some rest, and I was reminded very soon of the hour as the mandatory lights out was strictly enforced.

CHAPTER 10

THE MESETA

(DAYS 12–16)

We will come back changed. Of that I am certain.
But, of course that is why you go on pilgrimage
in the first place; to find the holy, stumble upon
God in action, and be changed forever by the experience.

Canon Trevor Dennis

[**Burgos**—[Hornillos del Camino], **Hontanas**, [Castrojeriz], [Alto de Mostelares], [Boadilla del Camino], **Frómista**, **Carrión de Los Condes**, [Terradillos de los Templarios], **Sahagún**, [Reliegos], **Mansilla de las Mulas**] *(163.6 kilometers—101.7 miles)*

The first third of my trip on the Camino concluded in the great cathedral town of Burgos at the start of the Easter weekend. I had been excited by the newness of the journey and in the changing landscape. By Day 12, however, not only had the novelty worn off, but the nature of the terrain to be traversed—the "dreaded meseta" to some—tested my mental resolve for the trip. Also, my commitment to press through this region more quickly challenged me physically. In the end, as it is with most things in life, you profit most by the investment you make. My time on this high plateau region proved to be a unique time for reflection, but most of all, the people I met and the friends I made—and some of the stories we can tell now—made this time both fruitful and memorable.

Saturday, April 19 (Day 12)

[Burgos to Hontanas]
(31.8 kilometers—23.7 miles)

Upon leaving the great cathedral city of Burgos, the pilgrim on the Camino de Santiago enters a region known as the meseta. I had read about the meseta in Camino guidebooks, and I heard about it from people who completed the Way and from Spanish pilgrims familiar with this part of their country. For many, this region is thought to be the most challenging on the Camino, not because of any physical challenge relating to the severity of the terrain (such as climbing through the Pyrenees), but as a result of the mental challenge relating to the monotony of the topography.

Meseta is simply the Spanish word for "plateau." *Meseta* then refers to the high plains of central Spain. While this tableland occupies a large portion of central and northern Spain, my walk on the Camino was in the northern portion, just below the Cantabrian Mountains and just west of the Pyrenees, extending across most of the northern edge of Spain to Galicia in the far northwest. The expansive region is windblown and largely treeless. It's hot in the summer as wheat and other cereal crops are grown. For me, the spring season offered just brown, dusty fields with green sprouts pushing through the soil in a uniform design. In some regions of the meseta, flocks of sheep graze and roam under large skies filled with billowing clouds.

This region is largely known politically as Castile or Castilla Y León. The word *castile* recalls how the enormous landscape was dotted with fortresses ("land of castles") to protect a region that saw significant conflict for hundreds if not thousands of years, specifically to preserve the region for Christendom after the Reconquista. (Technically, I had passed into Castile just after Grañón on Day Nine between Santo

Domingo and Belorado.) Castile plays a critical if not dominant part in the history of the Iberian Peninsula and the development of what is now Spain. The region is home of the Castilian language, which evolved to what we know today as "Spanish."

The Roman Empire extended its reach to this area largely because of gold discovered in the mountains to the north and west, which was mined and transported to Rome. Hence, most of the monuments, villages, landmarks, and surviving prominent, manmade features in the northern part of the meseta are remnants of either its Roman past or the later Reconquista, which involved the retaking of control over the region by Christians from the Moors. El Cid, the "George Washington" or national hero of Spain, is from just outside of Burgos. He gained that title and status as a Castilian nobleman and military leader in the eleventh century. He led armies successfully against both neighboring Muslims and competing powers in León and Galicia. Tradition holds also that El Cid traversed the Camino on his own pilgrimage. This landscape is also the setting for the most famous book and fictional character to come out of Spain—Don Quixote. With his sidekick Sancho Panza, the aging knight "tilting at windmills" traveled throughout La Mancha, the southern part of the meseta.

I was prepared for boring, flat, and open vistas. From a negative perspective, the landscape lacked definition or interesting landforms and, with endless fields of wheat, the colors were dominated by basic, dull hues with little variation or nuance.

From a positive perspective, the meseta recalls American landscapes like Montana and its "big sky" with brilliant cloud formations against a spectacular blue background and verdant green base. Yet preparing for long, relatively flat, straight pathways alongside roadways caused me to come up with a plan to reduce my time in this area. While I was averaging twenty to thirty kilometers a day, I determined that if I could add ten kilometers a day, I could turn five days on this high plateau into four days. Physically I figured that the flatter terrain would also make it easier to press out longer walks.

I started my assault on the meseta by leaving Burgos before sunrise. As I approached and then walked beside the cathedral on my way west, the moon still hung between the high Gothic cathedral spires. I had hoped to be hiking by 6:00 a.m., but the albergue was locked down (and we were locked in) until 6:30. After passing the cathedral, guided more by the artificial light of the city, I started looking for yellow arrows to show me the way out of the city and onto the Camino. Just ahead I saw a woman glancing around, like I was doing, for some indication as to which streets and what turns to take to leave the town and enter the meseta.

I caught up to Carmen, a young woman from the southeast of Spain, as she paused for some indication of direction. After saying hello, we worked together to find "the Way." We spotted some yellow arrows and, relieved, we finally moved along. A few minutes later, we ran into Lynn from British Columbia and the three of us left the city limits and headed out into the broad landscape as the sun was rising. Little did I know then, on Day 12 of my journey, that despite separating and reacquainting various times, the three of us would walk the final twenty kilometers together into Santiago seventeen days later. But such is the Way of the Camino.

The first two hours of the meseta lived up to its reputation. We met "Ricky" from Japan on his first day on the Camino. He had started that morning in Burgos, which reminds us that not everyone starts in St. Jean or Roncesvalles. I would see Ricky many more times over the next seventeen days and, remarkably, would see him the day Carmen, Lynn, and I arrived in Santiago. Many Spaniards start the Camino in Pamplona or Burgos or León.

Yet, I was reminded further that historically pilgrims started "their Camino" by leaving their hometown by foot and walking to Santiago whether they lived on a farm outside of Paris, or in the city of Munich, or the foothills of the Alps, or wherever. In Puente La Reina (where I bunked my fourth night), I had dinner with Frank from Austria who had actually started his walk—his Camino—from his home. Later I would bunk with new friends from the Netherlands who started in

Holland and walked the entire way over three years. The year I met them, they were finishing the final third and planned to arrive in Santiago about the same time I planned to do so (I saw them again in Galicia as we left the town of Molinaseca one morning).

After eleven kilometers, we stopped in Tarjados for coffee and ham/egg/cheese sandwiches. Amazingly, I saw the Italian Trio and my Aussie family friends there. Carmen and I continued on, walking among early wheat fields with no cover from the bright sun. After a brief lunch stop in Hornillos del Camino, we walked a long afternoon together talking about her family, her boyfriend, and her future. Wise and grounded, despite being out of work for three years (typical, unfortunately, of her age group in a country still suffering significantly from the credit crisis and housing bubble of the Great Recession), Carmen was nonetheless content, acknowledging that she was very blessed because of her family and community despite Spain's problems.

The hiking was comparatively easy. Good conversation provided considerable interest where the landscape offered little. As predicted, Day One in the meseta was a fairly long haul, made challenging mainly because of the sameness of most of the steps. Carmen said she enjoyed our conversation, at least in part, because she could practice her English. Late in the day, we neared the tiny hamlet of San Bol. We were tempted to stop, take off our packs, and drop our hot, dusty feet in the special fountain there to test the pilgrim legend that such a soaking would cure the weary traveler of all foot pain. Yet, when we saw that it involved a detour—even though it was just a half of a kilometer—we marched on because our destination, the small town of Hontanas, was just four kilometers ahead.

Tired and ready to stop, I was becoming a little distressed because I knew we had already walked over thirty kilometers and, unlike my walks through most of the towns in Rioja, I had not yet caught a glimpse of our destination. We finally eased ourselves down into the town that had been all but hidden from us because of how it sits low, below the horizon. Entering the interesting, pilgrim-friendly one-street town rewarded our long walk into Hontanas. Carmen headed for the municipal albergue, and I went to the private one directly across the street where I got the last bed at what proved to be my favorite hostel of the entire trip.

I cleaned up in the best shower I had on the Camino—the water was hot and did not turn off automatically every three minutes. Also, it had a dressing area outside the actual shower stall where you could lay your dirty and post-shower clothes, rather than trying to figure out how to remove your clothes while keeping your clean clothes dry, and then figure out how to shower without having any of the clothes get wet or slide off the walls or door of a stall where only a ninety-pound woman might be able to turn around.

Carmen met me for a beer at a café right on the main street in town to celebrate a long, hot walk that would have been tougher mentally if we had not enjoyed each other's conversation. I returned to my hostel, which had a beautiful courtyard with a large, covered picnic table where I sat, rested, worked on my journal, and met some new Camino friends: Tess from Colorado, Jen from Australia, David from Denver, and Frida from Germany. We had some interesting conversations about government, health care, and entitlements. I decided to keep my more conservative views to myself. I did not know these people (who seemed to know each other), and this was not the place to fight political or social battles. Yet, I couldn't help but note to myself that I thought most of the fruits and nuts came from California.

Later, I enjoyed a very pleasant, "family-style" paella dinner around a large dining room table with Frida, Jen, George from Arizona, two from France (who, for me would become, the "Frenchmen"), two from the Netherlands, and two older women from Pensacola, Florida. We all retired to the cleanest bunks and bunkroom on the Camino. Nothing would keep me from a good sleep after only my second day of hiking over thirty kilometers.

Sunday, April 20 (Day 13)

[Hontanas to Frómista]
(34.6 kilometers—21.5 miles)

After a good rest at my favorite albergue, as usual I woke early (4:45 a.m.) and as usual planned get an early start on the day's walk and my second day in the meseta. So as to not disturb those sleeping, I carried my gear downstairs and packed to leave. The Frenchmen joined me downstairs as they too were heading out early. We knew each other from other short visits on the Camino, but we shared little due to our language barrier.

I had rain on the very first day leaving St. Jean and climbing over the Pyrenees. Since then, the weather had been nearly perfect. Leaving Hontanas, it was cold and gray and raining lightly. The Frenchmen headed out before me as I grabbed a cup of coffee and croissant. Yet, I was still out before sunrise and due to the cloud cover, it was still dark. The path led through trees outside of town making the going slow as finding the Way marks was difficult. I actually stopped before exiting town to use the light from a street lamp just to find the next yellow arrow. I used this pause to put on my rain jacket, pull out my headlamp, and put the rain cover on my pack. It looked to be a challenging day.

Almost immediately after leaving Hontanas, the trail headed into forest. The path was earthen and widened into a narrow two-track lane, about the width of a car. It didn't appear to actually be a country road—maybe a rarely used trail for some farm equipment. Because of the previous night's rain, there was considerable puddling and in the early morning light I had to watch my steps. The day brightened a little. I turned off my headlamp after about thirty minutes. The trail was generally flat.

After a little over five kilometers that I covered in just over an hour, I turned left and came out on a paved road. Considering the remoteness of these towns and the early morning hour, I was surprised and just a bit concerned when I saw a car stop at the intersection of the road and the Camino path and seemingly wait for me as I approached. As I got closer, the passenger got out and walked toward me. I was relieved—very surprised (because I was certain that only the "Frenchmen" and I had started out early) but relieved—to be greeted by George, with whom I had shared the paella dinner the night before.

George directed his flashlight beam at my shoes as he said, "Somebody took my boots this morning."

I guess somewhat defensively I said, "Well, I can assure you that these [placing my foot into his flashlight bean] are mine."

He quickly agreed that the Vasque Mindbenders that I was wearing were not the boots he was looking for. He then explained that when he arose, got dressed, and went to put on his boots to start the day's walk, his boots were gone. He had convinced a cook arriving at the hostel for work to drive him out ahead on the Camino to catch up to those who had left before him. I explained about how the Frenchmen and I were the only ones out early and that they were probably twenty or thirty minutes ahead of me.

Lifting the boot on his left foot, George explained, "My boots are just like this, but these are older and a size smaller … and, my left boot was laced by skipping [pointing toward the toe] these two bottom eyelets."

Thinking quickly that only fifteen people were staying in the same hostel the previous night, I said, "I just can't figure who could have taken your boots." And then I repeated, "I'm all but positive that no one other than the Frenchmen are up ahead of me."

"Then," George replied, "the person must be somewhere between here [indicating where the trail intersects with and begins to follow the paved road] and the hostel."

I readily agreed that the alleged culprit had to be somewhere back the last five kilometers, but added, "I can't imagine someone took your boots, but I guess if they're that similar it's possible." I wished George good luck, turned right, and started hiking down the street toward San Anton.

My walk continued through San Anton and onto Castrojeriz, an interesting town with castle ruins still watching over its medieval streets. After a café con leche and a brief rest in Castrojeriz, I made the gradual but significant climb in a light rain up to Alto de Mostelares. Another dozen or so pilgrims were on the path with me hiking along at different paces. Some passed me, and I overtook others. I enjoyed a brief break at the summit in a shelter with Frida and Jen, both from the previous night's hostel, as they caught up to me just as I dropped my pack. Frida and I departed from the summit together and immediately had a very steep downhill to a relatively flat and mildly rolling path, which characterized the terrain for most of the rest of the day. I walked more quickly than Frida, but she caught up in the town of Itero de la Vega. We searched together for a lunch spot, but most places were closed, presumably because it was Easter Sunday. Finally, we had to double back to the albergue at the entrance to town, which was open and where we lunched on a *bocadillo* of ham and cheese. To our pleasant surprise, we again ran into Jen, Carmen (from the day before), and David (from Colorado—from the albergue the night before). I headed back out on the Camino alone after charging my iPod, which I used for the rest of day's walk all way to Frómista. It was a peaceful walk, with interesting lyrics causing me to reflect on the great questions of life. This truly was an inner journey.

Midafternoon the day started to clear. Rain gear came off and skies brightened. Most others I had spoken with were stopping in Boadilla del Camino, which would make for a twenty-eight kilometer day. I decided, however, to push on another six kilometers to Frómista as part of my plan to shorten my time in the meseta, making it a thirty-four kilometer or a twenty-one mile day.

The sun finally began to peek through as I walked through Boadilla. The trail then followed a canal that cut through an agricultural landscape, so the terrain was almost perfectly flat, which helped me to make good time heading toward and into Frómista. Low on euros, job one was finding an ATM. Standing outside a Santander branch, having been unsuccessful in extracting any euros from its ATM, I ran into the Frenchmen from that morning. They too had obviously ventured all the way to Frómista. George had caught up to them and checked out if they were wearing his boots—no luck. Fortunately an ATM across the street had an adequate supply of euros and I restocked.

I secured a room at the San Martin hotel and headed for an outdoor table to put my feet up and relax. While enjoying my afternoon *cervesa*, Ciaran from Ireland, another pilgrim about my age, joined me in the café. Two days before his son was to start the Camino, Ciaran decided to go as well. *Wow!* I thought, *How's that for planning?* His son was now a few days ahead of him, but they'd planned to meet up in Santiago. We enjoyed a beautiful late afternoon together sharing stories from home and the Camino. (I would see Ciaran several times in the days to come, and, we would finish in Santiago at the same time.)

Just across the courtyard from the outdoor café where I sat with Ciaran was the Iglesia de San Martin or Saint Martin's Church, which I learned was perhaps "the most brilliant example of Spanish Romanesque architecture." Completed in 1066, it featured many elements I had come to understand exemplified that pre-Gothic art form, including circular stone towers. This church apparently has among the best preserved decorative features—corbels—consisting of mystical, animal, vegetable, and geometric forms and designs. Here, as unfortunately in many Camino towns, the church was closed, even on Easter Sunday.

I showered and then walked around town. The sky had cleared and was bright and breezy. I stopped in church long enough to focus on the day (it was Easter Sunday), give thanks, and pray. Back at the hotel, I ordered some wine and pasta and worked on my photographs, journal, and blog. I called Cheryl and enjoyed a good night's sleep in a private room, my second one after thirteen days on the Camino.

My second day in the meseta had not been the monotony I had anticipated. The landscape had included traversing a high ridge, and the scenes had been more varied than the first day, including an interesting medieval town, a canal cutting through the agricultural plains, and the more modern town of Frómista. And the day had its intrigue, as I wondered what happened to George's boots.

Monday, April 21 (Day 14)

[Frómista to Carrión de Los Condes]
(20.5 kms—12.7 miles)

After a Sunday much like the first Easter weekend itself (beginning dark and gloomy but finishing with brilliant sunlight and joy) and being greeted by remarkable weather, I felt invigorated to my soul, like the promise of new birth. At its core I wondered, if this isn't ultimately what pilgrimage is all about—the hope, optimism, and expectation of change, of finding answers, and of finishing the journey as someone different than the person who started the adventure.

I was eager to get started by 6:00 a.m., but the front desk wasn't open until 8:00. I had planned to conserve euros and pay by credit card, but I was not going to sit around until 8:00. Worse yet, I did not know precisely what I owed. Unwilling to hang around for almost two hours, I made the best calculations I could and left enough euros (I hope) to cover the room, beverages, and dinner. I left Frómista in the dark and enjoyed one of my most spectacular sunrises as I walked away from the town.

After a brief search trying to identify the way out of town, I located a yellow arrow and headed out before the sun rose. Glancing back over Frómista, I saw that the rising sun painted a dramatic pink sky among scattered clouds. I followed a fairly major road (quiet, though, because of the hour) for fifteen or twenty minutes and then reached a decision point. My preferred approach was to always take the more rural route—the road less taken—because that route was usually more pleasant aesthetically and often quieter and prettier.

The path less traveled followed a small river (Rio Ucieza) west rather than follow the busy, main road to the town of Carrión de los Condes, the site of my first planned "nero day." The route was uncharacteristically overgrown. I was the first to walk that way that morning and perhaps the first in a number of days. The morning dew soaked my feet for the first time on the trip. Yet, I loved the removed setting and the solitude that accompanied it. I ran into a local Spaniard and his dog as he collected snails for his next Sunday paella. Before long I veered away from the river and followed the more rural path into a small town and then onto a hard dirt path along the main road. The terrain was very flat. I reached Carrión before noon.

If you hike the Appalachian Trail a "zero" day is a rest day (a day of no hiking—"zero" miles). A "nero day" is almost a zero day. I had planned to read, write, rest, and resupply in Carrión. I was the first to check into the albergue that is part of the Santa Maria church complex, one of the iconic stops along the Camino. The hostel is run by nuns who sing folk songs with the pilgrims each evening. At its height, Carrión had ten thousand inhabitants and fourteen pilgrim hostels. It was an important waypoint on the route to Santiago de Compostela. Today, the town has only two thousand inhabitants and three pilgrim hostels; however, all services are available.

As I enjoyed the sunshine and relaxed in the church courtyard, I met and greeted a remarkable number of fellow pilgrims I had seen previously along the Way, including JuanJo, Carmen, and Ricky. And George arrived—wearing his own hiking boots! I was heading out to do some resupply and he was heading over to check in at the hostel, but I told him, "I have to hear the rest of the story!" After running some errands to retrieve some euros and supplies, I rested by reading and writing in the beautiful sunshine while sitting on a bench in the church courtyard. My rest was planned. I had two more long days on the vast tableland. I was already excited about finishing the meseta and visiting another great cathedral town. Unless something unusual happened, I would reach León soon.

I joined in a communal meal preparation and sat down with almost twenty other pilgrims from all over the world, including Ken from Ohio and Jacob from Poland (with whom I'd spend the evening in Finisterre two weeks later). My sleeping quarters for the night was in the bottom bunk of a room filled with ten bunks, which were occupied variously by twenty-year-old college students from Japan, a sixty-five-year-old man from Austria, fifty-year-old George from Arizona, fifty-five-year-old Lynn from British Columbia, a thirty-year-old

German woman who hobbled into the albergue just after I did (she was suffering from a very bad leg injury), and a young Korean woman ("Lee"), who slept in the bunk just above me.

After the meal and singing, the *hospitalero* gave a talk about Jesus and a pilgrim's inner journey, which he concluded by giving everyone the gift of a painted star as a symbol of the spiritual aspects of their time on the Camino. Before lights out, George took me outside to the courtyard before the Church of Santa Maria and recounted the tale of the missing boots and their unlikely return.

Apparently, after George said goodbye to me the morning before, he somehow convinced the driver to take his car on the earthen path back toward Hontanas. Recalling that it was neither paved nor even hard dirt, I wondered how they got along trying to drive on a grassy, earthen trail after an evening's rain. George continued, "The car did get stuck in the mud a few times and we had to get out and push it out of some holes. Fortunately, some other pilgrims were on the trail and they helped push the car out of mud holes." He explained that as they got closer to town, he was able to check each pilgrim coming along the way for his boots but was not successful in locating them.

He got back to the hostel where his driver worked. "The inside of the car was a mess. I felt terrible. Every time we'd get stuck I'd get out into the mud to help push the car free. I tracked a lot of mud into the car," George elaborated. "I got my pack and started walking, wearing the other person's boots that were a half of a size too small," George explained. He walked all the way to Boadilla del Camino looking at the feet of all the pilgrims he passed, but never found his boots. He selected an albergue and, while checking in, explained his plight to the *hospitalero*, who helped him get settled and then offered to take him around to the other three hostels in the town to check further for his boots. George went on, "We went through the first two hostels, but didn't find my boots. But at the last stop I saw my boots lined up with everyone else's walking shoes. So my *hospitalero* explained the situation to the warden at that albergue and she let us walk back into the hostel to talk with the pilgrims staying there."

Eventually they ran into Shannon and a few others lying around on their bunks. George asked about the boots, noting that he had seen his boots out front and wanted to exchange them for the ones he was wearing. He told me, "I recalled Shannon from somewhere. We spoke because we recognized that we had met before. As we were inquiring with a few others, Shannon got up and left the room. When he returned, he came up to me and said he thought he probably had my boots. I walked out to the front of the albergue, picked up the boots that were mine and here I am."

All I could say was, "Unbelievable! It's lucky you were able to locate them." And then quickly I said, "We'd better get back to the hostel. It's after ten and the door may be locked."

Sure enough. But a friend was watching the door and let us in. What a day it had been.

Tuesday, April 22 (Day 15)

[Carrión de Los Condes to Sahagún]
(39.8 km—24.7 miles)

Similar to the stretch outside of Burgos, the path leading west away from Carrión was very straight, very open, and very uninteresting. The guidebooks said that it was the restored Via Aquitana, an ancient Roman way. In fact, this stretch remained very straight, very open, and very uninteresting for seventeen kilometers, over seven miles. The openness of Spain's central plateau allowed for a strong wind to meet us head on and, having started early, I was a little cold. I wore both an extra layer and my wind jacket, which were the most layers I had worn since the first day climbing through the notch in the Pyrenees.

The sun played hide-and-seek with large, cumulus clouds above. Here the warming sun was welcome. The path was a single lane of hard dirt and loose rock that was well-graded, useful for pilgrims but probably no one else. Other than the vast expanse of the meseta, there was little to see but the hard dirt corridor cutting through the scrub, leaving a permanent, linear scar on the landscape.

I saw and then leapfrogged with the lone French couple. Out of no-where a tractor-trailer came hurtling down the road. It surprised me initially and startled me in the way that we give thanks, after the fact, for surviving such a close call, not realizing while it was happening how dangerous the situation really was. Little room was available for me to get to the side and no way existed for me to get off the improved surface to give the truck a wider berth. Barreling by, in what had to be in excess of seventy miles an hour, the aftershock created a brief windstorm that took the hat off my head and deposited it thirty yards behind me. Thankful I was in one piece. Afterward, I found it actu-ally humorous as I walked back to retrieve my hat. When I later was passed by the French couple they laughed retelling the scene, with vigorous arm movements, of watching my hat come flying off as the truck raced by.

After three hours of sameness with no services, I reached the worn and tired town of Calzadilla de la Cueza. Ready for a break and some refreshment, I ordered eggs, bacon, and coffee. This bar had some local life and I saw Lee, who bunked above me the night before. She must have gotten an even earlier start than me. She left shortly after I arrived, but in a very sweet manner said she hoped we'd meet again (and, of course, as it is on the Camino, I would run into Lee again as we walked into Sarria ten days later).

Having defeated the Roman road and rested with a great breakfast, I was ready to press on. As I prepared to leave, I was unexpectedly greeted by a real sense of joy mixed with excitement and gratitude. I was unsure of its source, but it put a bounce in my step and I headed off enthusiastically to challenge the next part of the meseta. I made good time to Ledigos and the Terradillos de les Templarios and then to Moratinos and San Nicolás del Real Camino. The atmosphere as I passed through these mud brick towns was terribly quiet and some-what sad as the streets were lifeless and the buildings aged and worn. Other than the names of a couple of albergues, little is there to remind travelers that this was an area where the Knights Templar had been.

The day seemed to consist of two distinct parts, like the "outer/inner journey" theme of the Camino itself: first, a cold, cloudy boring slog over ten miles; second, joy and enthusiasm with bounce in my step and excitement in my heart. What explained the difference? Some would say the break after seventeen boring kilometers. Some would say the bacon and eggs. But I believe it was gratitude and grace.

While stopping for breakfast, I was able to use the bar's Wi-Fi and picked up a message from Cheryl. The message itself was not particularly noteworthy, but it reminded me of the joy of loving and being loved. I loved my time on the Camino, but I missed Cheryl. Not only did I have these thoughts at the time, but I was moved to capture them in my journal by writing: "Nothing explains the lightness of my pack, the strength of my legs, or the enthusiasm in my step other than being reminded that God is walking with me and bringing me along; and nothing reminds me of his grace like the love I have for Cheryl and our girls."

I decided to push on to Sahagún, which would be a long day—forty-one kilometers or almost twenty-five miles. The walk was mostly a lonely one with the coolness and the clouds increasing. The joy I experienced midday had begun to wear off with the miles and the unrelenting sameness of the terrain and vistas. The weather never cleared, so my afternoon walk was dreary, although I did use this time for some meditation with selected music.

When I finally arrived, Sahagún itself was tired and gray, and like many towns I walked through on the Camino, it was just a shadow of its former prominence. My Dintaman guidebook said that Sahagún had "great significance in medieval times." Apparently, it was the center of monastic development in the kingdom, second only to León in importance, and characterized by a very diverse population of Jews, Muslims, and Christians, which led to the Romanesque-Mudéjar architectural style still evident in modern-day Sahagún. I walked around to get a sense of that proud past, but very little was engaging about the historic buildings that remained. They just seemed tired and gray. I'm sure I was tired and, without the benefit of a docent to point out the finer details, I probably rushed by some items of interest.

I arrived in Sahagún later than most days, not surprising considering the distance traveled that day. I grabbed a beer, some supplies, and some dinner, which I ate alone in my hotel room. I saw few signs of life and only two other pilgrims while I was out and about. Late and tired, I had decided to stay in a private room, which may have been a mistake because the energy of most albergues might have shifted my mood. I seemed as though I always met someone interesting in the hostels. It just seemed late and quiet and gray and depressing when I entered Sahagún, so I grabbed a room and settled in fairly quickly. I did call Cheryl, which definitely helped my mood and perspective.

Wednesday, April 23 (Day 16)

[Sahagún to Mansilla de las Mulas]
(38.4 kilometers—23.9 miles)

A key point in my journey to Santiago was probably my days approaching and leaving Sahagún. I seemed to have outpaced my early friends on the Camino, and I had not really connected with a new group. Not only were the bedbug bites I had suffered a few days earlier in the "Hayloft" at Ages still present, the itch was ferocious, and just the idea of those bugs crawling on and biting me was a little disquieting. Those days I walked mostly by myself, which I enjoyed from time to time, but a combination of the aging towns, stark vistas, little companionship, and depressing weather conspired to create a modest and brief "damp, drizzly November" in my soul.

Brierley described these meseta towns as "delightful villages seemingly unaffected by the speed of modern life." Not to be mean, but most meseta "villages" were well past their prime and decaying. Their churches were boarded or locked up. There was little activity in the streets, few bars, and nothing of note historically or culturally. To my way of thinking, confirmed by having walked through it for four or five days, the meseta is aptly described by the following I read on a website:

The Meseta is sparsely populated. The scattered, earth-cultured villages are often camouflaged in the open plain, and only a church tower–or nowadays a grain silo—identifies their location. With mechanization of the land, many of the villages are now abandoned or inhabited only by older people, the younger set having either emigrated or moved to the large towns in the 1960s and 70s in search of work.

Sahagún was much more than a village, yet I remember it as a depressing town. As I departed the morning was cool and gray, doing little to lift my spirits. As the sun began to rise, the temperature actually got even cooler so I added a layer under my backpack. I was off, hoping for a better day.

The day's walk featured an inconsistent sky, shifting between sun, clouds, wind, and clearing skies, which even included a ten-minute rain shower as I walked from Calzada del Coto to Bercianos del Real Camino. Perhaps because the November in my soul lingered, I failed to carefully review my guidebook, so I overlooked the spot just before Calzada where routes split. Hence, I missed the detour and was stuck on the road more traveled, which meant I missed the more pleasant, rural walk and was confined to a hard dirt and gravel path parallel to the main road.

The walk was steady and easy as I reached El Burgo Ranero, which, as a meseta village, was particularly sad and depressing. From there I walked alone most of the day along a paved road and saw very few other pilgrims. This created a good opportunity to listen to some music, and not just listen to the melodies but to concentrate on the lyrics, what the writer was trying to convey, what meaning I might tease out of them, and how might they speak particularly to me. Fortunately, the traffic was more bicycle than vehicular, which helped make a mindless wander possible and permitted me to concentrate more on the music and lyrics.

I focused on some James Taylor lyrics, particularly what they said about life and many of the eternal issues I had been working through my mind with all of the time on my feet. In "Wandering," Taylor writes and sings, "I've been wandering early and late, from New York City to the Golden Gate; and it don't look like I'll ever stop my wandering." And Yusuf Islam (the artist formerly known as Cat Stevens) sings in "Maybe There's A World" that he has been seeking a special place, "a place and time where nobody gets annoyed"—but he notes that he's not there yet. I saw little difference in seeking that place and heading out on a pilgrimage. Islam's special "place" about which he sings is not just a place "where nobody gets annoyed" but is "borderless and wide" and no one is "taking sides." The song finishes by suggesting that all the wrongs of the world will be put right when that time comes.

Certainly for a medieval pilgrim, the song sounds much like the message of Christianity, which says the "wrongs of the world" are put right through the death and resurrection of Jesus. Even more, Islam sings, "Then, there'll be a new life to begin," which is also very consistent with Christian theology. And Santiago himself would tell us, through the death of Jesus, believers are given a new life.

The afternoon walk was a bit monotonous, but I did come upon a shepherd guiding a very large flock of sheep across the main road, a reminder of the past when Ranero was a much more important wool-producing town and flocks as large as forty thousand often wandered these vast fields. The weather was similar to the previous day—cold and cloudy, then much clearer and warmer with a big sky of blue interrupted by building columns of white cumulus clouds. I started to see mountains in the distance, which suggested I was nearing Galicia.

I stopped for lunch at a picnic spot before Reliegos and then pushed out the last six or seven kilometers before arriving in Mansilla de las Mulas. Brierley says the town's name is likely derived from its early prominence as a livestock market. I was again pretty tired when I arrived, but as I entered the town, I immediately ran into the Frenchmen who were standing in the Puerta Castillo—the "gateway" through the fortress walls—and I updated them on the story of George's boots.

Mansilla is a pretty substantial town that appears to have moved forward and modernized with time while still retaining a historic look and feel. The orientation of its streets recalls its origin as a Roman settlement and its well-preserved medieval walls date to Fernando II of León and the twelfth century. Brierley suggests that the walls "protect the town from the encroachment of modernity," yet, for the modern pilgrim, Mansilla had good services and offers good options. At the hotel restaurant I selected for dinner, the owner bought me a glass of wine and talked with me for quite some time before I enjoyed a particularly excellent pilgrim meal—lamb and potatoes starter, chunked beef and fries, flan for dessert, and the usual water, wine, and bread. I called Cheryl and then turned in for the night. Mansilla was a good Camino town. My mood had been adjusted, and I was ready to move along with renewed enthusiasm.

CHAPTER 11

CARMEN AND ERIC LIDDELL

I shall be telling this with a sigh
Somewhere ages and ages hence:
Two roads diverged in a wood, and I,
I took the one less traveled by,
and that has made all the difference.

Robert Frost

I met Carmen as I was leaving Burgos in the predawn light. We were both cautiously making our way down a street exiting the city but wondering if we were still on the correct path. Glancing about for a yellow arrow or two, we tried, now a team, to read the Way-markings and head off toward Santiago. Carmen was a twenty-six-year-old Spanish woman who started her own journey on the Camino in Roncesvalles, coincidentally, the same day Dan and I left the albergue in that town in a similar predawn light. Carmen and I, however, had not met before. Leaving Burgos, I walked a long day with Carmen and learned much about her and life in Spain. I was mostly taken and touched by her perspective on life: "I may have been unemployed for three years but I'm more blessed than most." She continued, "I'm rich in so many things. I live in a wonderful community, I have a roof over my head and I have a wonderful family." Even though Spain was continuing to suffer from a sagging economy and employment opportunities for her were few, she was content, she was happy, and she was comfortable that life would be fine. She seemed to have a trust in something unspoken.

We stayed together and conversed throughout the day. Yet we also enjoyed quiet moments while still having a walking companion. Refreshed by Carmen's attitude, I recalled a scene from the movie *Chariots of Fire* where Harold Abrahams says to Eric Liddell, "You're brave, compassionate, kind: a content man. That is your secret, contentment; I am twenty-four and I've never known it." After a brief, contemplative pause he adds to this realization, "I'm forever in pursuit and I don't even know what I am chasing." Later, Abrahams rendered judgment on his situation, "That was the miscalculation of my life."

Like Huck Finn and Ishmael, and like Chaucer's pilgrims, Abrahams in all of his running and racing, was searching for meaning, "forever in pursuit," on the road to find out. As he said, "When the gun goes off, I have ten seconds to prove myself." He lacked contentment because his hope, his sense of worth, his concept of meaning was based upon and bound up in his personal achievement on the racetrack. Abraham of the Bible trusted God; Abrahams trusted Abrahams. If he succeeded in his athletic endeavors, his life would have meaning, would be worth living. But ultimately, somehow he knew that his prowess in the sporting world would never be enough. Like Carmen's unspoken sense of trust, Abrahams seemed to *know*—"there must be something more."

For most, it's hard to have a sense of gratitude if you are not content. You are always looking for something else, something more. You are always wondering why some have more than you or some have achieved more—whether it is recognition, material success, or something else. The inability to be content with what you have, with who you are, or with where you are is a function of where you place your hope—where you, like Harold Abrahams, place your sense of worth and meaning. Like Liddell (and like Abraham, the patriarch), Carmen was content because she had not placed her sense of worth in a job or an accomplishment. She saw herself part of something much bigger and more important than merely herself.

I've said that among my reasons for being "on the Camino" was "to look forward" and "to look back." Time on my feet including long periods of solitude permitted me to think back in a meaningful way about my fifty-five years. Not being interrupted by the rush of life or the press of business helped me see more clearly that I have an enormous list of people for whom I am grateful.

Many would suggest that I have "succeeded" in life, however one may define that. I have had a successful professional career. I have achieved some things outside of the work environment. I have some great friends. And I have an extraordinary wife and children. So how do I assess that "success"? I could say that I pulled myself up by my own bootstraps. My Yankee heritage and Protestant work ethic would suggest that I had done just that—I worked hard and created opportunities for myself and by the dint of my smarts and the strength of my back, I became successful; hence, all glory and honor to me. Sadly, at one time that probably was largely my attitude about the secret of my success. Recalling that time, it sounds and feels much like the pathos with which Harold Abrahams was trying to deal.

But, I now know that such a narrative is not true. Rather, I am exceedingly aware of an extraordinary number of people who helped me become whatever "success" I may have achieved. Whatever I have achieved, whatever people point to as success, I now know was the work of many people, and inevitably the grace of God. So, when I take the time to think carefully about how I have been so blessed, especially as I walked through the somewhat monotonous fields of the northern meseta, even if I do not know why, I recognize that many people did a great number of things to get me to where I am today.

I also began to realize that many individuals have these insights late in life. We have great intentions to thank those who made a difference, but it is too often left unsaid and we are left only with regret. It is said that "regret is a terrible thing" because by definition you were in a position to avoid the disappointment. Unlike so much of life, you could actually control the outcome. As Carmen and I hiked along, my mind walked through the years of my life and noted those individuals to whom I owed so much. And, I noted that there really was not any good reason not to say so.

First and foremost, I am grateful to my parents for so many things, but certainly for the most important of life's values and for the sacrifices so I could attend the college of my choice. As I thought back honestly upon my life, I noted others to whom I am grateful:

> **Judge Shelley**, *my first professional mentor, who introduced me to the law and encouraged others to take a chance on a brash northerner.*

> **Butch and Burt**, *who thought I might be worth a risk as a new attorney.*

> **Tom**, *who provided an extraordinary amount of wisdom in two years, lessons from which have proved to be meaningful for almost thirty years.*

> **Tom** *(a different Tom)* **and Slate**, *who thought I might be able to contribute to a new practice team at a marquis law firm.*

> **Bonnie**, *who worked tirelessly for many years to see that my work product was complete, timely, and of high quality.*

> **Stan and Frank**, *who thought I might be able to stand on my own feet as a partner and develop a practice.*

> **Stan** *(a different Stan)* **and Gary**, *who took a still brash thirty-five-year-old in as a partner when I needed a home.*

> **Bill**, *who advanced our practice and supported my ego, while demonstrating extraordinary intellect and humility.*

> **Vern**, *for stepping up whenever I needed support.*

Lynn and Paula, *who, like Bill and Vern, advanced our practice by tireless effort.*

Chris, Kirk, Bill, Mike and Brandy *for handling matters better than I could.*

Kim, *who has handled so many matters and otherwise tried to keep me straight.*

Rob and Guy, *who consistently make me look better than I am.*

Jeff, *who trusted and supported me in the most important professional role in my career.*

Carl and Mike, *who have been alongside for most of the journey, always trying to keep me in the center of the road.*

John, Wally, Giff, Ned, Kevin, Dennis, and others *who have provided me with more fun and camaraderie than anyone could ask.*

Harry, George, Bill (and others I will regret that I failed to mention) *who have walked the walk to help me see the truth.*

And, of course, my "girls"—**Cheryl, Brooke, and Amy**—*without whom I do not think I would have the spirit, energy, or drive to continue in the race before us.*

I talked about many of these people and experiences as Carmen and I trudged into the meseta. Carmen shared as well about her boyfriend, her family, and about her hometown of Alicante in the southeast of Spain. She seemed to be at a crossroads with her boyfriend—time to make it permanent? She was frustrated with the economy in Spain and her inability to get on with a more permanent career path. It was a good time for her to be on the road to find out. She was definitely giving life a thorough thinking over.

Carmen loved where she lived. Her parents worked hard. Her father was the informal local "mayor"—knowing everyone and caring for anyone. By her voice and the way she talked about everyone, I could sense both the sincerity and the joy. Despite a twinge of frustration and even a hint of sadness, it was invigorating and encouraging. I hope I conveyed the same in talking about my family. She told me much about Alicante's wonderful climate and the joy of having both mountains and ocean within minutes of home. Better than any travel bureau, she made it sound so attractive I'm eager to visit. Carmen said she'd love to visit the United States and elsewhere, but I could tell if she never did she would be very happy among her family and friends in southeast Spain.

Like Carmen, I was grateful for many things—grateful to many, but also grateful for circumstances and conditions beyond the responsibility of any person. In making that statement, though, I am reminded of a question I heard Michael Ramsden raise more than a couple of times: "Are we not looking for someone to be grateful to?" The point is, I think, we cannot have a general sense of gratitude. Further, does this sense of gratitude within us, which often reveals itself as a mild command, point to something bigger, something beyond ourselves?

Merriam-Webster indicates that being "grateful" is "feeling or showing thanks; feeling or showing thanks to someone for some helpful act." Some very successful businessmen I have known feel no need to be grateful. In their mind, the opportunity to travel abroad or to enjoy a fine bottle of wine or to play golf in Scotland or to walk the Camino was something *they* created, something *they* earned by their hard work, ingenuity, or luck—why be grateful? They do not acknowledge any "helpful acts" along the way. But, I believe, if we have enough "time on our feet," the obligation to give thanks—that mild command—becomes compelling and inescapable.

So, to whom or what should we be grateful? Our parents, certainly. Our family and friends—certainly. But is there something more—something that transcends such temporal circumstances? Many of the things of life cannot be attributed to family or friends. Does it not seem odd to simply say, "I'm grateful," without having an object for the appreciation? For me, as much as I had proscribed to a "pull-myself-up-by-my-own-bootstraps" philosophy, I discovered that I was conveniently forgetting both the individuals who helped along the way and the circumstances into which I was set that put me in a position to be successful. But, even more, the real sense of gratitude—that internal voice—points to something beyond us. To God?

Like Carmen, I began to see that I had to trust in something beyond myself. We were on the road to find out, but here was something that, when given sufficient contemplation, rang loudly as true. On the road to find out, have we not found out something? One thing I did know with certainty, I was grateful to Carmen for the time we spent together and for our developing friendship.

CHAPTER 12

LEÓN, ASTORGA, AND THE ROAD LESS TRAVELED

(DAYS 17–19)

We are all pilgrims in search of the unknown.

Paulo Coelho

[**Mansilla, León**, [Virgen del Camino], [Villar de Mazarife], **Villavante**, [Hospital de Órbigo], [La Casa de los Dioses], [Crucero de Santo Toribio], **Astorga**]

(64.5 kilometers—40.1 miles)

My time from León to Astorga was among my most memorable. The walk was pleasant, but the sights, the heritage, the people, and the special times will preserve in me the most favorable connotation when I hear or recall my time around León or Astorga—some of which may not have been possible, like it often is in life, if I had not taken the road less traveled. These two days featured the magnificent cathedral city, another lesson in architecture, a perfect walk with my own thoughts, interesting historical landmarks, a great modern albergue, an iconic old albergue, a modest hotel room, wonderful new acquaintances, and a story of young love that may seem like it was written for a novel.

Thursday, April 24 (Day 17)

[Mansilla de las Mulas to León]
(18.1 kilometers—11.2 miles)

My guidebook confesses that the seventeen-kilometer walk into León is the "one place on the Camino where you might want to take the bus." I thought, *It must be pretty unappealing if even the guidebook suggests skipping a section.* At some level I'm a bit of a purist. One of my golf buddies says I was the last person to stop using persimmon drivers and gutta-percha balls—an exaggeration, but the point is made. Likewise, I dream of completing a "thru-hike" of the AT—hiking the entire Appalachian Trail in one calendar year. For most, for me, and certainly for purists, it's not a "real" thru-hike if you skip a section of the trail. I felt the same way about the ten miles between Mansilla and León. I never considered skipping the section. Yet, to make this part of the journey even more challenging, rain was forecasted for the morning I had set aside for this apparently disagreeable walk. My mental approach became singularly focused—try to get to León as quickly as possible, which might help avoid the precipitation, put the unpleasant walk behind me quickly, and give me more time to tour León, a city that seemed to offer much.

As billed, the walk was through commercial and industrial properties—uninspiring, if not just plain ugly. I was among a fairly large contingent headed into the cathedral city. I leapfrogged with three from Ireland and saw my two French buddies a few times during the otherwise uninteresting walk to León. Despite the forecast, by 9:30 the sky was partly sunny. Trying to counteract the ugly walk along busy roads, I listened to a Tim Keller talk about the "fruit of the spirit" and a variety of tunes by Bruce Hornsby, James Taylor, and Alison Krauss. As the old cliché goes, I fear we often hear but do not listen. Extended time on a long walk gave me time to think—to listen. No topic seems to consume songwriters more than a search for meaning. Someone might say that "love" is a more frequent theme. At some level, I'd have to agree, but at another level, the search for love is just a search for something that helps provide meaning. Love may feed our need for something that transcends us, but it also may point to something deeper and more significant.

In "Fields of Gray," Bruce Hornsby explores this great mystery of life as he lovingly looks in on his infant boys sleeping. He writes and sings about the difficulty in finding truth. There are ups and down ("sad scenes and bad dreams") and life is very uncertain. I thought much about whether that was true. Nuance appeared to exist everywhere, but I continued to believe that truth was worth pursuing and that some truths could be identified.

... *walking with a Hornsby song ...*
... *hiking with a Cat Stevens song ...*
... *sauntering with a Mary Chapin Carpenter song ...*

And, appropriate for the time of the Camino, I reminisced about decisions made or matters left undone and wondered about regret in "The Road Not Taken." Today, Hornsby is among my most favorite artists. Ironically, when I was a freshman in college, the school had a "pub night" each Wednesday that featured live entertainment. Hornsby is from my college town and he would play there often, apparently too often for me because I still can recall walking by a hastily hung flyer taped to a dorm wall announcing that the "Bruce Hornsby Band" would be playing that week at the pub. Turning quickly to my friends as we walked by, I said, "Can't they get anyone other than Bruce Hornsby?"

Although the walk into León was billed as very flat, we had one really good hill to climb around the halfway point. Like the walk into other larger cities, I needed some time to wind through city streets as scallop shells and faded yellow arrows led us through ancient Roman walls and into the historic part of León. The final steps of the day were up a slight incline that shielded and delayed a full view of a remarkable destination. I had certainly read about and seen photographs of the cathedral of León, but arriving around noon in its large, open square with a brilliant cobalt sky as a backdrop, I admit to being awed by the beauty and majesty of the historic Gothic cathedral.

Thinking that I needed a picture of myself in front of the grand church, I spotted a young man sitting nearby on a bench who, for whatever reason, looked American to me. I asked if he'd mind taking my photograph. With that request I was introduced to David—a medical student from Michigan. He assisted and I returned the favor. I did not see David again in León, but little did I know then that David would play a prominent role in a number of my future days on the Camino.

I checked into Boccalino Hostel and cleaned up. I then had almost half a day to explore León. The city is thought to have been settled by the Seventh Legion as early as 29 B.C. as part of the Romans efforts to protect the shipment of gold out of Galicia on its way to Italy. León was "run over" and conquered and re-conquered by Muslims, Visigoths, Asturians, and Christians. Just about the time that Santiago was being recognized as an important pilgrimage destination, León was rebuilt and became an important commercial center for the wool trade. That prosperity helped to fund the construction of its trademark cathedral.

León Cathedral was begun in 1205 and finished in just under a hundred years—apparently record time. Guidebooks explain that its most noteworthy feature is its large stained-glass windows that emphasize the use of light in the cathedral. One guidebook states: "Without a flashy retablo, the cathedral lets the streaming light steal the show." An excellent audio self-tour explained the history and architecture, including an extensive and risky but ingenious renovation in the late nineteenth century that probably saved the cathedral from ruin. El Cid, the national hero of Spain mentioned earlier, is buried in the center of the cathedral.

I also roamed the city and viewed its major historical and architectural highlights, including the eleventh-century Basilica de San Isidoro ("one of the premier Romanesque structures" in all of northern Spain, which was commissioned to house relics returned by Muslims after being defeated in the Reconquista), the more "modern" (nineteenth-century) Casa de los Botines, the cathedral's museum and cloister, and the ancient city walls. Interestingly, especially for someone on the road to find out or otherwise searching, just before I left for my adventure on the Camino, a book (*Kings of the Grail*) was published indicating that the "real" holy grail has been located in the Basilica de San Isidoro for over a thousand years. The forecast that had promised rain delivered instead a perfect day of moderate temperatures and beautiful sunshine.

Incredibly, as I cut through a public square to return to my hotel, I heard "Bruce! Bruce!" off to my right. And, in typical but amazing Camino style, there were Frida, Lynn, and Jen finishing a late lunch at an outdoor café. I sat with them and caught up on everyone's journeys—and I heard a supplement to "the rest of the story" about George's boots. I had not seen Frida or Jen since the rainy morning after Hontanas, and I last saw Lynn early in the morning at Carrión as we both stood by the front door to the hostel waiting for it to be unlocked. I mentioned to Jen, "Hey, did you hear? George got his boots back."

Not expecting this response, she said, "Yes, I was there when he got them back."

Amazed at how small the world seemed sometimes, including this adventure about George's boots, I said with a tone of incredulity, "Really? So, tell what happened. George made it sound as though things got pretty tense."

Jen responded, "Oh, I felt very bad for Shannon. He was so embarrassed by what happened."

"So you were really right there," I replied.

"Yes," Jen said, "I was lying in the bunk next to Shannon when George came in and confronted him."

I inquired, "But was Shannon at our albergue that night in Hontanas?"

"No, that's the point," Jen responded. "George and Shannon had met at Grañón. I was there that night, too. It's not surprising that their boots got confused because all of our hiking shoes were stored together but pretty much in a pile."

With Jen filling in more details and adding a different perspective, it now made sense to me, and I said so. "Well, that now makes sense. When George gave me the story in Carrión, he still was indicating that the boots had been taken that rainy morning just outside of Hontanas."

Still recalling with incredulity the story about driving the car back on the muddy Camino path, I inquired of Jen, "Hey, did you hear that George actually had a car drive right on the path trying to find his boots?"

"Did I hear?" Jen replied, "I was walking on the trail while the car was coming at me! It got stuck in the mud a number of times and I helped push it loose."

I could only smile and say to Jen, "Amazing."

Jen finished the story by saying how sorry she felt for Shannon. "He was feeling so bad and embarrassed. I think he's going to stay back a day so he doesn't have to walk among a group of people who know the story."

I added a final comment, "That's too bad, because it sounds as if the only story that makes sense now is that George had walked four days with the wrong boots and he didn't realize it until that morning in Hontanas." Jen nodded in agreement.

Frida then mentioned to me that Jen had just replicated one of the special events in *The Way*—the movie about the Camino de Santiago starring Martin Sheen. Like Sheen's character in the movie, after growing tired of hostel living, Jen treated the three of them to a night in the Parador—a five-star luxury hotel that served as a massive pilgrim hospital in the fifteenth century. The grand old building sat on the river at the edge of the city center and right on the Camino route as the Way-marked path heads out of León. I would pass right by it very early the next morning as I started my trek to the next destination.

Eager to find a "good meal" now that I was in a city that offered a wide array of choices, I walked around trying to decide upon Italian, Asian, or some other inviting fare that wasn't a "pilgrim meal" dominated by French fries. Despite my efforts, my inability to understand menus well or to speak with waiters or to order properly left me defaulting to my fairly typical (and now somewhat redundant) cheese, bread, fruit, and wine. Recalling my hat full of sardines and remembering that I didn't understand that "tomato macaroni" was pasta with spaghetti sauce, I had to acknowledge that occasionally I even had trouble at times ordering off of pilgrim menus. I thought, *Where's my friend Carmen? She could help me order something more interesting.* I resolved that I was going to find some way to decipher dinner choices before I ran out of time on the Camino.

Friday, April 25 (Day 18)

[León to Villavante]
(25.1 kilometers—15.6 miles)

Despite both my preference and my habit of starting to hike early in the morning, I did not leave León until almost 8:00 a.m. Perhaps not surprisingly, I routinely got more sleep when I had my own room as opposed to a bunk in a hostel. Leaving the city center just before crossing over the Rio Bernesga, I passed the five-star Parador Hotel. I was pretty confident that my friends Jen, Lynn, and Frida were still asleep in their five-star luxury. I did not dare to disturb them. No worries, though. I was excited to be walking again on a beautiful morning—and something told me I'd see them again.

On city sidewalks, I kept moving west and started to leave León behind. I walked with Hector, a Spanish gentleman about my age, while we were still in the city proper. He wore a golf shirt with a logo of the PGA of America on it—a logo with which I was very familiar. So I asked him if he was a golfer. Hector laughed and said, "Oh no. I have an American friend in Arizona who is a golf professional. He gave me this shirt." Hector had done portions of the Camino and was back out on it for a couple of weeks. We talked briefly about our work and our families, and then he encouraged me to walk ahead because our pace had been faster than he wanted to go and he didn't want to slow me down.

Despite an urban and somewhat industrial climb out of León, the magnificence of the morning prevailed. This uninteresting urban walk was broken up by meeting Henri and Alyssia, a couple from Brazil whom I had seen and waved to many times in walking the last couple of days. We thought it was long past time to make more of an acquaintance. Henri and Alyssia were "slack packing" the Camino. They had a tour operator arrange hotel rooms at the various towns, consistent with the number of days or stages that most pilgrims walked, and deliver their luggage to those hotels. The couple then would walk with just a daypack with snacks, water, lunch, and probably rain gear while on the day's walk.

As we did most mornings and as many others did this morning leaving León, I stopped in the first significant town—Virgen de Camino—for coffee. I walked into a café and as I set my pack down next to a table to ask if I could sit there, who was sitting there but Carmen with whom I had walked leaving Burgos and then all day to Hontanas! I joined her for café con leche. Svetlana, a thirty-two-year-old Indian woman from Toronto made it three at our table. To supplement my cup of coffee, I was introduced to a sugared Spanish breakfast treat, which Americans would recognize as remarkably similar to "French toast." Other than being introduced to French toast in Spain, what was remarkable about sitting down with Carmen was that I had just—coincidentally—said to myself that day, "I need Carmen." I needed someone to read and speak Spanish to help me order a dinner more interesting than another pilgrim meal of chicken and fries. I mentioned this to her, and we made a pact. Two days later, we would be in Astorga. Carmen's job was to find a nice restaurant and help me order a nice meal. My job was to pay for our dinners. With that, we finished up our morning coffee and a nice visit with Svetlana and headed back onto the Camino.

Just a few minutes later, on the outskirts of Virgen del Camino, not wanting a repeat of the mistake I made hiking into Mansilla, I took the alternative, more rural route (the "detour," or as I liked to say, "the road less travelled"). Most of my fellow pilgrims, however, stayed on the hard dirt path close by the roadway leading to Villadangos del

Páramo. Carmen also took the more direct route. (Later, when we re-united in Astorga, she told me how sorry she was to have made that choice because, as I told her how enjoyable the terrain, the path, and the scenery had been on the road less travelled, she said the fourteen kilometers to Villadangos was "the worst, the absolute worst" stretch of the Camino.)

As I headed off alone on the way less travelled, I almost immediately lost the path—I could not locate a scallop-shell sign or yellow arrow anywhere. After some map work and bushwhacking across a field, I finally located the Way and a familiar yellow arrow pointing across a bridge over an interstate highway, which I took as I headed toward some rural countryside ahead.

The use of yellow arrows was a modern addition to the Camino, but the scallop shell has been a symbol of St. James and the Camino de Santiago for thousands of years. While some debate appears to exist as to its origin, the scallop shell as a symbol does point to mythical, met-aphorical, and practical meanings related to the historic pilgrimage. Some tradition indicates that when the body of St. James was brought to Galicia, the ship scared a horse carrying a wedding groom who then fell into the ocean and, coming out of the ocean, was covered with scallop shells.

The *Codex Calixtinus* explains that the scallop shell represents fin-gers on a pilgrim's open hand, pointing to the good deeds expected of all of those on the Way of St. James. We do know that scallops are plentiful along the northwest coast of Spain, where the pilgrimage to Santiago essentially leads. The speculation that makes most sense to me, as an amateur historian, is that pilgrims returned to their home-towns with a scallop shell as an indication that they completed the journey. Others point to the manner in which the lines on a scallop shell converge in a single point—like the various Camino routes all leading to Santiago.

My guess is that the tradition is derived a little from all of these ex-planations. One thing is clear—the scallop shell (and various artistic interpretations of it) is a ubiquitous symbol of the Camino de Santiago today. Dan and I were each given a real shell at the official pilgrim office in St. Jean when we picked up our Pilgrim Passports. I carried my scallop shell to Santiago, and it remains an important keepsake of my journey.

On a Way-marked road, I climbed down a modest hill into the tiny village of Fresno where the only trace of the local population was a couple and their dog sunning themselves outside the town's convenience store—Fresno's lone commercial establishment. The trail then took me back up over a similar hill to a plateau that offered broad views, big sky, and a relatively flat walk. At this point, the Camino also left the paved road for a dirt path as it headed through open moorland.

Other than a couple in the distance, I was alone. The walk was beautiful and peaceful. After a couple of hours, I stopped in the small hamlet of Chozas de Abajo to get some water and eat the salami sandwich I had made before leaving León. In the town square, where pilgrims typically can find a reliable fountain, I sat with two sixty-year-old women—Mika and Elizabeth—from England, a pastor's wife and a Vicar in the Church of England, on their first day out on the Camino de Santiago. These ladies were engaging and delightful.

After our lunch break, my new "little while" friends from Great Britain and I pulled on our backpacks and headed out again on the Camino. Noting that their pace was probably too slow for me, Elizabeth encouraged me to move along without them if I wanted. I bid them goodbye and picked up my pace, not knowing that we would meet again at the same hostel in Astorga the next day. I sectioned and ate an orange while I enjoyed a quiet walk along the country road that led pilgrims out of Chozas and westward ho.

Energized physically and mentally by my lunch stop, I made very good time and arrived in Villar de Mazarife just before 2:00 p.m. I recall the time well because I helped some other pilgrims find a supermarket just before it would close for *siesta*. Villar de Mazarife had the look of an aging town. Its prominent church was the mud brick Iglesia de Santiago. Both observations reminded me that I really had not quite left the meseta yet.

I made good time and finished a thirty-one-kilometer day in the small town of Villavante. I checked into what appeared to be a fairly new, private albergue. It proved to be as it appeared, clean and modern with more services than most pilgrim hostels and with very welcoming hosts. A light rain started just as the hostel host showed me to a bunk.

Over an afternoon beer, I met Andy from Switzerland and two new friends from Holland who had walked all the way from the Netherlands over the last three years doing sections at a time. On this trip they would finally got to Santiago. I also met Harry, with whom I had discussed religion, faith, spirituality, and 9/11 conspiracies.

I enjoyed a good pilgrim meal at the hostel with Andy, Svetlana (whom I had met that morning over coffee with Carmen), and Karina (a nineteen-year-old recent high school graduate from Bavaria, who was doing the Camino before heading to university to study theology). All in all, I had a great day on the Way of St. James with old friends, new friends, tranquil moments of solitude, engaging conversation, and a beautiful walk.

Saturday, April 26 (Day 19)

[Villavante to Astorga]
(21.9 kilometers—15.6 miles)

The day was overcast and cloudy as I headed out of Villavante. Rain was threatening, but I was eager to see the Cantabrian Mountains even though Galicia was still five or six days of walking away. The fairly substantial town of Hospital de Órbigo was just an easy five kilometers farther along the Way of St. James. The route to Villadangos del Páramo and the route through Villar de Mazarife and Villavante re-converge right in the center of Hospital de Órbigo. As was typical, I got some walking under my belt and stopped in this first town for coffee. As I started to enter the café, and no longer surprised to constantly run into familiar faces, I saw Carmen (and others I knew who had taken the other route after León) lifting their packs and heading back out on the road of yellow arrows. We said a quick hello, but long enough to remind Carmen of our dinner pact. And long enough for her to tell me how much she disliked the section she had walked the prior day, when I took the more rural "detour."

After coffee and a croissant and a brief rest, I put on my rain jacket as a light rain had begun to fall. I regained the path and crossed the fascinating thirteenth-century Gothic bridge over the Río Órbigo, which has twenty arches and extends over two hundred meters. The bridge is often referred to as "El Paso Honroso"—the "passage of honor"—after a legendary jousting competition held 1434 to free Don Suero, a noble knight, from wearing an iron collar he imposed on himself as the result of unrequited love. Some believe that Suero was the model for Cervantes's hapless knight, Don Quixote. The legend also provides that after defeating all challenges and being freed from his collar, Don Suero proceeded then to Santiago on his own pilgrimage.

I ran into a busload of tourists from Japan at the western end of the very lengthy bridge. I spoke with a husband and wife—stragglers needing to catch up with their group. We took photos for each other, and then I found my way out of town. The sky was still dark, but the precipitation was holding off.

Leaving Hospital de Órbigo the route splits again—and again I took the "detour." And, again, instead of following a hard dirt path along a flat road into Astorga, I headed slightly north and west into the foothills of the Cantabrian Mountains as a light rain began to fall. The mostly earthen path rolled over hills and through orchards, oak groves, and forest. The rain lasted very little time and the hiking was great fun. The hills rolled through two small villages, and then we faced a more significant climb up to a plateau. Completing that steeper climb was rewarded, however, as we were greeted by some wonderful people manning a snack cart that offered complimentary fruit, baked items, coffee, and more to pilgrims. (On the Appalachian Trail, that would be called "trail magic.") I caught up to Andy from the previous night's dinner and we visited there for a little while.

The plateau on which we had walked came to an abrupt end as Andy and I came upon a very large monumental cross (Crucero de Santo

Toribio) that looks down on the village of San Justo de la Vega and from which the spires of the cathedral in Astorga can be seen. The sky had lifted and the sun was breaking through the clouds. Still feeling pain in my knee from the climb down the Alto de Perdon on Day Four, I eased my way down a steep hill into San Justo and then through town, across the Rio Tuerta and onto Astorga. The trip from Villavante is only twenty-two kilometers, about half of which is very easy hiking. The final walk into Astorga involves navigating a complex footbridge over railroad tracks, a small creek that resembles a maze, and then climbing a steep hill into the ancient city.

I made good time and was in town around noon. Astorga is an attractive town with a modern feel, but one that has not lost its historic past. In fact, arriving midday Sunday, I experienced a vibrant mood and much activity in the city, which has many well-maintained historic religious and governmental buildings. I stopped at Siervas de Maria hostel—a large, municipal albergue that housed up to 150 in rooms of four (two bunk beds per room). Two of my bunkmates were a father and son—devout Catholics from Poland—whom I would see a number of times in the next ten days, including in Santiago.

For four euros, the albergue took and cleaned my clothes. I showered and cleaned up. I ran into Carmen, who likewise was having her clothes cleaned. We had made a dinner agreement back in Virgen de Camino when I asked Carmen if she'd find a good restaurant in Astorga and that I'd treat if she'd help with selecting the restaurant and guiding me through the menu. After making plans to meet at 7:00, I headed out to see the town and find a *supermercado*. I bought strawberries, wine, cheese, and bread. I settled into a table and chairs on the back porch of the albergue and enjoyed a magnificent view (the sun was out brilliantly now) and a delicious lunch.

After a very relaxing lunch, I headed back out into the town and visited the cathedral, which is newer than the Burgos or León cathedrals, featuring a Baroque façade, having been built in the fifteenth century. I also checked out the Iglesia de Santa Maria (an earlier church, next to the cathedral) and the Palacio de Gaudi (the archbishop's palace).

Astorga was an important city on the historic Camino, offering up to twenty-one different hospitals for pilgrims at one time—including St. Francis of Assisi in 1214. (The guidebooks indicate that only Burgos had more pilgrim hospitals.) Upon my return to the hostel, I ran into Elizabeth and Mika, with whom I had enjoyed lunch in the small village of Chozas de Abajo on their first day on the Camino having started that morning in León.

During lunch, Carmen and David (the med student whom I met in front of the cathedral in León where we took photos for each other) sat nearby, so I invited David to dinner with Carmen and me. They knew each other from some earlier time on the Camino. Carmen had selected a nice Italian restaurant. The three of us looked forward to a great meal and good conversation.

As planned, Carmen helped me through the menu, and the three of us enjoyed a much-better-than-usual meal of the Camino. Toward the end of the meal, David explained that his girlfriend was coming to surprise him in Santiago. His excitement was palpable as he then told us of his plans to walk with her to Finisterre and propose marriage at the "end of the earth."

"Wow!" Carmen exclaimed, telling us that her boyfriend was just not that romantic. Just as she was telling us, "He would never do something like that," who walked into the restaurant (this is a true story) but Juanan, her boyfriend! In fact, Carmen's entire family—her father, mother, older sister, and younger brother—also walked into the restaurant as a surprise. They had driven eight hours from southeast Spain to reach Astorga!

After hugs and introductions, I wondered, *How did they find us?* Upon asking, through Carmen, we learned that the family had stopped in seventeen restaurants in Astorga before finding us!

David and I left Carmen with Juanan and her family. He and I continued our conversation that evening over a bottle of wine David insisted on sharing back at the albergue. This was my nineteenth day on the Camino de Santiago. The afternoon had been beautiful and the day had been lively and fun. I was still enjoying almost every minute of the journey.

CHAPTER 13

HAROLD AND G.K. CHESTERTON

*That's the way it goes; you have to expect
a physical and emotional low here and there.
Still, a pilgrimage has to be completed alone,
or at least begun alone.*

Hape Kerkeling

I met Harold as I sat down in the den of our pilgrim hostel in Villa-vante relaxing after the day's walk. Harold was from Germany. As we shared some space together with a cold beverage, he asked how my journey had been so far. And, with little hesitation or small talk, Harold inquired whether my time on the Camino was for "religious reasons." For a brief moment I wondered where this conversation with "Harry" might be going and how might I respond.

During most of its history, pilgrims on the Camino de Santiago were out for "religious reasons." They were focused on much more than a "sports adventure" or a walk of spiritual discovery. The primary mo-tivation was *orandi causa*—as one resource explained, medieval pil-grims headed out on the Camino "in order to pray, to seek forgiveness, to fulfill a vow, or to petition St. James for a certain blessing, such as healing." Completing the pilgrimage to Santiago earned a pilgrim an "indulgence" from the Church. It was a distinctly Christian pilgrimage. The infrastructure that supported pilgrims on their way to Santiago historically consisted of convents, monasteries, hospitals, and other Christian-run structures and organizations.

Today, indulgences are still available from the Roman Catholic Church (and possibly the Greek Orthodox Church), but most other Christians are not focused on obtaining an indulgence for walking the Way of St. James. I grew up in a Congregational Church in Connecticut. During college I attended a Lutheran church. Neither of those Protestant denominations taught anything about indulgences. When I recall something about "indulgences," I am reminded about a matter that had troubled Martin Luther and helped spur a revolution of change in the Church. All that said, I had to ask myself: What then is an "indulgence"? Why did medieval pilgrims seek an indulgence? Maybe I think too much, but these questions flowed naturally, including, "Why might someone today want or need an indulgence?"

According to the Church, upon death the soul spends time in purgatory where the person is punished for sins committed during his or her temporal life. After that, the soul is released to heaven and eternal life with God. An indulgence, as the Official Pilgrim website states, provides its recipient with remission of that punishment—reduction of time spent in purgatory for sin. Anyone who receives an indulgence from walking the Camino de Santiago during a Holy Year receives a "plenary" or "jubilee" indulgence, which provides "full" remission of punishment and immediate release from purgatory. Hence, for many then, reward of precious worth awaited some completing the pilgrimage to Santiago.

Critical then to understanding the motivation of a pilgrim seeking an indulgence is the belief in sin or an understanding of the nature of sin. Today, the word *sin* for many seems distasteful or is considered outmoded. For some it's a relic from the unenlightened past. Yet, before discounting its significance because modern people are uncomfortable with the term, someone seeking to live an "examined life" (and certainly someone on the Camino de Santiago) would want to ask, "What is sin?"—including whether such a thing as "sin" even exists.

Getting back to Harold's question about whether my time on the Camino was for "religious purposes," I responded, "In many respects." I decided not to get into a nuanced discussion about what "religion" is or isn't as opposed to faith. I thought I knew what he probably meant. Yet, perhaps because I delayed more than I realized, like a trained apologist trying to figure out what question to use in response to a question (or perhaps he wasn't really planning to wait for my answer anyway), he quickly indicated that he believed that "god was in everyone and that everyone was god." Harry was throwing a lot at me. I could change the subject and not engage, but I believed (as Pete might) I was there for a reason—I was on the road to find out—so I looked for a response, for an approach to this conversation.

Not prepared for a deep conversation, but curious, I paused, thinking, *How might I respond or should I engage?* Harry's views seemed in line with Pete's or at least some of the New Age thinking with which I had become familiar.

Yet, again, before I could decide, Harry launched on. "I think everyone creates their own world of rules and expectations. In creating your own reality, you are god." In my own experience, a deep consideration of how we decide what is right or wrong had proved to be effective at getting at the essence of how people thought about meaning and truth.

In light of Harold's comment about making our own rules, I decided to see where that type of discussion might go. Never being one to shy away from a good debate, I decided to test the waters and asked, "How do we decide what is right and what is wrong if everyone gets to create their own rules?"

Very quickly Harry interjected, "I think everyone decides for themselves what is right or wrong."

Equally as quickly I replied, "Doesn't that lead to everyone doing whatever they please without regard to any standard of right and wrong?"

He repeated, "Everyone decides for themselves. Each person decides what is right or wrong."

Recalling C.S. Lewis's discussion of the Law of Human Nature in *Mere Christianity*—where Lewis showed that regardless of what we might say, we all have a very real sense of right and wrong when applied to our own life and experiences—I tried a slightly different approach. "Let's see how that plays out in real life," I said. Continuing, I said further, "You have to acknowledge, do you not, that there are at least a few things we all agree are wrong?"

Having dealt with people committed to extreme relativism (and being convinced that certain things are clearly right and wrong), my strategy was to get my new friend to admit that at least some things we all acknowledge are good or bad. From there, I'd try to show him that such a belief required a universal standard, or as Blaise Pascal said, a "fixed point" of reference. I was thinking that if I could get him to that point, I'd try to suggest that such a standard had to be grounded in God, in one God. If there was one God, we all could not, as he had suggested, be god. And, here, I was not suggesting which "god" but just that logically there had to be "one" or "a" god.

Maybe Harry saw where I was going, because he insisted, "No, I think it's just up to each person."

"Well," I said, trying to think about how to react, "I know this is a sensitive topic for your country, but it's a common and useful example—wasn't the Holocaust wrong?"

Harry fidgeted a little and paused but finally replied, "I might not like it or agree with it, but I could not say that it was wrong because that's for everyone to decide on their own."

Surprised, but maybe not really surprised, I responded (probably with more emotion than the calm of a debate logician), "Really! You do not think what Hitler did was wrong?"

Harold did not waver, "In Hitler's mind, what he was doing was right, and we all have the right to decide those things for ourselves."

We had moved the conversation about God and sin to one about morality. For many, that is a distinction without a difference—to break the moral law is sin because the moral law is grounded both in God's nature and in His expressed will. Merriam-Webster is consistent with this approach; it defines "sin" as an "offense against the religious or moral law" or a "transgression of the law of God."

Many do not want to talk about sin (and may not even want to read about it here). Such a discussion makes some people uncomfortable. This is true even for Christians. But why? Is it because it recalls images of "an angry and wrathful God"–the God of the Old Testament, they would say? Do they dislike this God and believe He has been replaced by the loving God introduced to us by Jesus? Others are uncomfortable because they believe in the goodness of human beings—a notion incompatible with a realization that sin is real. Americans particularly adhere to a creed of self-reliance, more convinced that we can pull ourselves up by our own bootstraps than admitting that we, as human beings, might be flawed, or even broken and selfish.

But it seemed to me that if we are on the road to find out—if we really want to live an "examined life"—we should want to go where the evidence and reason takes us.

Christianity has, of course, traditionally asserted that sin exists, that sin is real. Starting with Adam in the Garden of Eden, his refusal to obey the will of God was the "original" sin creating the "Fall" of man. The various doctrines of the Christian faith have been debated and cross-examined for thousands of years. If sin is defined as violating God's will, then those who reject belief in God may think they have a reason to reject the notion of sin. If sin is defined as violating the moral law, people like Harold will continue to reject the idea of sin because they reject any existence of a moral law. But if sin is defined, as it is by a close friend, largely as "radical selfishness," does sin exist?

About sin, a well-known quip by Reinhold Niebuhr captures the truth of the matter for me. Niebuhr was an outspoken commentator on society as he lived through the crises of the Depression, the horrors of World War II, and the reckless tensions of the Cold War. In observing that human beings were free but finite, he said, "The doctrine of original sin is the only empirically verifiable doctrine of the Christian faith."

After one permits the words and then the meaning of that statement to settle in, its accuracy becomes troublingly clear. Niebuhr is saying that all we need to do is observe mankind now and through the ages to conclude that sin is very real. It's not just Hitler and Stalin, it's not just the killing fields of Cambodia or the Rwandan massacres—but it's Enron and Madoff, it's Armstrong and Sandusky, it's padding your expense report, cheating on your spouse, or plagiarizing a news story. I was reminded further of a comment I heard from Professor John Lennox. In commenting on the Madoff fiasco, he said, "The most surprisingly thing is that we are surprised." I understood Lennox to be saying just what Niebuhr was saying—if you honestly observe the years of human history, the most compelling observation is that we are radically selfish—we do that which promotes our self-interest, even at considerable cost to those around us. Or, as Niebuhr said, we observe original sin.

Like observations about gratitude, the road to find out had offered a compelling—a breakthrough—conclusion. Answers may actually exist. Truth can be known. In his search for truth, Plato initially asked, very logically and practically, whether *anything* could be identified as *true*—true in the sense that it was a valid and an unchanging correctness, true today and tomorrow and for all time. As Niebuhr suggested, here was something that was observably true, suggesting that answers to some or all of life's big questions about meaning, truth, and right and wrong might actually exist.

For someone then examining life, the obvious question next is whether we are guilty of such radical selfishness. Have I sinned?

Again, like the quip from Niebuhr, a famous tale about G.K. Chesterton helps to both clarify and amplify the point here. This story is not popular, however, with those who find goodness and generosity at the core of human existence. As the story goes, *The Times* (of London) posed this question to its readership: "What's wrong with the world?" In response Chesterton, a well-known British journalist at the time, sent a letter saying simply: "Dear sirs: I am." What Chesterton meant, I believe (and it is what I believe Niebuhr and Lennox meant), is that as human beings we are imperfect, we are broken—in fact, we are so flawed that despite our best efforts we not only make mistakes, but we stumble badly and do so often. We are not grateful for the good things in our lives, and we too often insist on selfish objectives over collective benefit.

This conduct for many really is sin—we reject the moral law and we seek to glorify ourselves. Yet, to use the word *sin* is often too distasteful today largely because it flies in the face of our wish that people might really be good. It mocks our hope that with enough education and benign government intervention, we can make a good society. But is man at his core any different today than in medieval times? I did not need very much "time on my feet" to realize that I was often selfish and even radically so. Far too often I placed my own needs, objectives, or wants above those of my family, friends, or colleagues, and above both the unnamed and the most needy.

Harry and I volleyed thoughts and arguments back and forth like a friendly tennis match. When I pressed him about some of the world's horrible atrocities and the idea that certainly some things were objectively wrong or evil, he remained resolute to his adherence to radical moral relativity. What I did not see coming was his reply to my mention of the horror of the 9/11 attacks on the United States as further evidence of evil and sin.

With all sincerity, Harry's reply to that terrible event was that he was not sure it ever occurred, that it may have been fabricated by the U.S. government to justify the military actions taken in the Middle East.

That took me back—and again, forgetting my need to be a statesman in such a debate, I pushed back pretty hard and pretty emotionally with more than a hint of incredulity, saying, "Really! Do you really believe—even if the government wanted to—that could even be possible?" I'm sure the tone of my voice had moved away from what had been a friendly conversation. He indicated he knew of credible websites with significant materials suggesting that 9/11 was a hoax. Recalling how very real that event was for my brother and other New Yorkers, I decided it was time to move on before the conversation devolved to something less cordial. But before moving on, Harry and I became Facebook friends, and he downloaded a copy of *The Race Before Us* (the marvels of technology!).

When Chesterton suggested that "we" are what is wrong with the world, he was referring to the Christian belief that the world is not the way it's supposed to be—that God created a perfect world in which people could live, but our insistence (Adam's original insistence) on having things and doing things our own way corrupted the world. Whether it is the Holocaust, a massive Ponzi scheme, cheating on a spouse, or padding an expense account, *we* are what's wrong with the world. That notion seems quite different from the New Age thought that focuses upon the individual creating his or her own reality. Both views can't be "true." But after my visit with Harold, I still had many more days to continue to saunter toward the holy land.

By the way, websites about 9/11 being a hoax do, in fact, exist. I'm still wondering what that says about the reality of sin in the world. It seems to say more about our willingness to suppress evidence—even facts directly presented to us.

CHAPTER 14

CRUZ DE FERRO AND DAYS OF PURE HIKING
(DAYS 20–22)

*The geographical pilgrimage is the symbolic
acting out of an inner journey. The inner journey is the
interpolation of the meanings and signs of the outer pilgrimage.
One can have one without the other. It is best to have both.*

Thomas Merton

[**Astorga**—[Rabanal], **Foncebadón**, [Cruz de Ferro], **Molinaseca**, [Ponferrada], [Camponaraya], [Cacabelos], **Villafranca del Bierzo**]
(76.8 kilometers—47.7 miles)

If I were to be pressed to select that part of the Camino I enjoyed the most, I'd have to say it was the walk from Astorga to Portomarín, which takes the pilgrims into the Cantabrian Mountains, through the interesting microclimate of the El Bierzo region, back up over another significant mountaintop that serves as a gateway to Galicia, and then down again into Triacastela and Samos before leaving the countryside for the final, more of a suburban, walk into Santiago. (This chapter is the first half of that walk, which concludes with Chapter 18.)

This was pleasant hiking, but it was certainly more hiking than walking. The pathways were mostly easy underfoot, but the terrain had tremendous variety, including rolling countryside through farms, modest hills, and forest land beside mountain streams, paved village streets, and significant ascents and descents that sapped energy and stressed the body. Seemingly spaced perfectly in these wonderful walks were interesting and attractive Camino towns and villages. Again, my time over these days—well into the journey—remain my fondest memories.

Sunday, April 27 (Day 20)

[Astorga to Foncebadón]
(25.9 kilometers—16.1 miles)

David cooked up a dozen eggs and a pound of bacon. I brought an orange, strawberries, and bread. We shared the crowded kitchen with a surprisingly large number of others also preparing a morning meal at the albergue, which was a particularly large one housing about 150 pilgrims a night. In fact, Siervas de Maria was probably the largest albergue I stayed in (along with the municipal hostel in Burgos and the converted convent the first night in Roncesvalles). The numbers were not shocking, but rarely had I seen so many preparing breakfast before heading out for the day's walk. If I have one regret from my trek to Santiago, it would be the lack of more opportunities to cook meals with my fellow travelers.

Some of the memoirs I had read and some of the observations shared with me by recent pilgrims indicated that small groups would often share shopping and cooking to enjoy meals together at the albergues rather than go out for another pilgrim meal. I would have enjoyed that camaraderie, but for whatever reason, most people I encountered and walked with were not planning meals in that fashion. Often larger groups, especially of Koreans, would gather to prepare and share meals—in some respects to enjoy foods from home rather than the local, northern Spain options. I commented more than once to some of my fellow travelers that these Korean groups might enjoy their experience even more if they either invited others to partake with them or otherwise interacted more with the wide array of travelers from around the world every day on the Camino. One friend I made from Korea, Lee, told me she had often been invited to join but avoided those group meals because she wanted to meet more people along the way.

There was far more food than David and I could eat, even after we ate far more food than we should have. David used the considerable leftovers to create a grand sandwich for later that day. David said he was going to linger a little at the albergue and insisted that I let him clean up. Having already packed, I was out the door around 7:30.

The morning was again beautiful and perfect for a hike—clear and cool, almost cold, with brilliant sunlight. I headed back up streets I toured the day before, past the town square where children's games and a temporary market had been set up the prior afternoon, past my *supermercado*, and then toward the cathedral where the Way-markings direct pilgrims to turn left and head out of town. Just before the cathedral as I walked past three different ATMs, something nagged at me to stop and pick up some extra euros. And, not wanting to be in a position where I would need to borrow money for room and board from a German high school student, I stopped. With the magic of plastic cards and telecommunications, I retrieved three hundred euros to help fund my way to Santiago. I quickly resumed my march out of town. A dozen other pilgrims were making their way west. I joined the slow parade through and out of town.

Based on notes from my guidebook and comments Carmen had shared, I prepared for a tough day of hiking. But the hike out of Astorga and up into the mountains began very gradually. Perhaps because of the elevation, the temperature outside did not warm as quickly as earlier days. And it was windy. Just as the rise of the ambient temperature had stubbornly stalled, my hands did not warm up even after starting the climb with twenty-four pounds on my back. Although it was one of those items I wondered if I should have left home, I had only worn my gloves one other time on the trip—I was thankful I had a pair to pull on. I continued the modest incline leading out of town and into the Cantabrian Mountains.

Just beyond Astorga, my recent dinner and very recent breakfast companion, David, raced by me yelling back that someone had stolen all of his money while he was sleeping at the albergue the previous night. He thought he knew who had taken his euros and he was running—literally running—with a twenty-pound pack and hiking poles determined to catch up to the person who had robbed him. After another fifty yards of running, David stopped briefly. Realizing he could make better time without his hands full, he asked if I would carry his trekking poles. I readily agreed and said we'd catch up down the trail. So David laid down his poles and resumed his considerable pace.

This morning more pilgrims seemed to be on the path than any previous day. Maybe that was because of the open terrain and the ability to see more of the trail ahead as it climbed or because larger numbers were heading off at the same time. Astorga, I learned, is a very common stopping or starting point for people of the Camino. Not only is it a wonderful little city to visit, it also marks a significant shift in terrain and even culture. Moreover, the final ascent up into Astorga is difficult, helping to convince one to stop there for the day. Finally, with fewer services available on the Camino for the next few days, Astorga is a good place to resupply, rest, and prepare for a section of the trail that includes climbing to the highest point on the Way of St. James.

Astorga, then, had a way of gathering pilgrims in one town, at least for a night. It often required the morning and the afternoon, if not even another day or two, for everyone's different hiking paces to spread the congregation back over the trail. So more pilgrims probably *were* on the way that morning. As I stopped in the small town of Murias de Rechivaldo for my morning café con leche after walking a cool but very pleasant five kilometers, the unusually large number of backpacks carried by unfamiliar faces confirmed that I had involuntarily joined a different and larger crowd heading for the mountains and Santiago.

Murias, I read, is a "Maragato" village. It was quiet but did not feel as aged and tired as many of the villages we had recently walked through in the meseta. To me, the stone buildings, as opposed to the mud brick of the high plateau, gave the town an "alpine" feel. As I came into town, I noticed a few bars open for morning sustenance and plenty of backpacks lined up along their outside walls. I spent some time in my guidebook reading about the region and looking at the kilometers planned for the day as I enjoyed my morning coffee. "Coffee" was almost always café con leche—which was consistently excellent in northern Spain—and it always hit the spot after an hour or two on the trail.

The day's planned destination was Foncebadón, a very doable 25.9 kilometers even though it was uphill the entire way. Just beyond Foncebadón, up into the mountains farther, was one of the much-anticipated, iconic physical and spiritual landmarks of the Camino—the Cruz de Ferro. Translated, it means the "Iron Cross," which consists of a Christian cross made of iron and suspended high at the end of a tall pole. This cross is located at what is routinely referred to as the highest point on the Camino. (Technically, however, we would pass through another mountain pass a couple of kilometers farther west that is a few yards higher.)

My objective was to be at the Cross for sunrise. To do that, of course, meant I could not have a long pre-dawn hike. The plan, then, was to get within six kilometers of the Cruz de Ferro by spending the evening in the tiny mountain village of Foncebadón, which offered four different albergues—a large number for a village of its size. I thought I would find plenty of room for pilgrims.

Having been refreshed by the coffee break, I was up and along the way again, passing quickly through a couple other Maragato villages (Castrillo de Polvazares, Santa Catalina de Somoza, and El Ganso). I passed some pilgrims and others passed me as we all were finding our rhythm for the day. Just outside of El Ganso, I struck up conversation with Roberto, an engineer from Madrid who is my age and has one daughter. His English was a little rough and confusing at times. I'd give him a C+, but of course my Spanish is an F-. Roberto and I worked hard at conversation and enjoyed the walk together.

After an hour or so, Roberto said our pace, or I guess my pace, was a little too fast for him, especially with bigger hills ahead. We were less than an hour from the town of Rabanal del Camino where I was to meet back up with David. Roberto stopped for some water and a rest. I decided to push ahead—"Hike your own hike." The last stretch into Rabanal featured a pleasant earthen trail and wonderful hiking through light woodlands. Dintaman indicated that we were near ancient gold mines that date back to Roman times and were a primary reason for the routes through these hills. I came upon and passed someone "carrying" their gear in a contraption similar to a backyard wheelbarrow—but apparently designed for this purpose, one that allowed the walker to "pull" the load as it followed behind.

A very pleasant one-street town, Rabanal is populated mostly by stone buildings and a prominent church—the Church of Saint Mary of the Ascension, which I later learned has been substantially reconstructed from its twelfth-century origins, reputedly built originally by the Knights Templar. The marked path of the Camino, the cobblestone main street in Rabanal, is only about five hundred yards long, but in that space it climbs significantly from the eastern entrance to its western exit. Just as I came into the lower end of town, I ran into David, who was half waiting for me. I'd been carrying his trekking poles since early that morning. During the four-and-a-half-hour walk, I had learned that others at the albergue in Astorga had been robbed as well. And, sadly, among the victims was Carmen's mother, who had gone to great lengths to convince the hostel manger to let her family stay there to help with their efforts to surprise their daughter after an eight-hour drive from Alicante. (Typically, you may only stay at the albergues if hiking the Camino with a Pilgrim Passport.)

David had run down the individual who had bunked with him and whom he thought had stolen his money. Yet, after a proper "cross-examination," David said he was fairly convinced that suspect had *not* taken his euros. David was staying in Rabanal for the night and headed off to see if he could get into the church and the albergue early. Before he left, I convinced him, after some insistence, to take a hundred euros from me so he would not be without money. Fortunately, and coincidentally, I had loaded up on euros just that morning. I climbed to the middle of town, found a bench outside the church on the main street, dropped my pack, and decided to settle in for a lunch break.

Across the street were a bar and a young girl outside selling homemade jewelry and Camino (scallop shell) souvenirs. I walked by her and stepped in the bar to purchase an orange drink but not without receiving a sales pitch both coming and going. Returning to my bench, I pulled out my lunch items and sat down to enjoy my baguette and the beautiful day. The local girl was very cute but also very persistent, yet somehow, without being annoying. She greeted half a dozen pilgrims as they came up the street but had trouble making a sale. I greeted a few peregrinos with whom I had been trekking, including Andy (from Switzerland) and Henri and Alyssa (from Brazil). As a father of two girls, I could not resist the sales tactics of this ten-year-old. Her English was no better than my Spanish, but after a few hand signals and smiles I bought a bracelet from my new friend.

I climbed the last hundred yards to the top of the main street and left Rabanal around 1 p.m. The path leveled for a while and the vista expanded. In the distance I could see the mountains, still snow-capped. I wondered if I might be heading into those peaks. The trail then began to ascend again, now more steeply, but the sun remained bright and the air cool. A modest breeze welcomed me as the views became ever more extraordinary. I was refreshed and exhilarated. I barely noticed the twenty-plus pounds on my back as I enjoyed the hike up toward Foncebadón.

Arriving in Foncebadón around mid-afternoon, I found a village that appeared old and worn. The guidebooks say that it was abandoned, but is now "stirring back to life with the reawakening of the Camino." It still appeared to be abandoned, and the only thing "stirring" were a couple of other pilgrims milling about the Monte Irago albergue, which greets you near the entrance to Foncebadón. Someone had mentioned, or warned me, that Monte Irago had a "hippy vibe" complete with yoga sessions and a communal vegetarian meal. I was not sure this was the best place for a boring American lawyer, so I had decided to stay at one of the other hostels.

My guidebook listed four albergues and showed their location on a small inset map, but I had trouble locating them. Even though there couldn't have been more than fifteen buildings in the whole village, I could not seem to locate the other hostels. I walked uphill to the far end of the village's main street and found the parochial hostel—closed. I headed off the main road toward where the La Cruz de Ferro private hostel was supposed to be located. I thought I found the building, but there was no sign of life. I headed back down the hill toward the "hippy vibe" hostel and ran into Andy. I saved him considerable frustration by telling him about my search for an albergue, so we headed to the Convento de Foncebadón, which was open but appeared to be pretty full with twenty to twenty-five peregrinos already registered. The innkeeper opened a new dorm room for us, so now the inn had room.

Much relieved that I had a place for the night, I settled in at a bunk and then grabbed a shower. Three more pilgrims joined Andy and me in our bunkroom. I found a quiet spot in the upstairs restaurant, reserved a place for dinner, and then worked on my journal and blog posts. I was pleasantly surprised when Juanan (Carmen's boyfriend who surprised her—and me—the previous night in Astorga during our not-a-pilgrim-meal dinner at the Italian restaurant) showed up and invited me to visit with Carmen's family, who was staying at the same hostel.

Chris, an in-house corporate lawyer from Australia, joined Andy and me for dinner. We were three, fifty-something men from three different countries each traveling solo on the way to Santiago. Our meal fell in the "fairly typical, but good pilgrim meal" category, but we had some great conversation about expectations and experiences on the Camino. We talked about the next morning and the final climb to Cruz de Ferro. I mentioned to Andy my original plan of trying to get up to the top before dawn. Despite the weather, we decided to leave early and try for a special sunrise. Chris thought we were nuts and declined to join us.

After dinner I joined Juanan, Carmen, and her family for a glass of wine. These were the warmest, most friendly people. I'm not sure why I was so readily included, but it was great fun. This family had driven eight hours from the southeast coast of Spain to spend a couple of days with their daughter, who I had the good fortune to run into leaving Burgos eight days earlier. Somehow the family and I communicated fairly well. The dad was the unelected "mayor" of their hometown back in Alicante. Even in this mountaintop village, through facial expressions, a few recognizable words, hand motions, and some translation, I was reminded that lawyer jokes apparently are part of a universal language. If Santa Claus was a prominent aspect of Christmas in southeast Spain, I was confident that Mr. Perez must have regularly played that role for his and the community's children.

Carmen's mother ran a woman's clothing shop there. Her sister was married and taught elementary school, and her brother was preparing for university. Carmen and her older sister spoke English fairly well. Juanan tried hard and helped make connections. I, of course, was pathetic, being barely capable of a simple greeting in Spanish. Before long it was time for "lights out." The Perez family and I took photographs, exchanged great hugs, and said our goodbyes. Sadly I knew I would not likely ever see them again, but they were now permanently part of my Camino.

Monday, April 28 (Day 21)

[Foncebadón to Molinaseca]
(20.3 kilometers—12.6 miles)

Andy and I had a fairly easy two-kilometer climb to the Cruz de Ferro. We were up early and quietly moved our backpacks and other items out of the bunkroom so we could pack without disturbing the others. We were greeted by the most pleasant surprise—the hostel manager was up early and had coffee and croissants available for us. This was a rare phenomenon in Spain along the Camino; as I have mentioned, the Spaniards just were on a very different clock, which did not seem to have an alarm before 8:00 a.m.

We glanced outside into the darkness. The outside lights of the albergue were surrounded by a yellow glow due to a heavy fog. I stepped out into the thickest air I may have ever experienced—no rain but humidity at 100 percent. We were sitting in a cloud. Our prospects for a mountaintop sunrise did not look good, but I remained optimistic. "Perhaps it will clear for us," I mentioned to Andy as we enjoyed a quick café con leche. Undaunted, we donned our rain gear, lifted our packs, and headed out into the pea soup of the early morning. A few fellow pilgrims (a group from France who had been up to the Cross the day before) suggested we take the road instead of the path due to the lack of any meaningful visibility. The Cruz de Ferro is a popular local attraction and readily accessible by motor vehicle. Realizing that finding and staying on a woodland path would be a significant challenge, we thanked them for the suggestion and headed for the road.

Despite the difficult weather and the thought that we would not be able to enjoy a sunrise, I was excited to be heading to this iconic site on the Camino. Halfway to the summit by way of the paved road, Andy and I crossed what appeared to be an earthen walking path so we took what appeared to be a continuation of that path, thinking it would lead us to the Cross. We moved along the well-worn trail near the mountaintop but saw no way-marks and did not find the destination. So we backtracked to the road and continued on.

Visibility was still minimal, but within ten minutes we finally arrived—still early morning. No other pilgrims were there. The area was completely fogged in, and it was cold and breezy. Our special planned sunrise visit looked very doubtful. Nonetheless, the forecast called for clearing, so I decided to linger at the top for a little while, but Andy moved on.

While waiting hopefully for the weather to clear, I glanced around the site. I was a little disappointed to see that the Cruz de Ferro was a well-worn roadside turnoff, like so many picnic spots along the Blue Ridge Parkway back in Virginia. The "Iron Cross" is at the top of a modest pole standing twenty-five or thirty feet tall. At its base is a mound of rocks, as well as other mementos left behind by pilgrims. Tradition holds that those on the way to Santiago should bring with them a stone from their home, carry it to this point, and leave it at the foot of the cross as a symbol of leaving one or more of life's burdens behind. Not one to challenge Camino tradition, I had brought a small stone from my hometown's James River, which I planned to leave at the mountaintop. It is symbolic, of course, not just because I brought it from Richmond, but because I took it from a place by the river where I had sat many times with my preschool-aged daughters, who liked to throw rocks in the river on Saturday mornings.

During the climb up to the Cross, I gave serious thought to what "burden" might be represented by my stone. I found myself focusing on my strong sense of self-reliance and independence, which I have learned can be as much a burden as an admirable quality. In fact, our culture generally glorifies these attributes—little is more "American" than pulling oneself up by our own bootstraps. And, regarding such independence, I was "all in." Yet, time and experience had shown me that if such individual focus and self-reliance is not tempered by humility and perspective, they devolve into egotism and selfishness. Hence, for me, such *uber* confidence may ultimately be one of life's biggest hurdles. I thought about this conviction that "I can do it myself" as I dug deep into my backpack for the sandwich bag that contained the rock I brought from home. I had concluded that life would be even more rewarding the sooner I recognized my limitations and my need for family and community. So with those thoughts, I approached the Cross with my stone.

I lingered at the top, apparently clinging to an irrational hope that any minute the clouds would part and the sunrise would reveal itself. I watched a couple of pilgrims come by the cross, stop for a few moments, take a few photos, and move along. Then another few came separately and moved on. When I saw an opportunity, I took a moment to approach the cross, climb the modest hill of stones, and deposit my rock. Distracted by the conflicting symbols of a Christian cross and miscellaneous items appearing to be mostly trash, I tried to reflect on the seriousness of the Cross, the most important symbol of my faith. I try to meditate on the sacrifice and atonement it represented. I moved off to the side where the tiny Ermita de Santiago sits and completed my thoughts before resuming my hike.

The weather did not improve. It became obvious that little reason remained for me to wait any longer for a clearing. I was also getting cold as the temperature began to work its way through my layers of clothing. As I got ready to hit the path and start down the mountain, a couple was at the cross tossing their stones. I came close enough on my way out for them to ask me to take a photo for them. I was happy to oblige and, as I came closer to get their camera, who was it but Carmen and Juanan! With the cold and the fog and everyone wearing rain gear, I could not make out that these visages were actually my newest best friends in Spain. I guess one might exclaim, "What a small world!" or, "What a coincidence!" Yet, I am reminded of C.S. Lewis's quip about no coincidences for those who believe in God.

We were ready to leave and I certainly could have walked with Carmen and Juanan, but they only had two days to be together, so I made up an excuse to linger at the Cross a little longer. So Carmen and Juanan headed off. I followed a few minutes later. As I started my descent, the weather worsened. The mist and fog turned to rain. The temperature dropped and the breeze stiffened. My hands got so cold I stopped to put on gloves. A few minutes later, the weather was no better, perhaps worse, so I stopped a second time. This time I pulled the rain cover over my backpack and slipped on my rain pants, which I needed both for warmth and as a shield from the rain. I walked down a well-worn, earthen path that descended gradually. I saw other hikers ahead, but with the weather I could not see much beyond twenty or thirty yards in front of me.

The path then leads pilgrims onto the road, which takes vehicles to and from the Cruz de Ferro. The road descends gradually, although with the thickness of the fog I could really only judge the severity of the slope as I was traversing it. Fortunately, we probably saw only two automobiles during an hour of road walking. I then came upon Villa-mayor de Monjardin—with a population of one. Despite the thick fog and light rain, the Spartan hostel run by Tomas was readily identifiable by sight and sound. A Georgian chant emanated from the old building and signposts pointing to most of the great world capitals greeted pilgrims passing by this eclectic albergue.

From there I was surprised that we had a modest climb. I had as-sumed that we would take the rest of the day to come down off this high spot, but we had an ascent to Alto Altar Mayor. At 5,036 feet it, rather than the Cruz de Ferro, is the highest point on the Camino. Then the descent became much steeper. It left the paved surface and returned to an earthen path, but the severity of the descent continued. The knee I injured on Day Four began to cry out as I moved slowly down the mountain.

My new med student friend David, who was a much more fit hiker with two healthy knees, came by as I made my way down the steep grade. Others also passed me as I cautiously eased myself along trying to nurse my knee. I started to see glimpses of blue sky and sunshine amidst the rising cloud cover, revealing magnificent mountain ridges off to my left, beautiful green valleys, and the outskirts of Ponferrada, the day's destination, down below and to my right. The beauty I had hoped for at the Cross was finally unfolding. I could see that the sky would probably soon clear. Still being high in the mountains, I wanted to take in what certainly, hiding behind the rising clouds and mist, appeared to be considerable physical beauty. I feared that I'd be off the highest points before the weather cleared and I'd miss some spec-tacular scenery, much as I missed the views when we were climbing over the Pyrenees on Day One. What to do?

A thought came to me rather quickly. I realized that I had all the time in the world and did not have to be anywhere, at least not any-time soon. I had no court appearances or client meetings. *Relax*, I told myself. I stopped my descent, took a few steps off the path, took off my pack, and plopped myself down on the hillside. I decided to have lunch to restore and refresh as the clouds continued to clear and reveal the beauty around me.

Stopping also allowed me to visit with a number of fellow pilgrims, including David the surgery nurse from Denver (whom I had met in Hontanas and had seen again in Carrión), Henri and Alyssia from Brazil (with whom I'd keep pace, and see, for each of the next nine days and finish in Santiago within an hour of each other), Bea from Brazil, Michael from Germany (who took some photos for me and with whom I'd walk again heading into Sarria in two days), Jen from Australia (whom I had first met in Hontanas and would later see again in León and Santiago, and then again in Finisterre), and Lynn from British Columbia (whom I had met with Carmen the morning we left Burgos, with whom I walked through the Bierzo wine region into Villafranca del Bierzo, and with whom I would walk the last day into Santiago).

Jen and Lynn decided to stop and have lunch with me, right there in the middle of the mountain, and watch the sky clear. The clouds lifted, and we enjoyed magnificent views. In brilliant sunshine, I moved on without Jen and Lynn and walked slowly and gingerly down and down through El Acebo and Riego de Ambros, two lovely "alpine" towns. The afternoon hike was wonderful, consisting mostly of good wooded trails and beautiful scenery. From time to time, like most afternoons, a modest pain developed in my back from carrying the backpack. I shifted the load around, trying to give the aching spot some relief. Despite some discomfort from the pack and although I needed to step carefully to protect my knee, I was exhilarated by the day and the great hiking.

I had no interest in or need for a distraction like listening to tunes, pleasant and thought-provoking as they might be. I was very happy doing just what I was doing. I continued down the mountain and into the valley. Having been lost, having come through the cold and rain at Cruz de Ferro but having watched the sky clear while still on the mountain, followed by a wonderful hike down into the valley created an elation matched only by what I had felt on Day Two. I loved my time walking through the forest pathways and modest farming villages.

I was headed for Ponferrada, but I really did not want this descent from the highest point on the Camino to end.

Eventually I came out of the woods and into the town of Molinaseca. The entrance to the town is across a medieval bridge (the Puente de los Peregrinos) over a clear mountain stream that had grown to the size of a river (Rio Meruelo) at that point, near the base of the mountain. Ponferrada had been my destination for the day, still another six or seven, mostly flat and easy, kilometers away. The day had been so great, I was tempted to stop and celebrate before something happened to ruin the experience. Molinaseca appeared to be both an attractive and well-resourced town. I decided to stop. Just across the bridge, I looked into the Hotel El Palacio and secured a private room for the night. I could say I was in a great mood, but those words fall short. I had enjoyed a wonderful day. My spirits were exceedingly high. I'm not sure how much better it could have been.

As was my habit, I dropped my pack in the room and, before taking a shower, headed into the restaurant below my hotel to have a beer. Except for a single party who appeared to be just finishing a meal, the restaurant was empty. I went up to the bar and ordered my *cervesa*. As I turned to take my beer outside and sit by the river, Carmen and Juanan and the Perez family greeted me! Small world? Coincidence? They were that lone party in the restaurant. I visited with them briefly. They were taking Carmen to an albergue in Ponferrada before getting on the road for a long drive to Alicante. So we had more goodbyes and I then headed outside to have another beer. And who was sitting there but Jen and Lynn!

After visiting with my two mountainside lunch companions, I walked around Molinaseca. I explored the seventeenth-century Church of Saint Nicholas or Iglesia San Nicolás. Its bell tower certainly exhibited architecture that was different from the Gothic or Romanesque we had seen so often on the Camino. Rather than having a spire, the church's tower looked as though it was capped by something resembling a military helmet from Imperial Germany. Upon investigation, I learned that this was "a neoclassical temple, a basilica." While I could understand the building itself being "neoclassical," I could not see how the bell tower and particularly its crown was that style of architecture, but then again, what do I really know. I met and talked with Rusty and Carol, husband and wife, from Pittsburgh (whom I would see again the day of arrival in Santiago). I enjoyed a dinner of pasta carbonara and wine at the hotel restaurant and enjoyed a night outside of a pilgrim hostel.

Tuesday, April 29 (Day 22)

[Molinaseca to Villafranca]
(30.6 kilometers—19.0 miles)

The morning walk into Ponferrada featured overcast skies with peeks of sun. Ponferrada dates back to a Celtic settlement of the Astures before the time of Christ. Gold in the surrounding mountains made the settlement more important as the Roman Empire extended its reach and grasp. In fact, the word *Hispanic* comes from *Hispania*, the word the Romans used to refer to the Iberian Peninsula. Today, Asturia is an autonomous community in northwest Spain, and Ponferrada is a vibrant, modern city and the last large town or city on the Camino Frances before reaching Santiago. As someone from Richmond, Virginia, I noted an interesting coincidence that the UCI World Championships (the most significant international bicycle race after the Tour de France) would be held in Ponferrada that year and would be in Richmond the following year.

The hike along suburban streets was modestly downhill, reasonably easy, and fairly enjoyable. I came to a point where I couldn't tell which direction to head, but as I was coming into the outskirts of the city, a local pointed me in the right direction. Off to my right were three fellow travelers who obviously had taken the "other" way and now appeared to be lost. I signaled to them. As they came by so I could tell them the directions I had received, I realized that the group consisted of Lynn, Jen, and my PGA Spaniard friend I had met on my way out of León.

Even after entering the city over an impressive medieval pilgrim bridge, the walk into the city center was otherwise long and uninteresting until I came upon the twelfth-century Templar Castle or Castillo de los Templarios—one of those iconic sites on the Camino—something most books and blogs feature for those seeking out information about walking the Camino de Santiago. Until Dan Brown's *The Da Vinci Code*, many had never heard of the Knights Templar or the Templar Order. Some assume that it was just a fiction created for the novel, but in fact, the Knights Templar had been a powerful military order of the Middle Ages. These Knights were endorsed by the Church early in the twelfth century and participated prominently in the Crusades.

Also in the twelfth century, as the popularity and importance of the Camino grew significantly, the Templars and other military religious groups appeared in northern Spain and were committed to protecting Christians on pilgrimage to Santiago. The restored castle in Ponferrada is the remaining prominent symbol of that past. It was built on the site of earlier fortresses on a bluff overlooking the confluence of the Rivers Sil and Boeza.

I caught up to a group that I referred to as the "German Boys" (even though it consisted of four college students—three from Germany and one from Denmark) and followed them into town. Way-markings in Ponferrada were the worst of the Camino so far. We found ourselves stopping often to look for yellow arrows and to ask citizens for help staying on the correct path through the busy, modern city. We finally found a supermarket and gathered some provisions. I then headed off alone and again had to seek assistance in finding the Camino. Various people, none of whom could speak English but who seemed to understand "Camino de Santiago" and who could point, showed me the way out of the city.

The "path" took me on city sidewalks for a long time and I had to maneuver through a couple of roundabouts with vehicle traffic. After a while, I sensed that I was lost—I had been in the city too long without seeing another fellow traveler for a half an hour. As I learned here and in a few other similar places, pilgrims were more likely to get lost in cities. A glimpse at my map suggested that I should not still be on city streets. I stopped outside a grocery store and, practicing what Father Jim mentioned on our way up the Pyrenees, I sat to rest, refresh, and think. I took out my map again to study it; I determined I must be in one of two places and that the Camino should be up ahead. I asked a woman coming out of the store if Camponaraya was straight ahead, pointing to the map and the direction I thought I needed to travel. She couldn't speak English but seemed to understand my plight and was able to affirm that the town of Camponaraya was straight up the busy road on which I had been travelling the last hour.

I realized that the well-intentioned citizens of Ponferrada had pointed me to the "road" to Santiago—if you were driving—but apparently did not know the way to the walking trail. Getting distressed would do me no good, and now that I knew definitively where I was, I laughed it off and headed west along the sidewalk of a very commercial four-lane highway. Twenty minutes later, I spotted some walkers with backpacks and then some yellow arrows as I picked up the proper trail again in Camponaraya. After a stop for lunch, the Camino headed through rolling vineyards and agricultural fields.

On the outskirts of town, I walked by a building, "VINO BIERZO CO-OP" and a "wine tasting" sign. Really? Wine tasting? *What's the rush?* I thought. So I doubled back a hundred yards to check out the winery. A fellow pilgrim from Germany joined me in tasting and discussing the region's wine with the resident winemaker there. I was particularly interested in learning more about this wine region. As an amateur vinophile, I knew a little but was burdened with the assumption that there was little in Spain by way of wine other than "Rioja" and the tempranillo grape.

The winemaker at the co-operative walked me through some details about the Bierzo area as a wine-producing region. Apparently near the mountains is a unique microclimate, despite its higher elevation, that permits the cultivation of the mencia grape, a new variety to me. Where the tempranillo grape is used for more full-bodied red wines typical of Rioja, wines made from the mencia grape apparently have been younger and lighter wines. There is an increase in the mencia grape, and some winemakers are now crafting more aged, full-bodied reds in this region. I purchased a bottle, which was a pretty heavy item to include in my backpack, but thought I could enjoy it that night in Villafranca with others.

The trail left the paved road and headed more into the vineyards and agricultural fields. I stopped at a picnic spot and decided to open the wine, which I shared with Orla from Ireland (whom I'd see again outside of Triacastela) and then with the German Boys, who had caught up with me after I left them at the *supermercado* in Ponferrada city center. Then Lynn came along. After we all shared the wine and enjoyed a brief rest, we walked the final thirteen kilometers through more vineyards and orchards as well as the modest Camino towns of Pieros and Valtuille de Abajo. The afternoon was warm and my feet were tired, but I enjoyed the El Bierzo landscape. We were glad to catch a glimpse of Villafranca—the destination for the day—as the dirt trail led us downhill into the valley where this picturesque town sat by the confluence of the Burbia and Valcarce Rivers.

Having planned to stay out after the usual 10 p.m. "lights out" curfew in the hostels, I got a private room for the night at the Posada Hotel Plaza. I showered and headed back into the town to get a tour. The town had much to see in terms of physical beauty, medieval charm, and interesting architecture. A lap around town took me past the Church of Santiago, the Castillo Palacio de la Marqueses, the Monastery of San Francisco, and the Church of St. Nicholas. I started to fade as my legs cried out for rest. My hotel sat in a pretty square at the western edge of town with a number of outdoor cafés. I needed to rest and have a drink. As I entered the square, I walked right into Carmen. I quickly explained that my legs were giving out but asked her to join me for a drink. We sat down outside and ordered our drinks. I had seen a sign on my stroll at a café with photographs of meals and thought I would order some *chorizo* (sausage) for us to share while we rested and enjoyed our beers.

I explained to Carmen that we should order some of that *chorizo* I saw advertised on one of the café signs. I asked her to do that because the language was a challenge and having her along made it much easier to ask questions, order, and pay. So we ordered the *chorizo*. Our beers came, and we enjoyed a peaceful late afternoon in a pretty public square in an ancient city nestled in a beautiful valley—with many other pilgrims sprinkled around the square in similar outdoor cafés.

Our tapas came. It was delicious but didn't look like I expected, not like the advertisement. I mentioned this to Carmen. She seemed surprised and confused as I tried to explain. I showed her the ad with the photograph of the spicy sausage bites I thought we were ordering. She responded with a laugh of surprise, and a hint of embarrassment. Then, with a big smile, she said to me, "Oh, you wanted 'chor—reeth—o.' I thought you said, 'chor–ras–co!'" We laughed, and I quickly assured her that I didn't really care. In fact, the *churasco* was delicious. (*Chorizo* is a type of salami or sausage in Spain. The problem was not in Carmen's ordering of our tapas but in my pronunciation of what I wanted. I learned that the "z" in Spanish is pronounced with a "th" sound—hence, "chor—reeth—o." But when I pronounced it with a "z" or "s" sound, Carmen thought I was saying, "chor—ras—co." It was all very funny and another reminder that Americans cannot expect to have the optimum experience on the Camino if they don't learn some Spanish.)

Andy from Switzerland came by and joined us. In discussing soccer and the current Champions League tournament back in our albergue in Foncebadón, we said we'd have to find a bar and watch the upcoming Madrid–Munich semi-final match, which would be on TV the night we expected to be in Villafranca. So Andy and I went inside the bar to have dinner and to watch "football," which was very exciting to watch in a bar in Spain because Madrid soundly upset Munich at Munich 4–0 to clinch a spot in the finals (which would turn out to be historic with two Madrid teams playing for probably the biggest soccer title outside of the World Cup or the Olympics).

CHAPTER 15

PETE AND SHIRLEY MACLAINE

No one saves us but ourselves.
No one can and no one may.
We ourselves must walk the path.

Buddha

I met Pete as he emerged, previously unseen, from some ruins at Zaraputz just as Clara and I were passing by. A tall, bushy-haired wanderer with a scallop shell dangling off his backpack, "Pete," I learned, was from Cornwall in southwest England. The lanky pilgrim had been investigating the broken-down stone walls and other remnants of a fifteenth-century hospital that had once served medieval travelers on the Camino de Santiago. As it turned out (as it often did on the Camino), Clara and Pete had met previously, during a bus ride into St. Jean a few days earlier. After a brief stop to make and renew acquaintances, the three of us moved on together—a little like Dorothy, the Scarecrow, and the Tin Man.

As we walked along, I had told Pete about how beautiful I found his corner of Great Britain when I had backpacked through Europe after college graduation. He agreed that his home region was very pretty, but he quickly wanted to inquire about U.S. foreign policy. At

189

thirty-two years of age, Pete had strong political views. He was not a fan of George W. Bush and was very critical of his own country's government for supporting the U.S. military initiatives in the Middle East. In fact, he found very little about the British government to be useful or appropriate.

I asked what Pete did back in the U.K. He explained he was "disabled" and drew on a stipend akin to the "dole" to support him. Perhaps recognizing the obvious confusion if not contradiction (of a "disabled" man walking fifteen miles a day with a twenty-pound pack on his back), Pete quickly added, "I'm not really disabled, but I have a doctor who says I am." This seemed not to trouble him.

Realizing U.S. and British involvement in the Middle East, despite Bush and Blair's friendship, was not likely to be the basis for creating close bonds, I changed the subject. "We're hoping to rejoin the other path in time to visit the wine fountain," I mentioned to Pete. I had read about "free wine" being given to pilgrims at the Irache monastery, which has become one of those "can't miss," iconic stops of any modern pilgrim's adventure on the Camino. Because Clara and I had taken the "detour," we were unsure if we might bypass this fountain before our chosen route rejoined the main path.

Pete replied simply, "If it was meant to be, it will be."

Without showing any surprise to this comment, I replied, "You think so?"

To which Pete came back, "Everything happens for a reason."

Something about Pete's comments caused me to hold on to them for a moment. Typically, they would leave as quickly as they came, but something caused me to pause and consider them longer, so much so that I asked myself: *What did he mean by this?* From our conversation, I would not have thought Pete might believe in God or anything transcendent. It may have struck me uniquely because I had also thought about this very question before. People often make similar statements: "It was meant to be," or "I'll keep you in my prayers," or "Everything happens for a reason." I wondered, *How often do we think about what it means?* Is it just a platitude? Is anything meant by it?

But, it *is* different than saying, "Whatever will be, will be," or the currently popular equivalent, "It is what it is." But it is much different to say that something is "meant" to be.

What then does it mean to say, "If it was meant to be, it will be?"

Pete's comments suggest, do they not, that everything (or at least *some* things) are "part of a plan." This same issue confronts us every day. In the popular television drama *Homeland,* Carrie says to Brody, "I believe one reason I was put on this earth was for our paths to cross." We often hear similar statements in an array of situations. Again, what do people mean in using them? Do they look behind the words and see the implications?

If we say we are "put on the earth" for something, or if something "is meant to be," it indicates that we recognize, even if we do not understand, that there is a plan, that these actions or events are part of a plan. And doesn't that require us to ask, "What plan?" (Isn't that what someone on the road to find out, someone examining life, would ask?) Or more accurately, "*Whose* plan?" Because, by definition, doesn't "a plan" require thought, intention, and action? Doesn't it assume a rational being? Would it be difficult to come up with a plan if we relied on whimsy or incoherence?

So I finally challenged him, "Pete, if something 'is meant to be,' it suggests, does it not, that there is a plan . . . out there? That there is some higher power that has a plan and that we are part of that plan?"

Without much thought, Pete replied, "Yea, I guess that's right." Then he added, "But it's not 'god,' at least not in any traditional sense." Pete explained that he had some general belief in things spiritual, but it was not defined or based upon any particular leader, thinker, or religious group—certainly not the Christian tradition of his homeland. "There's something bigger than us," he added, "but it is a reality that you create. You find your own way to that bigger something."

I had heard these types of expressions before, but I never felt that I could make them understandable in some tangible way. These notions of creating our own reality or an undefined embrace of spirituality appear to have gained traction in recent times and are sometimes referred to as "New Age" spirituality. They were popular with many on the Camino. I still wondered how there could be a plan without some entity–some thinking, rational being. In effect, how can you have a plan without a planner? Pete saw no contradiction in rejecting God, but believing there was a "plan," just as he was happy to collect payments from the government for a disability he did not have but to criticize the manner in which that same government interfered in his life back in the U.K.

For me, saying, "If it's meant to be," is similar to saying something like, "I will keep you in my thoughts and prayers." What do we really mean by that? Is it just something we say? I hope not, because we seem to reserve that expression for times that are most urgent in the lives of our family and friends. The expression indicates a promise to pray for them. Presumably it means we recognize that something or someone transcends us. Further it implies we must think such a someone or something is not only transcendent but might have some ability, and perhaps some willingness, to make a difference, to act in the present time to change circumstances or at least to comfort those who are grieving or suffering. Clearly it seems to point to something or someone we typically refer to as God. Pete would suggest that he's not so sure, but he'd embrace some generalized "spirituality." He would be likely to say, "I'm very spiritual, but not religious." In fact, he might well believe, as Ralph Waldo Emerson said, "Life is a journey, not a destination."

Pete's comments recalled New Age thinking and reminded me particularly of the actress Shirley MacLaine, who is prominent among New Age advocates. Coincidentally, MacLaine is one of the better-known Americans associated with the Camino because she wrote a book in 2000 about her own walk to Santiago in 1994 as part of her personal quest for enlightenment. *The Camino: A Journey of the Spirit* was one of the first books to introduce the Camino de Santiago to America. The book is an example of how some individuals head out on the "Way" for personal reflection and spiritual discovery without reference to or guidance from the traditional Christian aspects of the pilgrimage.

In her own way, MacLaine adopts Socrates's admonitions about an unexamined life. In *The Camino* she says, "Without the recognition of the soul's journey within us, we are lost and only part of what we were intended to be" (*The Camino*, page 10). While critical of traditional religion, she likewise challenges the modern adherence to science as the sole source of truth. Nonetheless, MacLaine blends words and concepts from different religious and spiritual traditions. Elsewhere in her book, MacLaine recounts, and attempts to draw meaning from, dreams and visions of prior lives as well as observations about lines of energy and karma as she traveled along the Camino. For example, about local, medieval churches she would pass by, she writes, "They were ornate and imposing and resonated with secrets of the past that I could feel" (*The Camino,* page 56).

About the Milky Way, she shares a belief held by many through the ages that the galaxy has a special relationship to the Camino—the Way of St. James is sometimes referred by many the Camino de las Estrellas or the "path of the stars." For some, the Milky Way appears to be directly over the Camino guiding pilgrims to their destination and leading others, including MacLaine, to extract spiritual meaning out of the coincidence. For others, like me, the Milky Way is just as much "above" Richmond, Virginia, as it is above northern Spain.

Perhaps the best-known New Age writer is Eckhart Tolle, often associated with Oprah Winfrey. When Tolle makes pronouncements like "the Truth is inseparable from who you are. Yes, you *are* the Truth. If you look for it elsewhere, you will be deceived every time," I keep asking, "What is he trying to say?" What does it mean? It remains elusive for me, like the proverbial effort to grasp and hold onto smoke. It seems to me that if *you* are the truth, then everyone is the truth—and if everyone is the truth, there can be no truth or at least nothing that is true now and for all times. Words and sentences need to have meaning, do they not? What are they trying to convey here?

For MacLaine and others, New Age thought is a real path to enlightenment. For others, like me, it is elusive as best, if not unintelligible. The words and concepts sound attractive, but I could not appreciate the connections or see how there was any coherence to the seemingly disparate observations about energy, divinity, enlightenment, karma, and spirit. At least MacLaine admits, "What I will attempt to convey and describe may take you off the Camino path and to the edge of reason." I could not figure out what it all meant unless they were proposing a highly egocentric, self-reliant process to understand what is "true" for each individual. If this is their focus, perhaps I could not grasp it because I had previously concluded that such an approach was terribly misguided—as Harold Abrahams said, such a self-absorbed focus was the "miscalculation of his life."

In classic New Age language, MacLaine concludes *The Camino* by stating, "We each create it all. And again, the absence of evidence does not mean the evidence of absence. Imagine that." When interviewed by Oprah (a present-day New Age devotee) just a couple of weeks before I headed out on the Camino, MacLaine explained more of her ideas about an "impersonal Divine" and the quest for spiritual meaning.

> *"Do you consider yourself a spiritual trailblazer?" Oprah asks MacLaine.*
>
> *"Oh, Oprah," MacLaine says, "That begs a huge question, which I've been thinking about rather seriously and intimately: We are all one. I am everybody who's seeking. And everybody who's seeking is me. So I make no differentiation."*
>
> *Oprah rephrases her question. "Are you pleased with the role that you've played as a spiritual trailblazer for our culture?"*
>
> *MacLaine answers modestly, "I'm pleased with the fact that I saw a trail and I walked down it, and didn't know what I was going to find."*

While comments about "creating it all" are, at least for me, all but impossible to grasp rationally, I noted that MacLaine used the seemingly universal language of pilgrimage—about walking a path and searching.

When I suggest that I just do not understand, Tolle, Oprah, or MacLaine would inevitably respond that everyone makes up their own truth and that I need to do the same. Further, these New Agers would add that everyone is at their essence their own "god." Like Clara and Socrates, understanding what is "true" is something every pilgrim seeks to discover. Does it answer the question if we say that we create our own truth? Yet, isn't the idea of creating your *own* truth contradictory—if you create truth then is anything true?

I could not help but recall a quip I heard a few years ago from a well-read, thoughtful colleague. In discussing how people seem to pick and choose the rules and doctrines (and "truths") they like in fashioning what they think God is like, my friend said, "You know you've created God in your own image when your God hates the same things you hate." The statement takes a moment to sink in, and then you chuckle, but as you walk away, you begin to see nuggets of profundity. Do we do the same thing? Os Guinness summarized these thoughts by noting that the fundamental problem with modern men and women is that human beings have become "both the source and the standard of their own meaning." That thought suggested to me what the New Age writers seemed to be doing.

The lawyer in me is accustomed to, but confident in, the use of reason and logic. Not only did I struggle trying to understand the New Age thoughts I sensed coming from Pete, I also wondered if everyone creates his or her own god (or *is* his or her own god), what might be left of the concept? Can we really have a "search for meaning" or "truth" if it is something we create for ourselves? I believe that for the words "God" and "divine" to have some meaning, they must relate to what is eternal, not be determined by any one of us to create or fashion God in our image.

When Pete says, "Everything happens for a reason," I can give a kindly affirmation, but if I ponder the statement for just a moment, I wonder what does it really mean? I cannot help but think that a "man with a plan" must be out there; otherwise the statement is simply a platitude that doesn't intend to convey serious thought. But, even if the latter is true, I still have to wonder what causes someone to make such an expression. Do even those not inclined to believe in God or something transcendent still have a sense that it is nonetheless real, and perhaps there are other things that suppress those thoughts from developing fully? Then again, what better reason might there be for being on the road to find out?

CHAPTER 16

GALICIA

(Days 23–25)

*I think everybody has their own way of looking at their lives
as some kind of pilgrimage. Some people will see their role as a
pilgrim in terms of setting up a fine family, or establishing
a business inheritance. Everyone's got their own definition.
Mine, I suppose, is to know myself.*

Eric Clapton

[Villafranca del Bierzo—[Vega de Valcarce], [La Faba], [Border: Castilla–Galicia], **Pedrafita do Cebreiro**, [Alto San Roque], [Triacastela], **Samos**, [Sarria], **Portomarín]**
(97.5 kilometers—60.6 miles)

Although I emphasized the wonderful hiking experience from Astorga to Portomarín featured in the last chapter, this chapter and these sections of the Camino also offered interesting and important highlights of the historic pilgrimage. These include the albergue run by the Confraternity of St. James in Rabanal, the Cruz de Ferro, the Templar city of Ponferrada, the Bierzo wine region and its important pilgrim town of Villafranca, and—featured in this chapter—the intriguing mountaintop village of O Cebreiro that was home to the modern father of the Camino, the massive monastery of Samos tucked away in a valley on a "detour" route, the busy Camino town of Sarria, and the reborn lakeside town of Portomarín.

Wednesday, April 30 (Day 23)

[Villafranca to O Cebreiro]
(30.1 kilometers—18.7 miles)

The early morning of my twenty-third day on the Camino was partly cloudy as the sun began to rise. I had been told (or warned) that this day's challenge would be one of the toughest of the entire trip. The Brierley guide counsels: "This stage represents one of the steepest of the whole pilgrimage, but the climb is rewarded with stunning views along the Valcarce valley that will keep spirits high." The objective was O Cebreiro, a mountaintop village just over thirty kilometers away but uphill the entire way. I was prepared for a very hard day, so I thought I should hike my own pace. During dinner the night before, I had asked Carmen to reserve a room at a hotel so when I crawled into town exhausted, I would have a place to toss my gear and myself. I had decided that the toughest day on the Camino justified a private room. I certainly didn't want to undertake the long climb only to find that I'd have to go farther because there was no room at the hostel.

Leaving Villafranca, I crossed a bridge over Rio Burbia and had a wonderful view east, back down into the town nestled in the folds of the mountains. I could see a variety of colors fighting through a light cloud cover. After a few more steps, I came to a decision point—as I had various times before when the Camino offered a "detour"—to take the path along the busy road or the more rural, wilderness path. As I stood wondering, a woman from Bordeaux I had seen before came by and headed up the inclined road to the right, toward the country ("Pradela") trail. I was already concerned about how difficult the day's hike would be, and I knew the detour would not only add kilometers to the day but three separate hills that had to be ascended and descended before rejoining the main path and the steepest part of the day's journey. So I chickened out and took the easier route, thinking I might need to conserve some strength. If I had read Hape's book beforehand, I might have endured more vigorous hiking because he described the route that I took as follows: "I'm flabbergasted to find that there is no sidewalk or separate footpath for pilgrims. Instead I have to walk along the shoulder, which is five feet wide, with hundreds of cars and trucks zooming along at top speed and making a deafening racket as they pass the poor hikers."

I was alone on a dirt path hard next to the paved road. The weather was partly cloudy and overcast with peeks of sun all day, actually quite amenable to walking. I met and then walked with "Sam," a thirty-something woman from Australia hiking solo, as the trail continued a long, steady climb through a variety of small fairly close towns. Thankfully, the traffic on the road is nothing like Kerkeling's experiences. In fact, the road was quiet as we made our way up through the narrow valley. In fact, we enjoyed the presence of a pretty mountain stream down the hill on our left all day. We made a quick stop for food supplies and a lovely old lady overcharged me for a baguette. I just smiled as I walked away and walked on.

Sam had news from David the med student and his efforts to arrange a proper wedding proposal at the End of the Earth. This was another great aspect of the Camino, certainly not one that I could have anticipated. Like the intrigue over George's boots, I was fascinated at how some stories developed over time and the details were passed up and down the Camino among people whose relationships are as disparate and changing/developing as the pace at which they were walking the Way.

When David first revealed the news and his plans, we were in Astorga. He had about two weeks to get the logistics sorted. At our dinner in Astorga, David had told me that he planned to speak to Juliana's father right away. He even had a plan to have Juliana (his girlfriend) unknowingly bring her own engagement ring to Santiago by smuggling it in a box of brownies from his mother. Three days after that dinner, I met

Sam. She had seen David the day prior. Apparently his future in-laws were not equally excited by the prospects of marriage.

After Sam finished our Camino gossip update, we stopped for a lunch break in Vega de Valcarce. Sam's friend Sebastian, from South Africa, was nearby and joined us for lunch. I often say "when in Rome," so I finally tried the local *cidre*—a popular local drink made from fermented apple juice. With her shoes already off, Sam lit a cigarette and sat back to visit with Sebastian, clearly planning for a longer break. Still a little stressed about the climb ahead (and having little use for the tobacco smoke), I thanked Sam for the morning companionship and moved along.

The hike along the main road continued for almost another hour, but I used the time to listen to some tunes on my iPod. The path eventually left the busy road and led into the hamlet of Herrerias on a more rural lane, which Brierley describes as follows: "From the Herrerias Bridge we wind our way through this quaint riverside village with its simple stone architecture." Just before leaving Herrerias to begin the ascent up to the mountaintop village, I passed a stable and saw that for twenty euros I could hire a horse to take me up the steep mountain to O Cebreiro. I did not seriously consider the option, but it reminded me of the serious hike ahead.

About half an hour after the horse stables, the yellow arrows—finally—directed me off the country road onto a rocky but earthen path and through chestnut woodlands pointing us toward the hillside hamlet of La Faba. Although I had completed less than half of the severe climb when I arrived in this pretty village, I was encouraged. I still felt strong and very prepared to continue on. At the pilgrim water fountain where I rested for a few moments, I spoke with one of the few Americans, a seventy-year-old man from Maine, I would run into during my time on the Camino. After a brief visit during which I shared my love of Maine, I headed out of La Faba. I still had a final five-kilometer climb to O Cebreiro, which I expected would be difficult.

Somewhat surprised, I not only enjoyed the final leg of the hike but also was invigorated by the broad, expansive, and magnificent views of the highest mountains I had experienced. Rain threatened as I continued toward the summit. I caught up with and then walked with two young women from South Africa and Namibia slack packing up this steep part of the Camino. I walked through a couple of light, brief showers, but streaks of sun also broke through helping to reveal large patches of purple heather growing on the mountain slopes. Shortly before reaching the goal for the day, I passed a stone marker announcing that I was leaving Castilla and entering the separate, autonomous region of Galicia. At the same time, I caught up with the father and son pair from Poland with whom I had shared a room at the albergue in Astorga.

Yet neither the challenge nor the beauty of the climb prepared me for the unique and remarkable mountaintop village. Today, O Cebreiro consists of a dozen buildings, each constructed almost completely of stone. In Roman times, this town helped protect the roads for gold shipments from Galician mines. The Camino helped the village develop. The first pilgrim hospital there was built as early as the ninth century. In the eleventh century, the church established a monastic settlement at the important mountain pass. In 1486, Queen Isabella (of Christopher Columbus fame) stayed here during her own pilgrimage to Santiago.

The church in O Cebreiro, Iglesia Santa Maria Real, was reconstructed in the nineteenth century, but on its medieval site. The church now houses the remains of Don Elias Valiña Sampedro, the local priest who in the 1980s helped promote and preserve the integrity of the Camino route, assuring it would continue through the town. He is credited with idea of using the yellow arrows to mark the way. In many ways, Elias is the "modern father of the Camino"—the Saint Dominic of his time.

Don Elias did his doctoral thesis in the mid-1960s on a historical and legal study of the Camino de Santiago. Commenting on how the tradition of the Camino had been lost, he wrote in that dissertation, "There survived only a remote memory of the Jacobean pilgrimage." Captivated by the ancient pilgrimage, Father Elias committed himself to recapturing some of its glorious past. He wrote the first modern guidebook for the Camino, which was published in 1982. Then, purely as a volunteer, Elias began, with the help of his family, to mark the route at which time he developed the idea of using yellow arrows as Way-markings.

In 1985, the government of Spain formally commissioned Elias to rebuild the Camino. New albergues were built; older pilgrim hostels were refreshed. Signage was improved and an official, modern route was established. In fact, in 1987, the Council of Europe named the Camino the first "European Cultural Itinerary." Attention was further drawn to Santiago by Pope John Paul II's visits to that city in 1982 and again in 1989. The modern Camino had been readied for a renaissance.

In 1972, only six pilgrims are believed to have received a Compostela, the certificate a pilgrim receives for completing the Camino. In 1985, after the initial efforts by Don Elias, about twelve hundred (1,245) pilgrims arrived in Santiago to claim their Compostela. The following year, Brazilian novelist Paulo Coelho walked the Camino and wrote about it in his autobiography, *The Pilgrimage.* On his journey in that book, Coelho has a guide named Petrus, who had the symbol of a scallop shell on his rucksack. A year later, Coelho wrote the now internationally famous book (the most translated book of a living author) *The Alchemist,* a novel about Santiago's (the book's protagonist) search for meaning and destiny or, as it's called in the book, one's "Personal Legend." Many credit Coelho's writings for helping to popularize the Camino in the late 1980s and early 1990s.

The number of pilgrims on the Way of St. James continued to increase every year (but one) since the official reestablishment or rebirth of the Camino and the publication of Coelho's books. UNESCO, the United Nations Educational, Scientific and Cultural Organization, has designated many sites along the Camino (Burgos Cathedral, Atapuerca, and the Old Town of Santiago) as "World Heritage Sites." This inevitably also helped increase interest in the Camino. In fact, after being named the first European Cultural Itinerary in 1987, the "Camino Frances"— the route itself—was also named a World Heritage Site in 1993.

Don Elias probably never thought his efforts would have the enormous impact they have had. Sadly, having died in 1989, Elias would never see the fruits of his passion, but even he never could have dreamed that a rebirth of such a magnitude would occur.

In the 1990s, the number walking the way to Santiago increased modestly, reaching thirty thousand in 1998. The year 1999 was a Holy Year, and over 150,000 arrived in Santiago to obtain their Compostelas. Very few of those peregrinos were from North America. In 1994, American actress Shirley MacLaine walked the Camino and then in 2001 published a book, *The Camino: A Journey of the Spirit,* about her experience.

Some suggest that, like Coelho's books, MacLaine's memoir had a significant impact bringing attention in the United States to the Camino de Santiago. Support for such a conclusion is inconclusive. In 2004 (three years after publication of MacLaine's book), another Holy Year, over 180,000 pilgrims arrived at the Pilgrim Office in Santiago; yet, only two thousand of that number were from the United States. The following year approximately 94,000 claimed a Compostela, which included almost the exact same number from the United States. Four years later, in 2009, approximately 145,000 arrived in Santiago—2,540 were Americans, less than 2 percent of the total and a smaller percentage than the prior year. (While participation continued to grow in absolute numbers, the percentage of Americans would not exceed 2 percent until 2011.)

In 2006, Hape Kerkeling published *I'm Off Then,* a book about his time walking the Camino in 2001, which sold well and boosted interest in the Camino, especially in Germany. For instance, in 2006 Germans earning a Compostela numbered 8,097. That number grew to 13,837 the following year. Similarly, at the same time, South Korean journalist Kim Hyo Sun wrote the first of his three books about the Camino, which coupled with a popular documentary shown in Korea, helped to promote interest in the Camino in that Asian country. Some sources suggest Korean pilgrims on the Camino increased seven-fold after these events. A prominent, South Korean businessman further drew attention to the historic "Jacobean" pilgrimage when Christopher Koo, president of LS Cable and the son of a significant multinational businessman, completed the Camino in 2011. (In 2004, less than twenty-five South Koreans received a Compostela, but by 2013 the number had risen to over 2,500.)

In 2010, Dee Nolan, an Australian journalist, published *A Food Lovers Pilgrimage to the Camino de Santiago*. The Camino has seen a dramatic rise in Australians on the Camino since the publication of that book. Some sources indicate an increase of 43 percent from 2010 to 2012.

In October 2011, many Americans were introduced to the Camino with the U.S. release of the movie *The Way*, starring Martin Sheen and directed by his son, Emilio Estevez. (The movie was first released in Spain in 2010.) The number of pilgrims continued to grow after 2010, but those from the U.S. grew disproportionately—the percentage of American pilgrims rose from 1.2 percent in 2010 to 2 percent the next year; 3.67 percent in 2012 and up to 5 percent in 2013.

My Camino was in April 2014. Now that 2014 is in the record books, we know that a record (for a non-Holy Year) 237,886 received a Compostela. Of those, 66 percent were male; 87 percent completed the Camino on foot; and 5.9 percent were from the United States. (As discussed briefly in the appendix to this book, the number of Americans showing up in Santiago will grow at a disproportionately large rate and should exceed 10 percent of those seeking a Compostela by the next Holy Year in 2021.)

After settling into my room in O Cebreiro, I toured the small village and walked to its far end where the Camino leaves town. Although clouds dominated the sky, the view was still extraordinary as I looked over the surrounding hills and below where the next day's hike would take me. A short block from my room was a reconstructed *palloza* that hosts a modest museum of Galician life. A *palloza* is a circular or oval pre-Roman building built with stone walls and slanted, conical thatched roof designed for housing people or cattle, particularly during harsh winters in northwest Spain. I also visited the church and commercial buildings, all made of layered stone. In the middle of this circuit through this small mountaintop hamlet, as the sun was setting, I ran into Sam with whom I had walked that morning—Sebastian and she had taken the horses to reach the mountaintop.

Thursday, May 1 (Day 24)

[O Cebreiro to Samos]
(30.5 kilometers—18.9 miles)

I was up early and focused on getting out and on the trail. The sun had not risen and a cloud sat softly over the top of the mountain and the town. I was eager in part because I wanted to move away from my "hotel," which, in reality, was just a collection of rooms above a bar. Unlike most towns on the Way, this place seemed more troubled by the presence of pilgrims on the Camino. Apparently, I had the misfortune of selecting what appeared to be a refuge *from* the Camino for locals. It was more of a place for those to crash after having imbibed too much. Yet, what probably set my mental state off was the owner banging on and shouting through my door (shouting something, of course, I could not understand, but probably related to paying my bill) and attempting to enter my room while I was on the phone with Cheryl and then again, after I was in bed. Not every moment on the Camino was sheer bliss. Yet, good things come to those who wait. Nothing about the prior evening or early morning indicated that this day would be one of my favorite and most memorable of my journey on the Camino.

I wasted little time rising and packing. The entire bar-hotel was dark and asleep. I left money with my key at the cash register as I groped to find a light and figure out how to unlock the front door and escape. Finally free, I walked through town, past the albergue (where, even there, I did not see anyone stirring) and onto the Way-marked path. I knew from the guidebook, and intuitively from looking down and around from the highest point on the mountain the day before, that today would largely be a day of descending. In fact, it looked as though I would be giving back as much elevation as I had gained the previous day. Yet, as I began walking down from mountaintop, despite its perch-like setting, initially the path out of town was surprisingly level and only modestly rolling.

I was decidedly in Galicia now. The green of the forested mountain and cultivated hills dominated replacing the brown and red hues of vineyards and tilled fields of Rioja and Bierzo. Galicia comes from a Latin word the Romans gave to the Celtic people they found living in this region. Perhaps a little like the Basques I encountered in the first few days of this trip, Galicia was also a region of proud locals, who also had their own language—*el gallego*—evidence of which I would see on some road and building signage.

But for brief climbs up Alto San Roque and, after a coffee break in Hospital de la Condesa up Alto do Poio, the morning's walk was a very pleasant, gradual descent. Thankfully, it was more gentle than the downhill after the Alto de Perdon or the Cruz de Ferro, the climbs that injured and then re-injured my left knee. A couple of hours of hiking brought me to Alto San Roque, another of the well-known, of-ten-photographed or iconic stops on the Camino. A prominent, over-sized statue of a pilgrim looking toward Santiago, holding his hat and leaning into and fighting the wind, looks out and down on the country below. This reminds us of the peaceful and humble image of St. James as a pilgrim as opposed to that of the warrior, "moor-slayer." The view was spectacular. When I stopped, the clouds still filled the skies, but the wind tried to replicate with me the image captured in the bronze statue. Getting a little cold from the early morning air and the wind, I did not linger long at Alto San Roque.

After almost fifteen kilometers and just before the tiny village of Bideudo, the sky cleared and I enjoyed magnificent views and idyllic hiking conditions. The earthen path below my feet was perfect for a long walk. As the mountain began to fall away more steeply, it shared much wider vistas of the Galician hillside farms and the distant moun-tains. Perhaps because the physical beauty distracted me and perhaps because the way was not well-marked, just after Bideudo, a fork in the road confronted me, but I saw no clear sign as to which way to go. I walked back a few hundred yards, but I still could not find a yellow arrow or any other Way-marking. I opted to go left down an apparently well-traveled dirt farm road.

My spirits were exceedingly high having escaped the prior night's lodging, both physically and mentally, and now delighting in a perfect day, walking through the Galician hills. As I worked my way down a fairly steep dirt track, I saw a tractor and three men working in a field where the path appeared to lead, but also, I noticed, where it appeared to end. I laughed within, noting, "Well, I guess I guessed wrong."

One of the men quickly realized I was a wayward pilgrim and, despite the usual language barrier, pointed me to a hillside that led to a road that would return me to the Camino path and on to Triacastela. I had to bushwhack downhill and slide down a very steep section onto the shoulder of a road. Once on the road, I had to walk for thirty minutes until reaching the hamlet of Villoval where I thought, based on my map reading, I could rejoin the Camino. I might have pulled out my iPod for this paved road walking, but I was still a little stressed that I had not yet caught back up to the yellow-arrowed path.

Villoval was just a couple of buildings, but I caught a glimpse of a sign confirming I was where I thought I was and could rejoin the path into Triacastela. The trail from there was a long, delightful downhill for three to four kilometers, which would take me a little over an hour to complete. Before reaching Triacastela, I continued to enjoy magnificent views as I descended through woodland and fields and through brief villages apparently devoted to farming the challenging hillsides.

When I finally arrived at Triacastela, I was immediately drawn to an attractive outdoor café with red-checked tablecloths. Thankfully it offered an easily understood menu with photographs and translations, clearly a stop meant for wanderers like me. Relieved that I was not lost for long and thinking I should celebrate both an exhilarating day of hiking as well as an important time on the inner journey, I selected a table, dropped my pack, and sat down to order a late lunch or a very early dinner.

In the early afternoon, many towns along the Camino have nothing open—siesta time. Triacastela clearly was a Camino stop open for business. A friendly waiter took my order: a full pilgrim meal of pasta salad, churasco, wine, water, bread, and rice pudding. I enjoyed a great meal and a fantastic rest. Before I finished, Henri and Alyssia walked by—the Camino headed straight down the street where I was enjoying my meal. They stopped to say hello, asked to take some photographs together, and then decided to join me for a similar late lunch.

I finished eating well before Henri and Alyssia because I was already on my second course when they sat down. So I excused myself and then walked down the main street and through the modest town where I saw other pilgrims settling in for the day. Sebastian waved from the second floor of his hostel as I walked by. I was determined to reach Samos for the evening, which was still six miles (10K) away. At the western end of Triacastela, the road ends at a T. Those heading for Samos turn left; those taking the more direct route to Sarria through San Xil head right. Although it added six kilometers to the trek, I crossed the river, took the detour, and headed toward Samos and one of the oldest and largest Benedictine monasteries in Spain.

Almost immediately I was on a paved road and the day was late—a perfect time to soften the hike with some music. I quickly arranged my iPod and selected some more Bruce Hornsby. He was singing about the Blue Ridge Mountains back in Virginia where hills are "so up and down." But he's really singing about regret and Frost's "road not taken."

   ... walking with a Hornsby song ...
   ... hiking with a Cat Stevens song ...
   ... sauntering with a Mary Chapin Carpenter song ...

After some distance on the road, fortunately with little traffic, the path entered a forest and provided a delightful environment for a late afternoon walk. The path was quiet. I saw very few pilgrims as I hiked through rolling countryside and intermittent woodlands and past the modest farming villages of San Cristobo and Renche. The walk was most pleasant and the music complimented the atmosphere. The songs played on—"The Show Goes On," where Hornsby warns us that time is passing. Again, the possibility for regret and, of course, one of the reasons I stepped away from the work world for five weeks—before life "passes me by."

I stopped briefly at a bar for a cold drink and ran into a woman from Great Britain I had met while tasting wine back in Cacabelos El Bierzo. We visited briefly while we enjoyed an afternoon rest. I finally reached the last part of the day's hike and caught a few glimpses of the huge monastery in Samos, which sits down in the river valley seemingly hidden away from time like Shangri-La. I still had to navigate a significant downhill climb into the valley before I could reach the town. I finally crossed the Rio Oribio, which I had been following much of the afternoon, and entered what appeared to be a most pleasant village, clearly dominated by the monastery to my right along the river.

... walking with a Hornsby song ...
... hiking with a Cat Stevens song ...
... sauntering with a Mary Chapin Carpenter song ...

Although the trail route I had taken is a detour from the primary, Way-marked path for the Camino Frances, I could understand why pilgrims would have taken this route in medieval times. Churches, convents, and similar religious organizations provided some of the principal support for pilgrims trying to make it to Santiago. The enormous monastery in Samos was first built in the sixth century. Thus, it would have been present and available for pilgrims to seek shelter, rest, food, and medical care during the eleventh, twelfth, and thirteenth centuries when the Camino was particularly busy with pilgrims.

Upon arriving in town, I followed my usual routine. I secured a room at a hotel, enjoyed a beverage outside, and used the local Wi-Fi. I walked through town and ran into Orla from Ireland and met her friend Andrew from Australia. Back at the hotel, I spoke with the lady from Bordeaux (who took the detour out of Villafranca when I took the easier route). She invited me to join her and a friend for dinner, but I decided to turn in early. Simply stated, I had enjoyed a remarkable day.

Friday, May 2 (Day 25)

[Samos to Portomarín]
(36.9 kilometers—22.9 miles)

Once again a magnificent morning welcomed me. I was amazed at how blessed I had been by spectacular weather for most of the journey of the Camino. I had a quick breakfast of coffee, juice, and toast with Henri and Alyssia, then I was off hiking alone, although a number of pilgrims were out ahead of me on the Camino. I had been told that this was a beautiful walk, but immediately after leaving Samos I was on a paved road for almost two miles. Fortunately, the path turned into the woodland and followed a mountain stream through the trees, spilling out into farmland and then back into the forest. I was excited to be walking again.

Perhaps because the trip was almost over, my inner journey was in full gear as I reflected on my life, looking back and looking forward without interruption. Moving down a steep section of the trail, I had to hold onto a tree to steady my descent. As I did, the back of my pack brushed the tree and one of my socks fell off. I had done some laundry the previous night and had draped my socks on the back of my pack to dry. I reattached the sock so it could finish drying out, but when I did, I noticed that its mate was missing. It must have fallen off sometime earlier that morning. Just then Eric, another lone pilgrim I had met a day earlier, came by. I asked if he had seen a sock on the trail. He responded, "Actually, I did, but it was back near Samos. Sorry." I was not going to backtrack the two or three miles just to get a sock. I had less than a week remaining in my journey and knew I could make what I had work, or I would be in towns most of the next five days and could buy some socks if I had to.

When I had left Triacastela the previous day, I had taken the road less travelled, but I regained the main path before lunch in a town called simply "Hospital." I stopped there for café con leche and had the pleasant surprise of running into Lee (the young Korean woman from Carrión), Michael (the young German man from Molinaseca) and Ricky (from our first day on the meseta). After coffee I walked with Lee and Michael into Sarria. When they headed into the business section of town to find an ATM, I climbed the steep staircase on the Camino up into the older part of town. I rested briefly there and enjoyed broad views of the surrounding countryside from this town perched high on a hill.

I arrived in Sarria with some anticipation about what the town might offer. I had been told a number of times that many pilgrims start their journey to Santiago from this spot, largely because it is the starting point closest to Santiago—110 kilometers—from which you can walk but still earn a Compostela. The fact that the town was a traditional starting point for many attempting a portion of the Camino was certainly suggested by the considerable number of albergues, bars offering "pilgrim menus," and shops catering to "pilgrims" and all things "Camino."

I had been warned that the feel of the Camino would change after Sarria, largely due to the increased numbers on the path as well as the fact that these new pilgrims would not have the shared experience of the last twenty-some-odd days. They had missed around 350 kilometers of time on their feet. They had missed tours of cities like Pamplona, Burgos, and León, the challenge of the meseta, and climbs like those to Cruz de Ferro and O Cebreiro. And they had missed an extended number of days and nights to deepen the experience with other pilgrims or with their own inner journey.

After climbing the last few uphill blocks on Sarria's main street, I had a very steep downhill as I left the famous Camino center, my left knee still reminding me of earlier steep descents. Despite the warnings, my first hour of walking after Sarria was very peaceful. I then did experience a busy path, especially with bicycle riders. Although the day's walk had been very pleasant, I clearly tired as the day wore on. My pack became heavy and uncomfortable with a nagging ache in the lower left of my back returning. I pushed along largely alone. *Perhaps a little music might distract me from the fatigue and modest aches*, I thought. I fished out my iPod and started listening.

When we take a few moments to really listen, not just hearing the music but focusing on the words, we learn that songwriters may offer a lot to digest. Often the lyrics have more to them than first appears. Maybe we hear what seems to be just a silly line, but like Winnie the Pooh getting a honey pot stuck on his nose, the line sticks and proposes one of life's great questions; and we need to turn to the owl for an answer. And, perhaps, we wander too far some days.

This would be my last time enjoying music on the Camino. I did not know it then, but I would have great, and very familiar, walking partners for my last four days on the journey.

I could see Portomarín—the destination for the day—but each step was more like one on a treadmill; I did not seem to be gaining on the day's final destination. It reminded me of the comedian who thought someone was moving the Eiffel Tower farther away from him as he walked toward it. Before reaching Portomarín, I had a very steep walk down to the reservoir that protects the city. Again, my knee reminded me of the damage I had done to it earlier in the journey. As I had done in a few other places, I turned around and walked backward down the slope, taking considerable stress off my knee.

I ran into my frequent Camino friends and breakfast companions, Henri and Alyssia from Brazil. We crossed the bridge over the expansive lake, climbed a steep set of stairs and, finally, entered Portomarín, or at least modern Portomarín. The town visited by medieval pilgrims now sits submerged on the bottom of the Belesar reservoir that was created in 1962.

I finished the long, Samos-to-Portomarín day by briefly touring the town, which has much more of a modern feel and fewer unique Camino attractions. Who would I run into during my brief tour? Carmen! Just as in Villafranca, I was walking the town after a long day's hike and we happened upon each other on the streets. We began to feel as if we were destined to be permanent Camino buddies or, as Pete might have said, "It was meant to be." After stumbling upon Carmen as we both tried to leave Burgos in the predawn light, I had walked with her on a few planned days, but "accidentally" ran into her in Itero de

Vega, Carrión, Virgen del Camino, Hospital del Órbigo, Foncebadón, Cruz de Ferro, Molinaseca, Villafranca, and now Portomarín! So we accepted the verdict of the fates and made plans to meet in a couple of days, walk together into Santiago, and finish our journeys together at the Cathedral.

Carmen and I stopped in one of the cafés along the beautiful colonnade at the city's center square. Ciaran, whom I had lounged with in Frómista eleven days earlier, was there and called us over to visit. We had a beer and enjoyed a pizza together while looking out at St. John's Church, which the guidebooks say exhibits a period of transition from the Romanesque style to Gothic architecture. Apparently, before flooding the old city, the significant historical buildings like St. John's were deconstructed, their stones numbered and the buildings reassembled in the "new" town. I did not have enough energy to tour this church, which had been reborn. I was bushed from a beautiful but long day of walking over eighteen miles from Samos. I did not know it at the time, but the magnificent hiking environment, including the interesting terrain, was about to end.

Chapter 17

Sue and Ravi Zacharias

We have come from seeking meaning to finding meaning in seeking.
Daniel Boorstin

I met Sue on a short hill as we climbed up and into the village of Sansol. "I teach religion at Florida International," she mentioned as we began to introduce ourselves. Although raised in a Christian home and culture, she volunteered quickly, "But I am not religious. The evangelicals have really ruined Christianity for me."

Intrigued, I pressed just a little more. "How so?" I asked.

Sue explained, as far as she was concerned, the "evangelicals" or the "fundamentalists," she used the words interchangeably, had turned the Christian faith into a political or social crusade. Further, Sue couldn't believe in God because of how she assumed belief played itself out. For her, it was a social issue. I couldn't tell if the key issue was climate change or abortion or gay rights or something else.

Sue was far from uneducated, but some of her logical fallacies were obvious. Despite my nature to rarely miss out on a good debate, I hesitated to engage in a substantive or meaningful way. For Sue, these positions were all but mathematical (Christian meant evangelical which meant fundamental which equated to right-wing conservative which meant opposed to abortion and gay rights). These positions seemed to have been either so hard fought or so hard-wired that engagement on the issues would likely ruin the opportunity to share as Camino pilgrims. I left the religion and politics alone, but I wondered to myself how those views developed. I have no doubt that the church has much to explain in its past—it certainly is responsible for some outrageously bad behavior, but this conduct seemed clearly at odds with Jesus' teachings (which recalls Gandhi famously saying, "I like your Christ. I do not like your Christians"). I could see a lot of room between the person and the institution.

Sue's rejection of belief in God because of her experience with fundamentalists reminded me of one of the more profound things I learned from listening to lectures and podcasts by Ravi Zacharias. He said, "Man's unbelief is not due to the absence of evidence, but because of the suppression of it." Zacharias sees belief in God as highly rational—there is considerable evidence upon which a person can rely in concluding that God really does exist, but some simply refuse to consider the evidence. They "suppress" the evidence because they seek to hold as sacrosanct [pun intended] certain other beliefs that might be inconsistent with belief in God if they let the evidence lead them to its rational conclusion.

Sue did not want to consider seriously whether belief in God was reasonable because, for her, the people who embraced that belief appeared to hold social and political views abhorrent to her way of thinking. Sue couldn't believe because it would lead to an apparent inconsistency. According to what I had heard from Zacharias, Sue was refusing to consider facts that might point to God, so she continued to maintain a value or belief more important to her than acknowledging God's existence. Stated differently, Sue suppressed anything that might move her away from that which she apparently valued above most anything else. In some respects, this "suppression" sounded a lot like the picking and choosing undertaken by New Age followers.

The more I considered this notion of turning your back on, ignoring, or actually suppressing evidence that conflicted with certain, strongly held beliefs, the more I started to realize the regular encounter with this type of behavior. It exists often in various aspects of our lives—the serious and the mundane. Sometimes we have so much invested in a relationship or a cause that we refuse to recognize that we ignore or suppress evidence contradictory to the way we want those things to be. For example, in the political sphere we may be so convinced of a position or a party that when someone from the "other" party makes a cogent, persuasive argument, we dismiss it without serious consideration because it's not "our" party or because it's adverse to "our" cause.

Likewise, strong personal relationships often cause us to trust or distrust the messenger without regard to the accuracy or truth of the message. Many divorced spouses have trouble ever accepting that their "ex" might actually be correct about something. As I walked and listened to music, Mary Chapin Carpenter sang about this same phenomenon—people clinging to the desire to be a happily married couple because "it's so hard admitting when it's quitting time." I see this propensity for all of us to suppress evidence to suit our objectives in almost every aspect of life.

As I got to thinking even more about how common this behavior is, I concluded that it probably explained George's actions about his "missing boots." Even though, as I observed, it was essentially impossible that anyone could have taken his boots the night we all stayed at the hostel in Hontonas, George *insisted* that he had them in his possession that evening. Yet when he finally recovered his boots, the person who had them definitively had not been at that hostel the night in question. Rather than admit that his boots had gotten switched four days earlier by accident (and that he failed to recognize the inadvertent swap for those days), George insisted on a set of facts that just could not be true. He was able to adhere to his version of what happened, despite its illogic, by *suppressing* compelling evidence that led to a conclusion he refused to accept (that he had actually been hiking in the "switched boots" for a few days without realizing it).

Getting back to Sue's comments, I had trouble believing or understanding how or why educated individuals who say they want to "examine life" would reject something out of hand without exploring whether it might be true. This reminded me of something else Ravi Zacharias shared, which was how Thomas Nagel famously said, "I don't *want* there to be a God. I don't want the universe to be like that," and, similarly, Aldous Huxley who said, "I had motive for not wanting the world to have a meaning. . . . For myself, the philosophy of meaninglessness was essentially an instrument of liberation, sexual and political." Hence, the desire that certain things be true or certain things be permitted form the framework for what might be believed—not whether it's true. If what appears to be real and true nonetheless conflicts with that framework, some other conclusion or belief would by necessity need to prevail—even if it is, in fact, not true.

Despite our professed open-mindedness and despite our professed desire for the truth, we appear to often have things that we cherish more than truth. I wonder how many of us refuse to go down certain intellectual roads because we fear where they might lead. Yet, should not we all agree that we should go where the evidence leads us? For example, we may suppress evidence because we want to worship or exalt something that disagrees or conflicts with the truth that otherwise appears to be revealed. Hence, we reject Christian truths when they interfere with our selfish quest to exalt ourselves or worship material things. Or we may suppress or reject evidence whenever we cannot get a satisfactory answer to one of life's troubling issues—such as pain and suffering, homosexuality, slavery, and so forth. We reject anything that conflicts with what *we* think is right or true or good.

Finally, this reminded me of a discussion I had with a friend who said to me, "Well, I couldn't believe in a God that would act like that."

I responded by saying, "Logically, if God exists, he is God. Don't we have to take Him as He is? We don't get to pick and choose the attributes we like and reject the attributes we dislike, do we?" My friend sat silent. Thinking of Pete and Shirley MacLaine, I continued, "Otherwise, aren't we just creating or designing our own God?"

It is hard to ignore the apparent "truth" that we want to know the truth, until it conflicts with something we want to hold on to, something we see as even more valuable. What might Socrates think?

Getting back to Sue's comments, it certainly appeared that she too was suppressing, or simply ignoring, facts and evidence that might suggest that God really does exist. A few years earlier, I had asked this very same question, so I may have focused on her comments more intently than most. I thought it was an enormously important question. I wanted to know the answer. I wanted to examine life, or at least I thought I did.

As mentioned earlier, I captured that spiritual quest in a book I wrote called *The Race Before Us*. I had learned about humanity's propensity to suppress facts or evidence, so I had tried exceedingly hard to remain open to any facts that might help lead me to a proper conclusion. I could not understand why Sue would not want to know whether something so profound might be true. Logically, she so much wanted or needed something else to be "true" that she did not want to even consider a set of facts or objective evidence that might challenge that "truth." This approach of adhering to something to the exclusion of other belief systems or other worldviews has been seen simply as worshiping that other "truth" as your "god."

It is the epiphany that Harold Abrahams (from *Chariots of Fire*) had when he realized what had kept him from being content in life. It is as Martin Luther said, "Whatever your heart clings to and confides in, that is really your God."

CHAPTER 18

HEADING FOR HOME
(DAYS 26–28)

*So we saunter toward the Holy Land, till one day
the sun shall shine more brightly than ever he has done,
shall perchance shine into our minds and hearts, and light up
our whole lives with a great awakening light, as warm and
serene and golden as on a bankside in autumn.*

Henry David Thoreau

[Portomarín, [Gonzar], **Palais de Rei**, [Melide], [Ribadiso], **Arzúa,
O Pedrouzo]**
(63.8 kilometers—39.6 miles)

Despite good companions, the final days of heading to Santiago
were not as memorable as my days of pure hiking from Samos to
Portomarín. The terrain was uninteresting and the scenery unspec-
tacular. Unlike so many of the unique stops earlier on the Camino,
I have trouble now recalling or differentiating Palais de Rei, Arzúa,
and O Pedrouzo—they run together in my mind. So, without a map
or guide, I cannot easily recall the sequence of when I visited each
of those overnight stops and cannot quickly recall an image to place
properly with those towns. Each one may have retained some vestiges

of their Camino past, but these locales feel much more like what they are—modern suburbs to Santiago, than what they were—historic pilgrimage villages.

Saturday, May 3 (Day 26)

[Portomarín to Palais de Rei]
(24.8 kilometers—15.4 miles)

The way out of Portomarín begins with a gentle downhill toward the valley but then requires a trip down the steep staircase at the entrance to town to the level of the reservoir. As I maneuvered the downslope, I walked alone, with numerous pilgrims ahead and behind. Looking down at the reservoir ahead, I could see groups and individuals crossing back over the water by the same way we had arrived the previous day. Low clouds hung against the surface of the water creating a beautiful, early morning tapestry as the sunrise worked through the shrouds and mist.

The day's first air was very cool, which had undoubtedly created this fascinatingly beautiful, early morning scene. The "clouds," an intermittent ground fog in the trees and along the trail, created a stunning atmospheric condition muting the morning colors like a pastel painting. I walked by an eighty-four-year-old woman from Ireland about whom I had heard at dinner the night before. Head down, she was hunched over and shuffling along at a slow but deliberate pace. She was getting very close to completing her seventh Camino.

As the mist and fog cleared, the sky and the surrounding colors became much sharper and the temperature began to rise. I stopped to zip off my pant legs and shed an outer layer. As I did, a young woman caught up with me while I was still "undressing"—Carmen, with whom I had shared dinner the night before. We decided to walk together, and we did all day with the usual stops for coffee, water, rest, and lunch. Although the volume of pilgrims on the path had increased, we saw a number of fellow peregrinos who had been moving along at a similar pace for many days, including Ciaran, Svetlana, and David. We had an especially fun visit with them when most of the Camino parade stopped for café con leche and croissants in Gonzar, eight kilometers out of Portomarín.

The day was pleasant as was most of the hike. We had a modest climb to Ligonde, where we rested and had a lunch at an albergue run by a Christian organization from England. The place had many visitors and a great spirit about it. (I was beginning to see that the volume of travelers on the Camino had increased, as predicted, since Sarria.) Between bites of my lunch, I kicked a soccer ball with a nine-year-old local boy. It was a little more than just passing the ball back and forth. He was determined that I not get the ball past him in this narrow area where we played. We could not converse, but everyone understood, "Goooaaal!"

After a reasonably pleasant afternoon of varied but not severe terrain that included considerable walking through forested hills, we arrived in Palais de Rei around 3:00 p.m. Carmen and I had picked up David, the med student from Michigan, and arrived in town with him. We later met for a beer and then dinner, which was a very bad hamburger. David brought us up to speed about his plans to meet his girlfriend and propose in Finisterre.

Carmen and I agreed to meet in the morning because my grand experiment with eating octopus was the next thing on the itinerary: lunch in Melide. Back in Villafranca, Carmen and I had discussed the rest of the itinerary—the towns best to stay in based upon her local Spanish guidebook, and the important sites to see. She emphasized that Melide was a special center for eating octopus—*pulpo*—a Galician delicacy very popular in Spain. We had a "deal" similar to our agreement in Astorga. She would help me through the language issues, select a good restaurant, explain the whats and hows of eating *pulpo*, and I would pay the bill. I was looking forward to this adventure the next day. We were scheduled to be in Melide right at lunchtime.

Sunday, May 4 (Day 27)

[Palais de Rei to Arzúa]
(25.6 kilometers—15.9 miles)

Day 27 was about food, something most days were not about—not because northern Spain does not offer some amazing varieties of fresh and prepared foods, but because the language barrier for me kept those delicacies typically beyond my grasp. But this day, like my day in Astorga, I had Carmen with me—my translator, but now also my dear friend who was almost like a daughter. She agreed to help me order and eat a Galician delicacy, *pulpo*, what Americans call "octopus."

I met Carmen for a quick breakfast before starting our walk. A bar outside her albergue was open early where we ordered toast and café con leche. The day's destination was Arzúa, but we had made plans for an important, intermediate stop in the town of Melide, one of Spain's major centers for *pulpo*. Melide is also where one of the other caminos (the Camino Primitovo) merges into the Camino Frances.

The morning was beautiful, again. Carmen and I made very good time and covered the thirteen kilometers to the outskirts of Melide in three hours. We crossed a medieval stone footbridge, snapped some photographs of each other on the bridge, and then climbed up into the bustling center of Melide, completing the morning trip to the town center by 11:30. It was Sunday morning. A few street markets were set up and the sidewalks were busy. A man behind glass snipping segments of octopus legs into bite-sized pieces with a pair of scissors drew us in to look more closely. The prospect was a little frightening for me. Was I really going to eat pieces of one of those long legs?

Carmen and I selected the *pulperia* next door to enjoy my culinary experiment. This wasn't an experiment for Carmen. Hailing from southeastern Spain, she was very familiar with and very fond of *pulpo*. The best comparison I can think of is that it's like lobster in the U.S., a fairly expensive, but widely enjoyed, treat.

The octopus tasted good. It was steamed and served with a little olive oil and paprika. I recalled the friendly barkeep in Nájera who had offered me a few bites of tapas, trying to say "octopus." The white, circular bites, edged in purple, had a fairly rich, seafood taste. (It did *not* "taste like chicken.") I was eating sections of an octopus arm (or was it a leg?). Each bite was about three-quarters of an inch thick and the size of a U.S. quarter or half-dollar. We complemented the *pulpo* with Shishito peppers and cold, local beer. I really did like the meal, but I couldn't ignore the fact that with each bite I was eating numerous tiny section cups that protruded from the otherwise smooth, purple skin. As Cheryl commented after I returned home, "It sounds like you were eating pieces of a bathtub mat."

After our lunch, and with the weather warming up, we moved through crowded streets and headed back out onto the Camino. Brierley recommends stopping in Ribadiso for stage 32, but Carmen and I decided to walk through that riverside town and press on to Arzúa. To accomplish that, because Ribadiso lies in a valley, we had a stern climb up into Arzúa. As it did most afternoons, my back called for some relief from the weight of the pack, which I tried to solve by adjusting where more of the weight would lay. Sometimes, releasing the hip belt would help, allowing me to carry the twenty-three pounds with only my shoulders.

After a couple weeks of trial and error, I determined that the chronic pain centered in my lower left back quadrant appeared to be caused by the manner in which the hip belt, not the shoulder straps, was focusing the burden of the weight. While this uphill portion was only three kilometers, I was hot and tired and ready to call it a day. I thought that after twenty-six days, this day may have been the first hot one on my Camino, but even at that, it was far from hot for people experienced with summers in Alicante and Virginia.

Before the day was in the record books, Carmen helped me find a better evening meal, just as we had done in Astorga when her boyfriend and family had surprised her. We went to a fairly non-descript bar that had been recommended to Carmen (because she could speak with the locals). They did not serve dinner until 8:00, so we had a drink as Carmen tried to take me through the menu, written of course entirely in Spanish. In honor of our walk through that region outside of Villafranca (and my visit to the winery in Cacabelos), I ordered a decent bottle of Bierzo wine, which I now knew featured the Mensa grape (not tempranillo as was dominant in most Rioja wines).

For dinner, we shared red peppers stuffed with *langostinos*) as an appetizer—maybe my favorite dish of my entire visit to Spain. (A *langostino* is sometimes called a "squat lobster" and is like a cross between a lobster and a prawn.) It had great flavors with the peppers, seafood, and cream sauce. I then ordered a real steak—rare and thick and served on an intensely hot stone plate with a side of olive oil and orange slices, both of which are used to finalize the cooking of steak to one's preferred temperature and finish. It was fabulous. A fairly uninteresting walk had become a special culinary day with two special meals, confirming again that being able to solve the language barrier can significantly improve a pilgrim's experience on the Camino. (Aspiring American pilgrims—study your Spanish!)

Monday, May 5 (Day 28)

[Arzúa to O Pedrouzo]
(22.8 kilometers—14.2 miles)

My next-to-last day on the Camino had me headed for the town of O Pedrouzo. Lynn, Carmen, and I had agreed to meet there and walk into Santiago the following day. Although Carmen was in Arzúa the prior night (we had that fabulous dinner together), I did not want her to think she *had* to walk with me another day, so I headed out just before sunrise. On a fairly dark, woodland path, I ran into my friends from Brazil—Henri and Alyssia, whom I had seen almost every day since meeting them the day we walked out of León together. A few minutes later David, the med student, came bounding by. (I rarely walked any significant distance with David because he had a much more vigorous pace.)

The weather unfolded better than the forecast. The walk was very pleasant—a cool saunter through rolling woodlands interrupted only by passing through various small villages and the usual morning stop for coffee, orange juice, and toast. Fewer pilgrims appeared to be on the Camino this day as opposed to the previous day, or maybe I was out a little earlier, ahead of the crowd. Just after breakfast, however, I ran into the father and son from Poland with whom I had bunked in Astorga. They wanted to take some photographs, and I'm grateful now we did. At noon, I found a picnic table just off the trail and stopped to rest and eat an orange. I was in an especially buoyant mood. I felt great physically. I had enjoyed my solitude that morning. I rested in the warm sunlight, reading through my guidebook and planning the final stages of this great adventure. While I was sitting there, back at the trail I saw Ciaran (my Irish friend from back in Frómista) and Carmen walk by without seeing me.

The day warmed as the sun got higher but stayed hidden behind an overcast sky. As I walked along, I ran into an impromptu lunch as various pilgrims gathered around a picnic table right next to the trail. "Bruce! Bruce! Come join us," Ciaran yelled. And why not, I thought. These spontaneous gatherings had always been some of the most wonderful moments along the way. I sat down with Lorrie and Ann (both from Canada) who were walking with Ciaran, a father and son from Australia, and two others whose nationality I cannot recall, but they were not from the United States.

I continually found that Americans were in a small minority whenever I got into one of these groups at an albergue, a pilgrim meal, or some other, spontaneous gathering. I joined Ciaran's group as they passed around cheese and bread, both of which were in great supply. I pulled out a large chocolate almond candy bar from my pack, which was received eagerly as it made its way around the table. Ricky came by, so just as Ciaran had called to me, I yelled, "Ricky! Ricky! Come join us." He was reluctant because he didn't know this group and was always concerned about his English, but I convinced him to sit with us. No one seemed ready to get back to the hike, but finally, after a good visit where I heard many new great Camino stories with many good laughs, I excused myself, broke from the pack, and set out to complete the trip to O Pedrouzo.

Upon reaching town, I booked a private room at Pension Plantas next to a municipal albergue. I enjoyed the late afternoon routine— cold beverage, shower (always in that order), journal writing, and a walk through town. Without Carmen, I was again frustrated by my dinner options so I took a typical pilgrim meal at the bar next to my hotel. Serendipity—Lynn and Carmen walked into the same place to get something to eat and joined me for dinner. We needed to catch up anyway because the plan was for these wayward pilgrims, who had first met nineteen days earlier in Burgos, to walk the final day together into Santiago.

Serendipity II—while Lynn, Carmen, and I enjoyed a basic pilgrim dinner, Eric (a young pilgrim whom I had asked about my missing sock in the woodlands between Samos and Sarria) walked by and saw me as he glanced into the restaurant. He stopped and waved, somewhat excitedly. He then came in and told me that he found my sock! (Actually a woman he was with found my sock.) He left and returned quickly with his friend. We had a great laugh about my prodigal sock. When we made arrangements for the physical return of the sock, we discovered that she was also staying at Pension Plantas, in the room next to me! As they say, you can't make this stuff up.

Lynn, Carmen, and I made plans to meet at the same place for an early start in the next morning. We had 19.8 kilometers (a little over twelve miles) to cover. We wanted to finish in time to attend the Noon Pilgrims Mass at the Cathedral, so we said good night—we were all staying in different places. I was excited about heading into Santiago. As I pondered the fact that the journey was about to end, I was neither disappointed to be finishing nor overly eager for it to be done. I was content with and grateful for, the opportunity to travel to Spain to undertake the walk. The next day would be fun. I did not expect any regrets.

CHAPTER 19

DAVID AND JESUS CHRIST

I am the way and the truth and the life.

Jesus Christ

I had met David on my first day on the Camino at Pic D'Orisson, a well-known, grand overlook halfway up the Pyrenees. David was walking the Camino de Santiago with his father, Gale. Standing at the overlook, we strained for some glimpse of the mountains beyond or the valley beneath, but the heavy mist and rain made even a brief "peek" of the majesty around impossible. Father Jim, my hiking partner for the day, and Gale spoke to one side and walked around the overlook as I visited with David. As we spoke, I learned that earlier that morning they had met Dan (my original travel companion) as he climbed along the path of the Camino. Apparently, Dan had recounted the story of our Marx Brothers' routine earlier that morning, but in his version Jim and I had left without him and he was trying to chase us down—something he couldn't do because we were behind him. Even worse, his hurried pace attempting to do so would cause him injury that would impact his entire time on the Camino.

Jim and Gale joined back up with David and me at the perch of the overlook. We still had no visibility, but much to my astonishment, as

229

I visited with Gale, he mentioned that David was blind. He wondered if I had noticed. I had been speaking with David for twenty minutes and commented to Gale that I had not noticed his handicap. "He does really well," his father commented. "Don't you think?" he continued.

All I could say was, "It's unbelievable!"

I recalled this encounter with David as I entered O Pedrouzo on the evening of my twenty-eighth day on the Camino. The contrast between the fascinating, medieval town of St.-Jean-Pied-de-Port I had left that morning I met David and the plain, modern town of O Pedrouzo was stark. I had come a long way. I had seen a lot. The following day I planned to reach Santiago de Compostela and its great cathedral, the final destination of the pilgrimage. I was coming to the end of my walk, an end to my journey. If I had been on the "road to find out," what had I found out?

As planned, I had taken many opportunities to walk alone and think about life's great questions and, as I've said, to look back and to look forward—to look back on over fifty-five years at what I've accomplished and where I fell short and to look forward and consider how to finish well. In addition to the changing and varied landscapes, I had used the music and lyrics of songwriters to stimulate my thinking, noticing how those big questions of life persist from classic antiquity through the world's great novels and into modern music.

... Clara, like Socrates, was examining life.

... Gordon Lightfoot asked about the "wherefore and the why."

... Victor Frankel inquired into man's search for meaning in a post-Holocaust world.

... Ishmael was wandering, seeking rest for his soul.

... Huck "lit out for the territory," and Dorothy walked to Oz for the same reason.

... Carmen was walking to set priorities straight for her life. In many ways like Eric Clapton, Hape Kerkling and Jean Valjean, she was wondering about "who am I?"

... James Taylor sang about the "secret of life."

.. Alfie was famously asked, "What's it all about?"

... Frodo Baggins' quest to destroy the Ring of Sauron and Sir Gala-had's search for the Holy Grail were the same journey.

In fact, were these not all different formulations of the same quest or question? (And note the root of the word *question*.)

As I went back over my thoughts—the accumulation of many days on my feet—I became more and more convinced that, despite sounding different, featuring different words, using different illustrations, and employing varied metaphors, these questions seem to be the same question. While writing the final chapters of this book and looking for some coherence in these seemingly disparate philosophical journeys, I continued to be confronted with yet other examples—including more modern ones—of how persistent and timeless these questions are, or how eternal this one question is.

While editing this book, I watched *Begin Again*, a movie that featured a song called "Lost Stars." I saw in its lyrics the same cry for answers to life's essential question: "What is true?" And where do we go for answers? And, again, that *search* for meaning is what *pilgrimage* is all about. In "Lost Stars," the singer asks, like so many other songwriters I listened to during the Camino, if there are answers ("God, tell us the reason"). The song captures not just the eternal quest, but the skepticism and ambiguity of the modern age, as it also asks the more troubling question: "Is the effort futile?" In asking whether we are all "trying to light up the dark," Lost Stars suggests there is a darkness—a meaninglessness or an ultimate fog of ambiguity—that cannot be overcome. While suggesting there are no answers and no meaning (that we cannot "lighten up the dark"), I wondered if "Lost Stars" might also be questioning the New Age notion that we can create our own reality or meaning.

When one pauses long enough—when one has an extended time for contemplation (such as a prolonged time on your feet)—these examples of journey and quest appear to cohere as much as they appear to continue almost *ad infinitum*. I noticed the same cry for answers when I listened, really listened, to Steve Winwood's song "Higher Love." I had heard this song many times over the last twenty years, but now with my thinking focused on the inner journey, I saw this same longing for pilgrimage in the lyrics. Winwood writes about the way many of us feel—there *must* be "higher love"—or in other words, there must be meaning and truth, or else life is "wasted time." (Winwood's concern about "wasted time" is a more modern, popular reference to Camus's musing that in a world without meaning the only true philosophical question is whether or not to commit suicide.)

Socrates had it right from the earliest times—don't we really all want to know what is true? Without it, as Steve Winword sings, is life wasted time? Like a newborn child who learns the love of its mother, we want to know what is true so we can know on what we can rely and in what we can place our trust. Knowing what is true provides a reference point—a "fixed point"—by which we can judge conduct. And, don't we want to know where to go for answers? And might the answer be the same?

I became ever more convinced that all of these great questions are really just different versions of the same question. Dorothy's longing to get home is the same desire—has the same impetus—as Socrates's search for truth and the same as Augustine's journey to find rest for his soul.

There really is no difference among Ponce de León seeking the Fountain of Youth, Sir Galahad searching for the Holy Grail, and Siddhartha trying to find enlightenment. This is equally true for Buddha's search for Nirvana, Christian's journey in *Pilgrim's Progress*, and Harold Frye's trip to visit Queenie. In each of these stories, people are looking to find themselves, seeking meaning and truth, or trying to reach "home" or the Promised Land. Whether it's the words of Adam Levine's "Lost Stars" or Gordon Lightfoot's "Wherefore and the Why," or James Taylor's "Secret of Life," or whether its Bunyan or Melville or Thoreau, they all represent a longing for pilgrimage deep in the human soul. Whether it is called a search for meaning, purpose, truth, a noble path, the Holy Grail, nirvana, enlightenment, peace, home, or rest, that quest is a search for answers to the same eternal question.

If these questions are all just the same question, then likewise they should have the same answer. Hence, could all of these longings, questions, and desires have a single answer, and could we have just confused the answers because the words and the speakers are different? And maybe there is not infinite nuance or endless iteration. Maybe there is one place to go for answers; maybe there is one way to that truth; maybe the answers we all seek are the same answer—the ultimate reason for pilgrimage.

My thoughts returned to my days on the Camino. I reflected upon the many people, places, and things I had experienced. I thought about David and his father, who were "on the Camino" for a fairly traditional reason—to worship God each day along the way, culminating with a special visit to the great cathedral in Santiago—where I hoped to be the next day. For David and his father, "God" was decidedly not "everyone" or an "impersonal divine" or some cosmic energy, but the Christian God of the Bible—the Father, Son, and Holy Spirit. Despite the intense fog at Pic D'Orisson, in a very real sense spiritually, David could see as much or more than I could see. David may have been blind, but he walked by faith. He *knew* what was true. He lived by the words of the writer of Hebrews: "Faith is the assurance of things hoped for, the conviction of things not seen" (Hebrews 11:1, ESV).

Even if you are not David or Gale or Father Jim, you cannot be "on the Camino" and not be confronted constantly by reminders that the "Way of St. James" is a *Christian* pilgrimage. Some "pilgrims" may be pursuing their own notions of "God" or an "impersonal divine" or may simply be on a "sports adventure," but the Camino de Santiago is, from the beginning, a pilgrimage offered to and for Christians, for whom the Way is much more than a long walk and much more than the grand cathedrals of Burgos, León, or Santiago.

The path Way-marked with yellow arrows and scallop shells takes even the modern, secular adventurer past churches, crosses, monasteries, monuments, and various other Christian institutions and signs— and does so, every day. In light of the history of the Camino and the constant reminders, it would be hard for anyone "on the road to find out" not to ask (or at least wonder) what Jesus might have to say about the great questions about meaning, purpose, or truth.

More to the point, using words seemingly tailored uniquely for pilgrims on the Camino (yet relevant for anyone seeking), Jesus said, "I am the way and the truth and the life." In the age of skepticism in which we live today, many either do not really want answers or they think that there are no answers, so the endless questioning and the endless searching to them are itself worthy objectives, if not the only objective. They subscribe to the thinking of Buddha who is reputed to have said, "Life is a journey." More to the point, these modern pilgrims confirm Boorstein's observation that "we have stopped searching for meaning because we find meaning in searching."

When Socrates set out to "examine life," he was not seeking to find meaning in the examination itself. Rather, he sought something he thought was attainable. He believed that truth did exist. In my core, I believed that truth did exist. It was an objective worth the journey. In light of the observations about the heart's longing for pilgrimage and the fact that I was following an ancient Christian pilgrimage I was particularly struck by Jesus' actual words about being the "way" and the "truth" and His statement, "I will give you rest" (Matthew 11:28, ESV). His reference to "rest" resonated as many have couched these eternal questions about the search as a desire to be at peace or rest or home. For David and his father, then, not only are these questions the same question, but there is a single answer to the question(s), and they were confident in what that answer was.

For me then, time on the Camino was not a pilgrimage to achieve a partial indulgence or to discover the meaning of life. For me, I pursued the Camino primarily for the extended time to disconnect from the everyday world to permit me to give considerable thought to where my life has been and how should I spend the time remaining. By itself, that explanation is accurate and adequate, but without more it is likely to be both superficial and misleading, even if "safe" in these modern times, as to the dimensions of the introspection. (Many admire the search, but dare you not to suggest that an answer—

truth—exists, because to acknowledge truth means by definition that other things are excluded, certain other things cannot also be true.)

A few years earlier, I had gone on another pilgrimage of sorts—it too involved a physical as well as a spiritual journey and resulted in the book, *The Race Before Us: A Journey of Running & Faith*. Asking many of these same questions about meaning and purpose—and particularly focused on the truth of Christianity—I had come to see that the religion of my culture was in fact true. Jesus is the "way and the truth and the life." I agreed with David. Jesus answers life's eternal questions about meaning, morality, origin, and destiny. For me, the person of Jesus Christ and the tenets of Christianity that flow from His life provide the best explanation for everything I see and feel every day. For me, conclusions about truth and meaning require pilgrimage. My time on the Camino was mostly about confirming these beliefs and trying to absorb on a deeper level how those truths are supposed to play out in one's life.

Pilgrims are on the road to find out. They "saunter toward the Holy Land." Jesus both asks and answers life's ultimate question: "What do you want?" (John 1:38). In the Gospel of John, that question is Jesus' first words, which are directed to John and James (the St. James of the Camino de Santiago). As he does with Peter and Andrew in Matthew's Gospel, Jesus tells them to "come"—to follow him.

Pilgrimage can provide answers—it is neither a journey without a destination nor the destination itself. In fact, immediately upon learning what is true, like the first apostles, we are faced with a new pilgrimage of sorts—how do we respond? ("Follow me.") I was on this second pilgrimage. Hence, for me, the time on the Camino was essentially an extended, relatively uninterrupted time with God. I viewed my thoughts about my past and my future much as a conversation or mediation—if not a prayer—with God as I tried to digest the first fifty-five years of my life. And, more importantly, how is it that I should live my life now? How should I run the race that has been set out before us, how should I follow Jesus? How might I live so that I may honestly say at that ultimate day: "I have fought the good fight, I have finished the race, I have kept the faith" (2 Timothy 4:7, ESV).

I may have arrived a couple of hours sooner than David, but when I stopped that first night in Roncesvalles, registered at the albergue, and received the first stamp on my Pilgrim Passport, like David, I checked the box on the form that I was walking the Camino for "religious reasons."

CHAPTER 20

SANTIAGO DE COMPOSTELA
(DAY 29)

The LORD has told you what is good, and this
is what He requires of you: to do what is right,
to love mercy, and to walk humbly with your God.

Micah 6:8 NLT

[O Pedrouzo, [Lavacolla], [Monte del Gozo], **Santiago de Compostela]**

(19.8 kilometers—12.3 miles)

The final day was an early start followed by strong walk. While I was departing the cathedral town of Burgos in the pre-dawn light twenty days earlier, I met Carmen and, a few minutes later, we joined up with Lynn. I would see and walk with them many times thereafter. They became an important part of my trip. Like we had back on that morning in Burgos, we headed out of O Pedrouzo together in the dark. We pressed hard to make it to Santiago for the daily Pilgrim Mass and, while we did, we tried to reflect upon and share our thoughts about the month-long journey we were about to complete.

Tuesday, May 6 (Day 29)

[O Pedrouzo to Santiago]

I met Lynn and Carmen for breakfast. We opened the bar at 6:00 a.m. and were hiking by 6:30. Our forecast was poor: 30 percent chance of rain. We started out in cool, humid conditions walking on an earthen path through low, forested hills. We were early and we could not see well, especially with the heavy clouds and the dense woods. Lynn's headlamp was most handy, so she took that out and led us along. It was only the third time in thirty days I needed to use a headlamp for walking.

After a month of walking, of following yellow arrows and scallop shells west, this day would finally bring us to the destination that seemed like an elusive dream when I began climbing up into the Pyrenees on my first day out. Our goal was to get to Santiago by 10:30 a.m. To do so, we had to maintain a strong pace. The Pilgrim Mass at the Cathedral started at noon, but we needed to first get to the Pilgrim Office to get our Compostela. We thought we might have to stand in a line there for an hour or so.

The hike that morning was mostly a gentle uphill with a few short, steeper climbs— enough to make me sweat. I removed layers so I could hike in shorts and one shirt. We kept up a good pace and walked by Lavacolla (the Santiago-area) airport, which was just beyond the one-third mark for us this day. We resumed gentle climbing up to Monte de Gozo, well known for being the first place pilgrims can catch a glimpse of Santiago and possibly the cathedral. When we arrived at Monte de Gozo, we were still on schedule. We took off our packs, got a cold drink, and rested briefly as we visited the large monument there and took the obligatory photographs.

The air was still thick and seemingly colder. Low cloud cover obscured any view of the destination. Without a glorious view to enjoy and a creeping chilliness in the air, we had little to do but move onto our final leg, our home stretch. The Way-marked path heads down a very steep slope just beyond Monte de Gozo, so steep that my knee,

which had recovered substantially from its ordeal on the Alto de Pardon on Day 4, provided me with a parting reminder of the inclines traversed and the miles traveled over the last five hundred kilometers. After surviving the relatively brief but severe descent, we had five kilometers or less to go to reach the cathedral. We still appeared to be on time.

After coming down off Monte de Gozo, we were immediately at the outskirts of the city. City sidewalks, commercial buildings, and vehicular traffic replaced the earthen trail and the woodlands. From the base of Monte de Gozo, however, we still had a long walk on roadways into the old part of town where the cathedral has sat for well over a thousand years. The newer or more modern outskirts of Santiago, which we entered first, had little or no visual interest. The final approach to the historic cathedral seemed to take forever—similar to my entrance into Portomarín. Every time we turned a corner or got around a city block, I expected to see what we had been walking toward for a month, but each time we were frustrated with more of the same. As we approached the older part of the city, the older buildings provided not only more visual interest but helped anticipate our final arrival at the historic tabernacle.

Lynn, Carmen, and I stayed together, and we finally eyed the portal that led to the cathedral square—the finish line of the Camino de Santiago. Just before passing through that final gate, much like the one we passed through in St.-Jean-Pied-de-Port a month earlier to start the journey, I waived to Ciaran and other pilgrims who had positioned themselves well to greet pilgrims such as us as we finished. I had Carmen and then Lynn go ahead so I could take their photographs.

Then, finally, I walked into the Plaza del Obradoiro. I had done it.

Looking to my left I saw the ancient shrine to St. James, now celebrated by the grand Cathedral de Santiago. Lynn, Carmen, and I stopped briefly in the cathedral square, looked upon the famous church (which unfortunately had one of its two towers covered in scaffolding), and gave each other a congratulatory embrace.

To our right, as we entered the square, was the historic Parador Hotel. In the sixteenth century, the same monarchs who had commissioned Christopher Columbus to try to find a new route to Asia had ordered the construction of a hospital for pilgrims in Santiago close by the Cathedral of Santiago. That hospital, now the Parador's "Hostal dos Reis Catolicos," is the oldest building on the Camino. Upon presentation of their Compostela, pilgrims could stay at this hospital for three days of recuperation. The hospital looked after pilgrims' health needs and became the most important hospital in Galicia. Later it was the offices for the faculty of Medicine at the University of Santiago de Compostela, and more recently, in 1954, the building was converted to the high-end Parador Hotel. While today you cannot secure three days at the five-star, luxury hotel simply by presenting the reception desk with your Compostela, as a remnant of the original commission by Ferdinand and Isabella (who themselves walked the Camino), the hotel continues the tradition of pilgrim hospitality by providing free meals each day to the first ten pilgrims who queue up.

Carmen signaled for us to move on. She knew where we needed to go next. We hustled around the side of the cathedral and down a narrow street to the Pilgrim Office to collect our "Compostela." We joined a fairly long line to wait for the official certificate for completing the Camino de Santiago. Henri and Alyssia, and many others we knew, were also there. Jen showed up to greet us as well. She had completed a fifty-kilometer walk (over thirty-one miles) the prior day to get to Santiago the night before!

When our turn to receive our Compostela finally came, the volunteers took time with each of us, asking us about the journey—where we were from, where we started—and offering sincere congratulations. Like they did on that first night at Roncesvalles, the volunteers asked us if we had taken the journey for "religious" or some other purpose. As I had on the evening of Day One, I indicated that I had set out on the Camino for religious purposes.

After we finished, Jen showed us where we could store our backpacks, then we ran to the Pilgrim Mass. Remarkably, we found some room in a pew and got settled at 11:55. Not only was our timing fortunate, but also we quickly learned that during this mass the priests would be swinging the *botafumeiro!*

The cathedral was packed with almost a thousand pilgrims, visitors, and tourists—standing room only. Although the atmosphere seemed to anticipate entertainment more than worship, the occasion and I tried to treat it as such. Because we were able to check in at the Pilgrim Office before 11:00 a.m., during the mass we heard the priest provide blessing for "a pilgrim from Alicante who started in Roncesvalles," one from British Columbia who started in St. Jean, and another "from the United States who started in St. Jean," for having completed the Camino de Santiago. Lynn, Carmen and I knew those words were meant for us because of the proximity of the references.

At the end of the service, a group of priests hoisted the *botafumeiro,* literally "smoke expeller"—an enormous incense chamber that was used historically to moderate the stench created by a church filled with pilgrims living on the road for weeks and months to reach Santiago. Today, it is more symbolic with much more pageantry. The Dintaman Guide reveals that the chamber is the largest censer for incense in the world, weighing 175 pounds, standing five feet tall, and requiring eight men to operate its pulley system that allows it to swing at great lengths and heights in the nave of the cathedral. We were excited because the guidebooks indicate that the *botafumeiro* is not put into use except for special occasions (or when someone pays a fee of three hundred euros).

After the Pilgrim Mass, Jen, Lynn, Carmen, and I stopped to share a pizza and to enjoy a glass of wine together. Then we separated to check into our respective hotels. We agreed to meet back up at 6:00 for drinks and dinner. I had a ten- to fifteen-minute walk to my Marriott hotel, the AC Palacio del Carmen. Yes, that really is its name—I guess just another coincidence.

I took a shower, ran some errands, and then met the ladies for dinner. We saw a number of other pilgrims near the cathedral, throughout the old part of the city, and around the restaurant district. We saw Ricky and Lee (from Carrión and Sarria); the German Boys (with whom I got lost in Ponferrada); Svetlana (with whom I had dinner in Villavante), Rusty and Carol (with whom I had shared a late afternoon beverage near the river at Molinaseca); the American volunteer (who helped me get settled—and who had done my wash—at the albergue in Astorga); Michael from Germany (with whom I walked into Molinaseca); and others from the Camino.

At a tapas bar that had a lively and fun atmosphere, we shared a great meal sampling cod, scallops, shrimp, *pulpo*, clams, cheese, and sirloin—all washed down with red wine and sangria. It was a pilgrim gathering, but we ignored all the "fixed price" pilgrim menus. After crème brûlée/cheesecake and chocolate lava cake, we walked to Cathedral Square and listened to "La Tuna," a well-known, Spanish folk band performing outdoors next to the Parador Hotel.

I returned to my hotel by midnight, both exhilarated and exhausted, if that's possible at the same time. What a day. What a journey. My Compostela stated I have walked 491 miles.

My formal Camino was over, but I had a few things still to do before returning to my old routine. . . .

Epilogue: The End of the Earth II

One's destination is never a place,
but a new way of seeing things.

Henry Miller

Finisterre, the narrow spit of land projecting into the Atlantic Ocean that gives the nearby town its name, has been known as "land's end" or the "end of the earth" for thousands of years. And long before St. James came to the region to share the gospel of Jesus Christ, this part of the northwest corner of the Iberian Peninsula was a destination for pilgrimage. At an earlier time, when the earth was flat, people looked to Finisterre as the very edge of the world—again, the end of the earth. In pre-Christian times its unique setting gave it significance (evidence of early Druid worship remains today) and made it a site to which people would journey. As we do today for different reasons, this place caused people to think about life, meaning, and possibility of the unseen. It has, then, for untold history been a worthy destination—a holy place—to which pilgrims could undertake an inner journey as well as an arduous walk.

After finishing my 491 miles on the Camino Frances, I took a day to tour Santiago. I ran into my favorite Aussie family—Andy, Jan, and Matt—as they were completing the journey. We had kept a very similar pace. I finished just a day before them. Then, I was off to Muxia and

Finisterre. Dan and I had decided, like many pilgrims do, to make a trip to the "end of the earth" as a capstone to our trip. Injured, Dan had gone back to the United Sates early. I promised to go to Finisterre for both of us. [Continued from the Prologue]

Jacob pointed to me and offered with a devilish grin, "I think it's time for our American friend to offer us his toast for the Camino." I had committed myself to join in. Everyone was taking part. It was great fun, and nothing could dampen the spirit. I stepped up onto the rocky stage and—now, with the benefit of editorial assistance, spell-check, and hindsight—here is something close to what I said:

> *I offer a toast to the Camino and to my friends from the Camino. I enjoyed every step of the way. I enjoyed time alone, and I enjoyed time getting to know fellow pilgrims. The time I spent on the Camino was extraordinary, for which I am grateful to God. I pray that it guides me in taking further steps in the race that has been set out before me.*

Endnotes

Religion points to that area of human
experience where in one way or another man
comes upon mystery as a summons to pilgrimage.

Frederick Buechner

Chapter 3

Among the good resources for information on the Camino de Santiago are these guidebooks:

A Pilgrim's Guide to the Camino de Santiago by John Brierley

Hiking the Camino de Santiago by Anna Dintaman & David Landis

Also, the Confraternity of St. James offers a wealth of information about the history of and planning for a pilgrimage on the Camino. It is accessed at: http://www.csj.org.uk. The information available in Wikipedia appears also to be generally accurate, comprehensive, and helpful.

Chapter 4

Codex Calixtinus. The *Codex Calixtinus* is a twelfth-century manuscript, consisting of six volumes, believed to have been written and/or compiled by French priest Aymeric Picaud, later named in honor of or attributed to Pope Callixtus II. The *Codex* is also referred to sometimes as the "Book of St. James," as it contains background and advice concerning St. James

("Santiago") and pilgrimages to Santiago. The sixth volume is a guide to actually walking the Camino with directions, references to roads and geographic features, and places for food and rest.

Much of the history and tradition concerning St. James, his presence on the Iberian Peninsula, the return and discovery of his body, and miracles attributed to him are found in the *Codex*. One of the few remaining ancient manuscripts of the *Codex Calixtinus* was stolen from the Cathedral of Santiago de Compostela in 2011, but recovered about a year later.

Basque region. The Basque region is an area in the western Pyrenees Mountains in and around southwest France and northern Spain, which includes the autonomous Basque Country. The Basque people have their own language, customs and traditions. In 1959 and for fifty years thereafter a separatist group, which sometimes resorted to violence, pressed for autonomy for a wider region than just the independent country that had been carved out of northern Spain and officially recognized. After a number of aborted ceasefires, a "permanent" ceasefire has held since 2010.

Hape Kerkeling. In 2006, Hape Kerkeling, a popular comedian in Germany, wrote and published a book entitled *I'm Off Then*, which is a memoir about his time on the Camino. Hape Kerkeling, *I'm Off Then* (New York: Free Press, 2006), pages 20 and 61.

Stephen Curtis Chapman is an American, Christian singer-songwriter. Among his many songs is "Long Way Home," which is about God being along with us despite life's ups and downs. The song begins, "I set out on a great adventure, the day my Father started leading me home."

Chapter 7
The quotations are taken from *I'm Off Then*, pages 4, 31, and 330.

Chapter 8
American "Pilgrims." William Bradford led the Separatists that arrived at Plymouth Rock. About their journey, he wrote in his journal

("Of Plymouth Plantation"): "So they left that goodly and pleasant city which had been their resting place near twelve years; but they knew they were pilgrims and looked not much on those things, but lift up their eyes to the heavens, their dearest country, and quieted their spirits." This was an intentional allusion to Hebrews 11:13-14.

The Archetype of Pilgrimage: Outer Action with Inner Meaning by Jean Dalby Clift & Wallace B. Clift (Paulist Press, 1996), page 9.

Thoreau and "Walking." Among the many essays written by Henry David Thoreau was one titled "Walking," which was first published in the *Atlantic Monthly* in 1862 after his death.

Surprised by Joy. C.S. Lewis's autobiography of his conversion to Christianity is titled, *Surprised by Joy.* Lewis saw certain inexplicable moments of joy in his life as signposts pointing him toward truth.

Chapter 10
John C. Lennox. *God's Undertaker: Has Science Buried God?* (Oxford, England: Lion Books, 2009), page 201.

Of Miracles. Section 10 of David Hume's work *An Enquiry Concerning Human Understanding* is titled "Of Miracles."

Chapter 11
Unjust Hanging & the Chicken Dinner. John Brierley, *A Pilgrim's Guide to the Camino de Santiago* (2014), page 112.

Atapuerca. Some of the oldest known human remains are found in certain caves in the hills near Atapuerca, Spain. This archeological site was designated a UNESCO World Heritage site in 2000.

Chapter 12
The *Meseta*. The website from which the quotation about the meseta is take is *"Spain: Then and Now,"* which can be accessed at: http://www.spainthenandnow.com/spanish-travel/the-meseta/default_25.aspx

Chapter 14

Kings of Grail. *The Kings of the Grail: Tracing the Historic Journey of the Holy Grail from Jerusalem to Spain* by Margarita Torres Sevilla and Jose Miguel Ortego del Rio (London, England: O'Mara Books, 2015).

Chapter 17

Shirley MacLaine. Her book about the Camino is *The Camino: A Journey of the Spirit* (New York, N.Y.: Pocket Books, 2000). Quotations are found at pages 10, 56, 187, and 297. The interview excerpts are taken from a story in the Huffington Post on March 21, 2014. http://www.huffingtonpost.com/2014/03/21/shirley-maclaine-oprah_n_5008946.html

Eckhart Tolle. The quotation by Eckhart Tolle is from his book, *A New Earth: Awakening to Your Life's Purpose* (New York: Dutton Books, 2005), page 71.

Chapter 18

The quotation from Hape Kerkeling's *I'm Off Then* is on page 279

The quotation from John Brierley's guide is on page 233.

Don Elias. Don Elias Valiña Sampedro, born in 1929, was the parish priest at Santa Maria Real in O Cebreiro in Galicia from 1959 until his death in 1989. He took it upon himself to restore the church and the ancient hospital (now the Hostal San Giraldo de Aurillac). During his studies at la Universidad Pontificia de Salamanca, he wrote a thesis on the Camino's history. He attempted to walk the ancient Camino and found it was nearly impossible, which led him to write the first modern guide to walking the Camino de Santiago.

http://www.galiciaguide.com/Stage-27-2.html

https://de.wikipedia.org/wiki/Elías_Valiña_Sampedro

Statistics. The statistics for this chapter (and the Appendix) were obtained from the Official Pilgrim Office website, which can be accessed at: http://peregrinossantiago.es/eng/pilgrims-office/welcome/

APPENDIX

In every walk with nature one receives far more than he seeks.

John Muir

I. Itinerary

Below is a listing of each town or city where I stopped and stayed for the night. I did not ever take a complete rest day or spend two nights in the same town.

1. Roncesvalles (from St. Jean = 25.1 kilometers)
2. Zubiri (from Roncesvalles = 21.9 kilometers)
3. Pamplona (from Zubiri = 20.3 kilometers)
4. Puente La Reina (from Pamplona = 24.2 kilometers)
5. Villamayor de Monjardin (from Puente La Reina = 25.3 kilometers)
6. Viana (from Villamayor de Monjardin = 29.8 kilometers)
7. Navarette (from Viana = 22.7 kilometers)
8. Azofra (from Navarette = 22.2 kilometers)
9. Belorado (from Azofra = 38.1 kilometers)
10. Ages (from Belorado = 27.9 kilometers)
11. Burgos (from Ages = 22.8 kilometers)
12. Hontanas (from Burgos = 31.8 kilometers)
13. Frómista (from Hontanas = 34.6 kilometers)
14. Carrión (from Frómista = 20.5 kilometers)

15. Sahagún (from Carrión = 39.8 kilometers)
16. Mansilla (from Sahagún = 38.4 kilometers)
17. León (from Mansilla = 18.1 kilometers)
18. Villavante (from León = 31.7 kilometers)
19. Astorga (from Villavante = 21.3 kilometers)
20. Foncebadón (from Astorga = 25.9 kilometers)
21. Molinaseca (from Foncebadón = 20.3 kilometers)
22. Villafranca del Bierzo (from Molinaseca = 30.6 kilometers)
23. O Cebreiro (from Villafranca del Bierzo = 30.1 kilometers)
24. Samos (from O Cebreiro = 30.5 kilometers)
25. Portomarín (from Samos = 36.9 kilometers)
26. Palais de Rei (from Portomarín = 24.8 kilometers)
27. Arzúa (from Palais de Rei = 25.6 kilometers)
28. O Pedrouzo (from Arzua = 22.8 kilometers)
29. Santiago (from O Pedrouzo = 19.8 kilometers)

II. Statistical Growth in Pilgrims on the Camino de Santiago

We are pilgrims, our life is a
long walk or journey from earth to heaven.

Vincent Van Gogh

Most historical accounts of the Way of St. James suggest that the number of pilgrims walking the Camino de Santiago in the twelfth and thirteenth centuries annually exceeded 500,000 (and quite possibly in excess of one million). After the Reformation and the "Enlightenment," interest in the Camino dissipated almost completely; however, a rebirth began in the 1980s. (See discussion in chapter 18, "Galicia," of Don Elias, the priest from O Cebreiro, who almost single-handedly sparked the rebirth of the Camino.) In 1985, approximately 1,250 pilgrims made their way to the Cathedral de Compostela. The number of pilgrims has increased every year since then with a significant temporary increase or "spike" each Holy Year (and each Holy Year the number of pilgrimages has increased over the previous Holy Year).

The Official Pilgrim Office notes that thousands walk parts of the Camino each year. The records it maintains report only the number of individuals completing the minimum requirements to receive a Compostela. In 1995, less than 20,000 pilgrims received a Compostela. By 2000, 55,000 pilgrims received one. By 2005, the number was approximately 94,000. By 2012, the number exceeded 192,000. And the year that I completed the Camino (2014), the number was 237,886.

Similarly, the years 1993, 1999, and 2004 were Holy Years, and the numbers obtaining a certificate of completion were approximately 100,000, 155,000, and 180,000, respectively. The Holy Year in 2010 saw 272,000 receive Compostelas. (Holy Years have always seen an increased interest in completing the Camino. In part, this is likely the result of increased attention as well as the possibility of receiving a "plenary" indulgence.)

The number of Americans arriving in Santiago never exceeded two thousand until the Holy Year of 2004, which was just over 1 percent of all arriving to claim a Compostela. Similarly, for the first decade of the twenty-first century, the number never exceeded three thousand or 2 percent of the total in any one year. In the Holy Year of 2010, 3,241 were from the U.S., but that was but 1.3 percent of the total. The following year (2011), the number increased to 3,670 (2 percent of the total), then 7,071 in 2012 (3.67 percent), 10,125 in 2013 (4.69 percent of the total), 11.577 in 2014 (4.86 percent), and 13,658 in 2015 (5.20 percent of total). Clearly, a significant change began in 2012. The number of Americans heading out on the Way is increasing at much different rate during the recent past.

Almost certainly with the interest that has been created in the United States and the relative affluence of Americans, the Camino will continue to see a material rise in the number of individuals from the United States walking the Camino de Santiago, which increase will more than likely be exponential rather than incremental. Statistically, we have tried to analyze this trend and to project what participation by pilgrims from the U.S. will look like in the near future and beyond. As illustrated on the charts below, the number of Americans claiming a Compostela should exceed 25,000 as early as 2019, exceed 33,000 in 2020, and by 2021—the next Holy Year—the number should exceed 37,000. (Hence, it appears that in just five years after I walked the Camino, the number of Americans heading to Santiago on the ancient pilgrimage route will have tripled—a growth of 300 percent! By comparison, five years after country-specific statistics were first maintained [2004–2009], the number of Americans grew by 20 percent.)

In a similar vein, statistical analysis of the trends concerning all pilgrims on the Camino, as demonstrated below, suggest that by 2020 over 350,000 pilgrims will arrive at the Official Pilgrim Office in Santiago to claim a Compostela. And, in 2021, the next Holy Year, over 500,000 pilgrims will arrive in Santiago completing the minimum requirements for a Compostela.

(Following are statistical charts illustrating these future growth projections that have been extrapolated from the current data.)

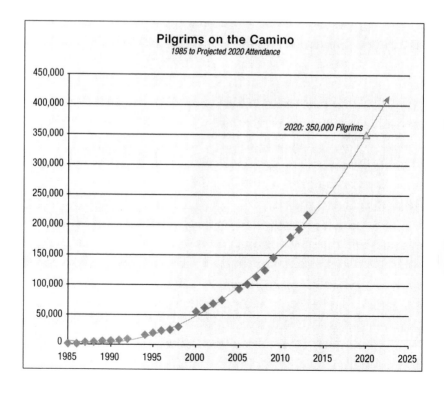

Pilgrims on the Camino
1985 to Projected 2020 Attendance

2020: 350,000 Pilgrims

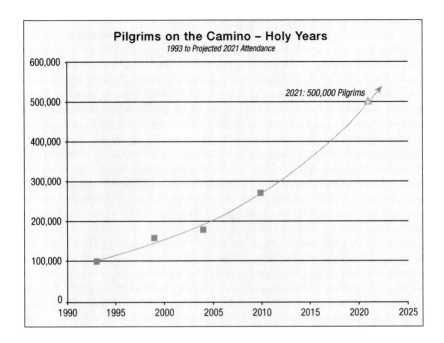

Pilgrims on the Camino – Holy Years
1993 to Projected 2021 Attendance

2021: 500,000 Pilgrims

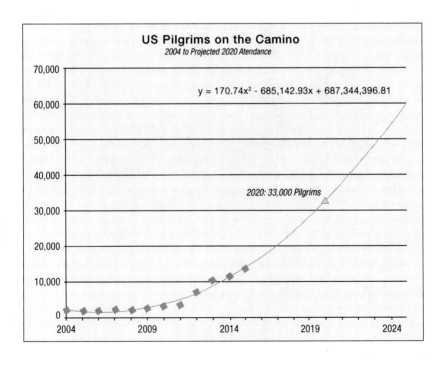

US Pilgrims on the Camino
2004 to Projected 2020 Atendance

$y = 170.74x^2 - 685,142.93x + 687,344,396.81$

2020: 33,000 Pilgrims

Also by the author . . .

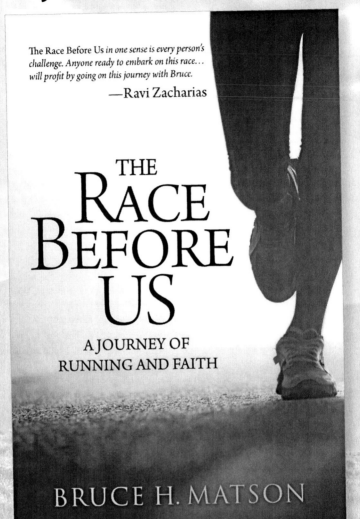

The Race Before Us *in one sense is every person's challenge. Anyone ready to embark on this race... will profit by going on this journey with Bruce.*

—Ravi Zacharias

THE
RACE
BEFORE
US

A JOURNEY OF
RUNNING AND FAITH

BRUCE H. MATSON

The Race Before Us: A Journey of Running and Faith
is available from:

- Amazon
- Barnes & Noble
- christianaudio.com
- and personalized copies can be obtained from the author
  (bruce.matson@comcast.net)

What people are saying about
The Race Before Us:

What follows is a very personal expression of an exceptional running journey back to spiritual, mental and physical health after staring into his own personal abyss.
— **Frank Shorter,**
Winner – 1972 Olympic gold medal
in the marathon

I believe very strongly in the power of sharing the stories of one's life, which is why as a professional marathon runner I always am eager to here the stories of breakthrough from other runners because after hearing their story it releases something in me to walk in that same breakthrough. In The Race Before Us: A Journey of Running & Faith, Bruce Matson shares his incredible story of breakthrough that is sure to inspire you to further breakthrough in your own life.
—**Ryan Hall,**
Olympic Marathon (USA)

A good book tells a compelling story. The Race Before Us is a two-for-one gem that clearly lights the path to both spiritual and physical wholeness. Bruce's parallel journeys of faith and fitness will inspire you to examine your own walk with Jesus—and perhaps to lace up a pair of running shoes along the way.
—**William C. Mims,**
Justice – Supreme Court of Virginia

I experienced and enjoyed The Race Before Us *on two levels. As a runner, I loved reading Bruce's efforts to prepare for running a marathon and his challenges along the 26.2 miles. His detailed descriptions of his personal journey are engaging and informative and will be helpful for those aspiring to complete a marathon. As a committed Christian, I appreciated Bruce' s journey to faith, his careful and detailed investigation of the evidence for God and case for Christ. Those searching for truth will learn from this excellent analysis.*
—**Dave Veerman,** Author
The Runners Devotional; Senior Editor of
the *Life Application Study Bible*

CPSIA information can be obtained at www.ICGtesting.com
Printed in the USA
BVOW03s0607070916

461356BV00007B/46/P

9 780972 461696